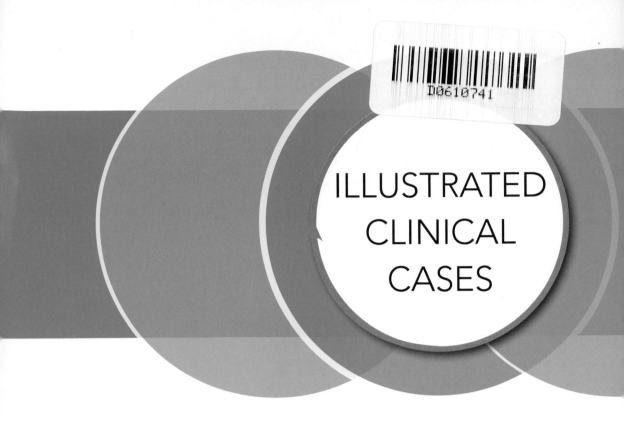

ILLUSTRATED CLINICAL CASES

Diagnosis of Non-accidental Injury

VINCENT J PALUSCI
MD, MS, FAAP
Professor of Pediatrics
New York University School of Medicine
New York, New York, USA

DENA NAZER
MD, FAAP
Assistant Professor of Pediatrics
Wayne State University School of Medicine
Detroit, Michigan, USA

PATRICIA O BRENNAN
FRCP, FFAEM, FRCPCH
Honorary Consultant Paediatrician
Children's Hospital, Western Bank
Sheffield, UK

CRC Press
Taylor & Francis Group
Boca Raton London New York

CRC Press is an imprint of the
Taylor & Francis Group, an **informa** business

CRC Press
Taylor & Francis Group
6000 Broken Sound Parkway NW, Suite 300
Boca Raton, FL 33487-2742

Printed and bound in India by Replika Press Pvt. Ltd.

Printed on acid-free paper
Version Date: 20150824

International Standard Book Number-13: 978-1-4822-3013-0 (Paperback)

Visit the Taylor & Francis Web site at
http://www.taylorandfrancis.com

and the CRC Press Web site at
http://www.crcpress.com

CONTENTS

Preface	xv
Broad Classification of Cases	xvii
Contributors	xix
Image Contributors	xxi

Case 1 1
VINCENT J. PALUSCI

Case 2 3
PATRICIA O. BRENNAN

Case 3 5
DENA NAZER

Case 4 7
VINCENT J. PALUSCI

Case 5 9
MARY LU ANGELILLI WITH ELLA HONG

Case 6 11
DENA NAZER

Case 7 13
PAMELA WALLACE HAMMEL

Case 8 15
CARL J. SCHMIDT

Case 9 17
TOR SHWAYDER

Case 10 19
NICHOLAS BISHOP

Case 11 23
VINCENT J. PALUSCI

Case 12 27
PATRICIA O. BRENNAN

Case 13
CARL J. SCHMIDT
29

Case 14
DENA NAZER
31

Case 15
DENA NAZER
33

Case 16
MARY LU ANGELILLI WITH NATALJA STANSKI
35

Case 17
TOR SHWAYDER
37

Case 18
MARY E. SMYTH
39

Case 19
MARGARET T. McHUGH WITH ANASTASIA FEIFER
AND LORI A. LEGANO
43

Case 20
PATRICIA O. BRENNAN
45

Case 21
VINCENT J. PALUSCI
47

Case 22
CARL J. SCHMIDT
49

Case 23
DENA NAZER
51

Case 24
NICHOLAS BISHOP
53

Case 25
MARY LU ANGELILLI WITH ALI SAALEEM
57

Case 26
TOR SHWAYDER
59

Case 27
PAMELA WALLACE HAMMEL
61

Case 28
VINCENT J. PALUSCI
63

Case 29   65
DENA NAZER

Case 30   69
MARGARET T. McHUGH WITH ANASTASIA FEIFER
AND LORI A. LEGANO

Case 31   71
MARY E. SMYTH

Case 32   73
TOR SHWAYDER

Case 33   75
ALAN SPRIGG

Case 34   77
PATRICIA O. BRENNAN

Case 35   79
DENA NAZER

Case 36   81
PATRICIA O. BRENNAN

Case 37   83
DENA NAZER

Case 38   85
VINCENT J. PALUSCI

Case 39   89
CARL J. SCHMIDT

Case 40   91
MARY LU ANGELILLI WITH JULIE GLEESING

Case 41   93
MARY E. SMYTH

Case 42   95
VINCENT J. PALUSCI

Case 43   97
MARGARET T. McHUGH

Case 44   99
DENA NAZER

Case 45   103
VINCENT J. PALUSCI

Case 46   105
DENA NAZER

Case 47   107
DENA NAZER

Case 48   111
VINCENT J. PALUSCI

Case 49   113
MARGARET T. McHUGH

Case 50   115
MARY E. SMYTH

Case 51   117
PAMELA WALLACE HAMMEL

Case 52   119
ALAN SPRIGG

Case 53   121
PATRICIA O. BRENNAN

Case 54   123
TOR SHWAYDER

Case 55   125
VINCENT J. PALUSCI

Case 56   127
PAMELA WALLACE HAMMEL

Case 57   131
VINCENT J. PALUSCI

Case 58   133
DENA NAZER

Case 59   135
MARY E. SMYTH

Case 60   137
TOR SHWAYDER

Case 61   139
TOR SHWAYDER

Case 62   141
DENA NAZER

Case 63   143
ALAN SPRIGG

Case 64   145
PATRICIA O. BRENNAN

Case 65   147
PATRICIA O. BRENNAN

Case 66   149
TOR SHWAYDER

Case 67   151
VINCENT J. PALUSCI

Case 68   153
CARL J. SCHMIDT

Case 69   155
VINCENT J. PALUSCI

Case 70   159
NICHOLAS BISHOP

Case 71   161
DENA NAZER

Case 72   163
DENA NAZER

Case 73   165
MARGARET T. McHUGH WITH ANASTASIA FEIFER
AND LORI A. LEGANO

Case 74   167
DENA NAZER

Case 75   169
TOR SHWAYDER

Case 76   171
PATRICIA O. BRENNAN

Case 77   173
DENA NAZER

Case 78   175
VINCENT J. PALUSCI

Case 79   177
VINCENT J. PALUSCI

Case 80   179
DENA NAZER

Case 81   181
MARY E. SMYTH

Case 82   183
VINCENT J. PALUSCI

Case 83   187
ALAN SPRIGG

Case 84   189
MARY LU ANGELILLI WITH SARAH HIRSCHBECK

Case 85   191
DENA NAZER

Case 86   193
MARGARET T. McHUGH WITH ANASTASIA FEIFER
AND LORI A. LEGANO

Case 87   195
TOR SHWAYDER

Case 88   197
MARY E. SMYTH

Case 89   199
PAMELA WALLACE HAMMEL WITH KENNETH COHRN

Case 90   203
ALAN SPRIGG

Case 91   205
PATRICIA O. BRENNAN

Case 92   207
CARL J. SCHMIDT

Case 93   209
VINCENT J. PALUSCI

Case 94   211
VINCENT J. PALUSCI

Case 95   213
VINCENT J. PALUSCI

Case 96   215
CARL J. SCHMIDT

Case 97   219
MARY LU ANGELILLI

Case 98   221
PAMELA WALLACE HAMMEL WITH SALWA ATWAN

Case 99   223
ALAN SPRIGG

Case 100   225
PATRICIA O. BRENNAN

Case 101   227
PATRICIA O. BRENNAN

Case 102   229
DENA NAZER

Case 103   233
VINCENT J. PALUSCI

Case 104   235
CARL J. SCHMIDT

Case 105   239
DENA NAZER

Case 106   241
VINCENT J. PALUSCI

Case 107   243
DENA NAZER

Case 108   245
VINCENT J. PALUSCI

Case 109   249
DENA NAZER

Case 110   251
DENA NAZER

Case 111   253
PAMELA WALLACE HAMMEL

Case 112   255
NICHOLAS BISHOP

Case 113   257
PATRICIA O. BRENNAN

Case 114   259
NICHOLAS BISHOP

Case 115   261
MARY E. SMYTH

Case 116   265
MARY LU ANGELILLI WITH PRIYANKA NANJIREDDY AND
AUTUMN ATKINSON

Case 117   267
MARGARET T. McHUGH

Case 118   269
DENA NAZER

Case 119   271
VINCENT J. PALUSCI

Case 120   273
DENA NAZER

Case 121   275
TOR SHWAYDER

Case 122   277
VINCENT J. PALUSCI

Case 123   279
DENA NAZER

Case 124   281
VINCENT J. PALUSCI

Case 125   283
MARGARET T. McHUGH

Case 126   285
MARY E. SMYTH

Case 127   289
CARL J. SCHMIDT

Case 128   291
PATRICIA O. BRENNAN

Case 129   293
MARY E. SMYTH

Case 130   295
MARGARET T. McHUGH, WITH ANASTASIA FEIFER
AND LORI A. LEGANO

Case 131   297
MARGARET T. McHUGH

Case 132   299
VINCENT J. PALUSCI

Case 133   303
VINCENT J. PALUSCI

Case 134   305
VINCENT J. PALUSCI

Case 135   307
CARL J. SCHMIDT

Index   311

PREFACE

Recognition and diagnosis of child abuse and neglect within private and public healthcare systems have become an important foundation for the safety and protection of children throughout the world. Over the past century, physicians and other healthcare providers have increasingly identified the sentinel signs and symptoms which, if properly evaluated, can provide clues to the often hidden injuries of child maltreatment within families and in the community. Failure to properly intervene may lead to disastrous outcomes for the child, the family and society.

This self-assessment book provides a varied collection of cases and images which can be used to test the diagnostic knowledge and skills of medical practitioners acting as primary care providers, emergency responders and consultants in a variety of specialties. It covers a wide spectrum across types of injuries, causes and locations within and on the body to challenge the reader with several common and not-so-common presentations of findings that may result from child abuse and neglect.

Not all the cases in the book are the result of child maltreatment, however. Many may be considered 'look-alikes' or 'mimics' which can arise from underlying medical conditions, other medical causes, or non-abusive trauma. The authors believe it is equally important for the clinician to recognize these given the need to provide treatment based on accurate diagnosis of non-abuse, as well as the potential harm to the family from unneeded investigations by authorities.

This book is designed to simulate clinical scenarios, with a brief clinical history and images followed by questions which focus the reader's attention on the important concepts to be learned. The answers are revealed after a turn of the page, sometimes with additional images to explain critical aspects of the case, diagnosis, 'ruling out' of abuse or neglect or further diagnostic options and treatments which may be helpful. Seminal references are offered for additional reading as needed.

The editors would like to acknowledge the invaluable contributions of those writing the cases and providing the images for educational purposes. We would also like to thank the children and families for teaching us how to help future children and families coming into our care. Steps have been taken to mask identifying information for the cases presented, and the identities of those involved are known only to the contributors or the clinicians caring for the children contained herein.

Vincent J. Palusci
Dena Nazer
Patricia O. Brennan

BROAD CLASSIFICATION OF CASES (CASE NUMBER)

Anal: Crohn's disease 121, 128; dilation 73; fissure 21; laceration 78, 110; rectal prolapse 101; trauma 59; venous distension 133

Bites: adult 84, 107; dog 89; foot 108; foot 27, 79; paediatric 51; spider 81

Blunt trauma: abdomen 72; back 32, 75; automobile 92

Burns: caustic 113, 129; cigarette 53, 60; drip 103; fork 93; with fractures 115; garlic 58; genitals 4; hand 36; immersion 85, 116, 126; iron 55, 67; scalp 5; splash 88; stocking 97; whisker 56

Complementary and alternative medicine: cupping 57; maqua 14; moxibustion 69

Craniofacial: blunt trauma 96; cephalohaematoma 94; drowning 127; ear bruises 74; facial bruises 105; perinatal 132; skull fracture 33, 40, 47; strangulation 8; subdural 90; subgaleal 71; sudden infant death 135

Dermatologic: abdomen 22; bamboo 1; cord marks 18; cutting 82; dermatitis artefacta 76; erythema nodosum 31; fixed drug eruption 54; haemangioma 41; Henoch-Schönlein purpura (HSP) 50; iatrogenic 48; leg bruises 109; loop marks 29, 46; mastocytosis 20; mongolian spot 3, 106, 120; phytophotodermatitis 87; sentinel bruise 16; sibling 62; striae 34; suction mark 37; trichotillomania 9; vitiligo 26, 91

Fractures: femur 77, 80; humerus 99; hypophosphatasia 70; metabolic 38; multiple 10; osteogenesis imperfecta 24, 104; osteopenia 108; prematurity 112; ribs 63; rickets 83, 114; skeletal survey 25; skull 33, 40, 47; spiral fracture 11; tibia 23, 119; ulna 52

Genitourinary: buried penis 45; clitoral hood enlargement 49; hymenal septum 125; hymenal tag 6; hymenal transection 19; labial adhesion 134; labial haemangioma 43; lichen sclerosus 61, 122, 130; normal exam 15; penile injury 123; penile laceration 131; scrotum 68; straddle 30; thin hymenal rim 28; ulcer 95; urethral prolapse 64, 86

Infections: carbuncles 124; herpes 118; human papillomavirus 66; impetigo 117; lice 12; streptococcus 17

Ingestions: heroin 39; lidocaine 13

Neglect: crush injury 100; failure to thrive 102; malnutrition 18

Ocular: black eyes 35; subconjunctival haemorrhages 2, 44; vitreous 65

Oral: caries 98; forced feeding 42; frena 7; palate 111

CONTRIBUTORS

Mary Lu Angelilli
Wayne State University School of
    Medicine
Detroit, Michigan

Autumn Atkinson
Children's Hospital of Michigan
Detroit, Michigan

Salwa Atwan
University of Detroit Mercy School of
    Dentistry
Detroit, Michigan

Nicholas Bishop
Children's Hospital
Western Bank, Sheffield, United Kingdom

Patricia O. Brennan
Children's Hospital
Western Bank, Sheffield, United Kingdom

Kenneth Cohrn
Heritage Dental
Lady Lake, Florida

Anastasia Feifer
Maimonides Medical Center
Brooklyn, New York

Julie Gleesing
Children's Hospital of Michigan
Detroit, Michigan

Pamela Wallace Hammel
Children's Hospital of Michigan
Detroit, Michigan

Sarah Hirschbeck
Children's Hospital of Michigan
Detroit, Michigan

Ella Hong
Wayne State University School of Medicine
Detroit, Michigan

Lori A. Legano
New York University School of Medicine
New York, New York

Margaret T. McHugh
New York University School of Medicine
New York, New York

Priyanka Nanjireddy
Children's Hospital of Michigan
Detroit, Michigan

Dena Nazer
Wayne State University School of Medicine
Detroit, Michigan

Vincent J. Palusci
New York University School of Medicine
New York, New York

Ali Saaleem
Michigan State University School of
    Medicine
East Lansing, Michigan

Carl J. Schmidt
University of Michigan
Ann Arbor, Michigan

Mary E. Smyth
Oakland University William Beaumont
    School of Medicine
Rochester, Michigan

Tor Shwayder
Henry Ford Hospital
Detroit, Michigan

Alan Sprigg
Children's Hospital
Western Bank, Sheffield, United Kingdom

Natalja Stanski
Cincinnati Children's Hospital
Cincinnati, Ohio

IMAGE CONTRIBUTORS (IMAGE NUMBER)

Mary Lu Angelilli: 5a,b; 16; 25a–c; 40; 84; 97; 116a,b

Salwa Atwan: 98

Patricia O. Brennan: 2 (Brennan, Yassa, Ludwig 2001, Fig. 68); 12; 20; 34; 36a (Brennan, Yassa, Ludwig 2001, Fig. 122); 36b; 53 (Brennan, Yassa, Ludwig 2001, Fig. 134); 64 (Brennan, Yassa, Ludwig 2001, Fig. 91); 65 (Brennan, Yassa, Ludwig 2001); 76 (Brennan, Yassa, Ludwig 2001, Fig. 130); 91; 100 (Brennan, Yassa, Ludwig 2001, Fig. 93); 101 (Brennan, Yassa, Ludwig 2001, Fig. 170); 113 (Brennan, Yassa, Ludwig 2001); 128 (Brennan, Yassa, Ludwig 2001, Fig. 30)

Kenneth Cohrn: 89a–d

Pamela Wallace Hammel: 7; 27a (Palusci & Fischer 2010, Fig. 393); 27b (Palusci & Fischer 2010, Fig. 403); 51a,b; 56a–e; 111a,b

Aparna Joshi: 24a (Palusci & Fischer 2010, Fig. 287); 24b (Palusci & Fischer 2010, Fig. 288); 24c (Palusci & Fischer 2010, Fig. 289); 114a Palusci & Fischer 2010, Fig. 283); 114b (Palusci & Fischer 2010, Fig. 284)

Margaret T. McHugh: 19; 30; 43a–c; 49a,b; 73 (Palusci & Fischer 2010, Fig. 479); 86 (Palusci & Fischer 2010, Fig. 457); 117; 125a,b; 130a,b; 131a,b

Dena Nazer: 3; 6a,b; 14a–c (Palusci & Fischer 2010, Figs. 245–247); 15a,b; 23a–d; 29a–d; 35a,b; 37; 44a–c; 46a,b; 47a–d; 58 (Palusci & Fischer 2010, Fig. 248); 71a–c; 72; 74a–c; 77a,b; 80a,b; 85a–d; 102a–e; 105a–d; 107a,b; 109a–d; 110a–d; 118a,b; 120a–c; 123

Vincent J. Palusci: 1a,b; 4a,b; 11a–f; 21; 28 (Palusci & Fischer 2010, Fig. 464); 38a–e; 42; 45a (Palusci & Fischer 2010, Fig. 442); 45b (Palusci & Fischer 2010, Fig. 443); 48; 55a–c; 57a,b; 67a,b; 69a–g; 78a (Palusci & Fischer 2010, Fig. 491); 78b (Palusci & Fischer 2010, Fig. 490); 79a,b; 82a,b; 93a–d; 94a,b; 95 (Palusci & Fischer 2010, Fig. 478); 103; 106; 108a–d; 119a,b; 122; 124a–c; 132a–d; 133 (Palusci & Fischer 2010, Fig. 448); 134a,b

Carl J. Schmidt: 8a,b; 22a,b; 39a,b; 68a,b; 92a,b; 96a–c; 104a–c; 113; 127a,b; 135a,b

Tor Shwayder: 9a,b; 17; 26a,b; 32a,b; 54a,b; 60; 61; 66; 75; 87; 121

Mary E. Smyth: 18a–e; 31; 41 (Palusci & Fischer 2010, Fig. 207); 50a–d; 59; 81 (Palusci & Fischer 2010, Fig. 243); 88a,b; 115a–d; 126a–d; 129

Alan Sprigg: 33; 52; 63; 83; 90; 99

REFERENCES

Palusci V, Fischer H. *Child Abuse & Neglect: A Diagnostic Guide for Physicians, Surgeons, Pathologists, Dentists, Nurses and Social Workers.* 2010. Boca Raton FL: CRC Press.

Brennan PO, Yassa JG, Ludwig S. *Paediatric Emergency Medicine: Self-Assessment Colour Review.* 2001. Boca Raton FL: CRC Press.

CASE 1

Vincent J. Palusci

This Asian 6-year-old boy was removed from his mother's care when police were called to his house by the neighbours. They reported hearing him screaming and saw his mother running after him with 'a stick'. He was brought to the emergency room where lesions were found on his body (Image 1a). There was no medical history available from the child or protective services worker. He refused to disclose what happened. His mother was taken into police custody, where she said that she was punishing him for poor marks on his first-grade report card. She reported that she and her child recently emigrated from China and she believed in physical discipline, having used this several times before to modify his bad behaviour. She reported that he has no chronic diseases, did not bleed easily and did not take any medication. She also denied using any home remedies or other alternative treatments at home.

    i. What does the image show?
   ii. Does the reported physical discipline explain the lesions?
  iii. Are there cultural factors present that would modify your assessment about whether this child was abused?

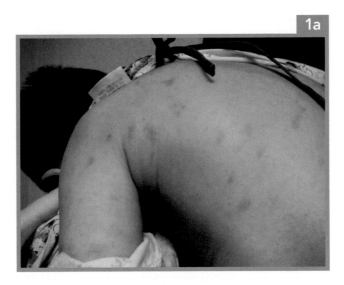

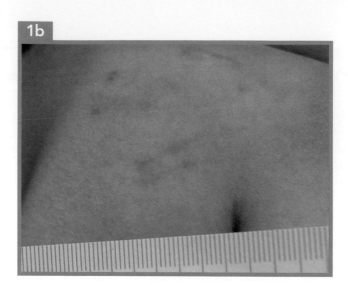

1b

   i. There are multiple marks of varying colour depicted over his back. Most are irregularly shaped bruises with red and yellow colour and some have thin eschar suggesting healing abrasion or laceration. While the image is limited, it does not appear that the child is malnourished or has other chronic skin conditions or scars. The remainder of the examination is normal.

  ii. The marks as initially depicted are difficult to characterize as to cause. An object such as a stick is possible. Further information is obtained from closer inspection of one of the lesions (Image 1b). This shows two lines evenly spaced with some erythema. The police also bring you the 'stick' which was being used which appears to be a stalk of bamboo with similar diameter. This led you to conclude that the reported discipline was consistent with the lesions.

 iii. Different laws and regulations in different jurisdictions govern the legal interpretation of responsibility when injuries arise from physical discipline, also called corporal punishment. As guidance for the medical assessment, the American Academy of Pediatrics (AAP) has noted that corporal punishment is of limited effectiveness and has potentially deleterious side effects.[1] The AAP recommends that parents be encouraged and assisted in the development of methods other than spanking for managing undesired behaviour in children. Using time-out, removal of privileges and punishment are common discipline approaches that have been associated with reducing undesired behaviour. These different strategies, sometimes confusingly called 'punishment', are effective if applied appropriately to specific behaviours. In this case, the mother reported that bamboo is often used for this purpose among people from her culture and that she had not learned about other techniques. To the extent that these lesions were inflicted upon the child, they constitute physical abuse. However, any treatment or remediation plan should take these cultural influences into account.

1. American Academy of Pediatrics Committee on Psychosocial Aspects of Child and Family Health. Guidance for effective discipline. *Pediatrics*. 1998;101(4 Pt 1):723–728.

CASE 2

Patricia O. Brennan

This 3-year-old child was brought to the emergency department in the middle of the night by her grandmother. She said the girl was fine when she went to bed. She heard the child coughing in the night and when she checked her, the girl looked like this (Image 2).

    i. What signs do you notice?
   ii. What history would you take?
  iii. What is the differential diagnosis?

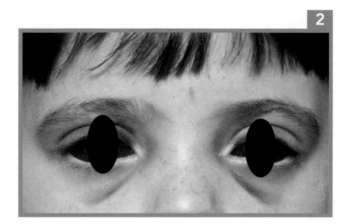

i. The girl has bilateral subconjunctival haemorrhages with ecchymoses of the upper and lower eyelids and a slight degree of congestion and oedema of the orbit. She also has fine petechiae of the face.

  ii. The doctor needs to take a full medical history, in particular asking details of the nature of the cough. A social history should also be taken and health and social care records checked for previous safeguarding concerns.

iii. Child abuse has been recognized as a cause of subconjunctival haemorrhage. Cases with non-accidental intracranial injury and fractures have presented with a single small unilateral haemorrhage when further investigations such as brain imaging and skeletal survey are done. Other causes of subconjunctival haemorrhage include blood dyscrasias and coagulopathies, malignancies such as metastatic neuroblastoma or rhabdomyosarcoma and leukaemia, conjunctivitis and traumatic asphyxia from severe chest compression. Bouts of violent coughing in pertussis, as in this case, were well recognized as a cause of severe subconjunctival haemorrhages when the infection was more common. However, the presence of pertussis does not rule out non-accidental injury, so appropriate assessments should still be undertaken in suspicious cases.[1–3]

1. Lowe L, Rapini RP, Johnson TM. Traumatic asphyxia. *J Am Acad Dermatol.* 1990;23(5 Pt 2):972–974.
2. Paysse EA, Coats DK. Bilateral eyelid ecchymosis and subconjunctival hemorrhage associated with coughing paroxysms in pertussis infection. *J Aapos.* 1998;2(2):116–119.
3. Spitzer SG, Luorno J, Noel LP. Isolated subconjunctival hemorrhages in nonaccidental trauma. *J Aapos.* 2005;9(1):53–56.

CASE 3

Dena Nazer

Child Protective Services referred this 9-month-old baby girl to the emergency department. She started at a new daycare that morning, and they were concerned about multiple bruises on her back. She has been previously healthy and is asymptomatic. Image 3 shows her back and buttocks. The remainder of her examination was normal.

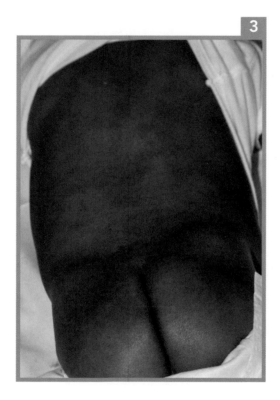

i. What is your diagnosis?

This child has dermal melanosis (commonly called Mongolian spots) on her back and buttocks. They were thought to be bruises inflicted by her daycare provider. Dermal melanosis refers to congenital hyperpigmented lesions more commonly seen in black, Asian, Latino and Native American infants but can occur in any infant. In most cases, lesions are located on the buttocks, lumbosacral region, back and shoulders as in this infant.[1] The spots have variable sizes, shapes and colour but are typically blue-grey or blue-green patches with irregular borders and, thus may be confused with bruises.[1] In this infant, they were documented at birth on her delivery records and her mother stated she had these since birth. Mongolian spots may be confused for bruises, especially when on unusual locations or when seen by a new caregiver. Unlike bruises, they do not change and fade colour over weeks. They are also non-tender.[2] It is very helpful to ask the parents about the presence of these marks since birth and to obtain birth records for documentation. They need to be documented in newborns and children to alleviate future confusion with bruises should physical abuse be suspected.

1. AlJasser M, Al-Khenaizan S. Cutaneous mimickers of child abuse: A primer for pediatricians. *Eur J Pediatr.* 2008;167(11):1221–1230.
2. Gupta D, Thappa DM. Mongolian spots: How important are they? *World J Clin Cases.* 2013; 1(8):230–232.

CASE 4

Vincent J. Palusci

A 9-year-old boy disclosed to a friend at his school that his mother had burned him 'on the pee pee'. The teacher was notified and the boy confirmed that this had occurred a week before with a hot iron used to press clothes. Social services were notified and he was brought to the emergency room, where his penis demonstrated these findings (Image 4a).

    i. What does the image show?
   ii. Is a pattern visible?
  iii. Can you estimate when the injury occurred?

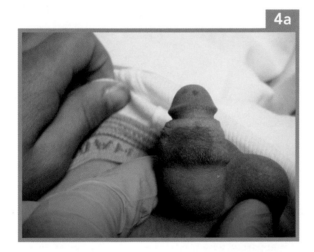
4a

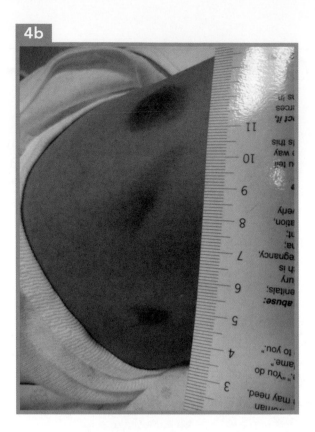

i. Image 4a shows a prepubertal circumcised penis with erythema and hyperpigmentation. There are also nevi present on the glans. No lesions are visible on the scrotum or more proximal shaft.

ii. There is a rectangular area on the dorsal shaft which extends to the foreskin, which would usually have a different colouring than the shaft. The area is homogeneous and no other particular pattern is apparent which would suggest the tip of an iron or steam holes. The bottom of a hot iron, if flat, could contact with the cylindrical shaft of the penis in such a way as to cause a rectangular lesion as shown. The findings on the penis are consistent with burns from an iron as described by the child.

iii. Given the presence of pigmentary change, some time has passed since the injury occurred. The presence of erythema can suggest more recent injury but can also be associated with irritation and hygiene. Additional information can be obtained from lesions identified on the thigh during examination, which were initially not disclosed (Image 4b). This shows three patterned, hyperpigmented marks which could represent other parts of the hot iron. The child disclosed that this had occurred at the same time and in the same manner as did the penis injury. These injuries have been described as patterns from physical abuse.[1]

1. Maguire S, Okolie C, Kemp AM. Burns as a consequence of child maltreatment. *Paediatr Child Health*. 2014;24(12):557–561.

CASE 5

Mary Lu Angelilli with Ella Hong

A 16-month-old boy was brought unresponsive to the hospital. His mother reported that soon after she put him to sleep, she found him 'stiff as a board' and unable to be awakened. Later, the mother added that the child fell from a single step and injured his head. The mother also stated that 2 days prior to admission, she was in the bathtub with the child when he accidentally turned on the hot water and burned his face. She did not seek medical care at that time.

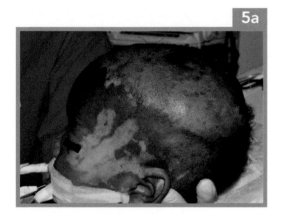

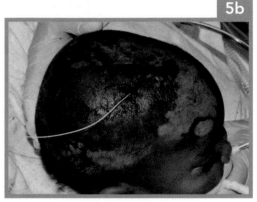

   i. What do the images show?

  ii. What tests and imaging are important to further evaluate the aetiology of this injury?

i. This child has an 8% burn on his scalp with a finger-like pattern on the left side of his face (Image 5a). The burn is well demarcated over his forehead and the top of his head as shown in Image 5b. This pattern is compatible with a head–first, scalp–down sink immersion burn.[1] The handprint on the left side of the face matched the baby's hand.

ii. Given the likelihood of inflicted trauma, full imaging of the axial skeleton using a skeletal survey was indicated as well as head imaging especially considering his neurologic status. His skeletal survey showed a proximal humeral fracture with no explanation. His head MRI scan showed subdural haemorrhages and hypoxic–ischaemic brain injury. His funduscopic exam showed retinal haemorrhages. This child succumbed to his head injuries. It is important to evaluate patients with suspected abuse for other types of abuse as there may be many different kinds of abusive injuries in the same patient.

1. Daria S, Sugar NF, Feldman KW, Boos SC, Benton SA, Ornstein A. Into hot water head first: Distribution of intentional and unintentional immersion burns. *Pediatr Emerg Care*. 2004;20(5): 302–310.

CASE 6

Dena Nazer

A 6-year-old girl had been referred to the children's advocacy centre for a complete medical evaluation for suspected sexual abuse. She disclosed that her mother's boyfriend put his 'private parts' into her private parts. The last time the mother's boyfriend was at their home was 4 months ago. She was initially seen by her paediatrician who described her hymen as 'not normal'. Examination reveals the finding seen (Image 6a).

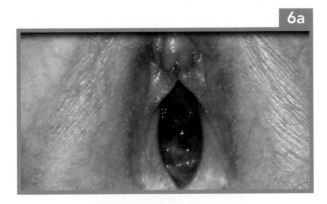

6a

i. What are the genital finding?
ii. Would this finding be consistent with her disclosure of sexual abuse?

i. Erythema and urethral dilation are seen. Examination as shown in the photo revealed otherwise normal labia majora, labia minora, clitoral hood and urethra. A persistent septal remnant was suspected at 6 o'clock. To further assess this, the labia were gently separated, revealing that the suspected septum was a hymenal tag (Image 6b). In prepubertal girls, the hymen is sensitive to touch, thus different exam techniques are used to confirm findings. Labial separation and labial traction may be used in the supine position. Examination in the prone knee-chest position may be done as well. In menarchal females, the estrogenized hymenal tissues are less sensitive and a Q-tip or swab may be used to demonstrate the septum to confirm the findings. In the presence of a septum, it is important to differentiate the finding from a vaginal duplication, which will require additional intervention.

ii. A hymenal tag is considered a normal finding and may be present in normal female newborns.[1,2] Tags are commonly located in the superior and inferior positions and tend to resolve spontaneously. New hymenal tags may appear postnatally as a result of extension of an intravaginal or external hymenal ridge. This examination is consistent with the child's disclosure of sexual abuse. This may be due to either the sexual abuse not causing any injuries or the initial injury healing at the point of examination especially in this child where sexual abuse last occurred 4 months prior to her examination.

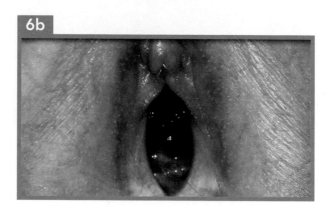

6b

1. Berenson AB, Grady JJ. A longitudinal study of hymenal development from 3 to 9 years of age. *J Pediatr.* 2002;140(5):600–607.
2. Heger AH, Ticson L, Guerra L et al. Appearance of the genitalia in girls selected for nonabuse: Review of hymenal morphology and nonspecific findings. *J Pediatr Adolesc Gynecol.* 2002;15(1):27–35.

CASE 7

Pamela Wallace Hammel

This oral injury was found on a post-mortem examination of a child subjected to long-term, severe abuse. The injury was not visible without lifting the child's upper lip (Image 7). Additionally, there were patterned lesions over the buttocks and legs which the parent explained occurred when they disciplined him by spanking him with a stick. There was concern that the child succumbed to intracranial injury. An autopsy determined the cause of death was drowning; the parents held the child under a water faucet with massive brain swelling due to abusive head trauma.

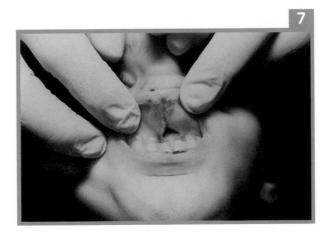

i. What does the image show?
ii. What are the potential causes of this injury? How does this affect this case?

i. Histologically, granulation tissue was present in this wound of the frenum, indicating an injury previous to the fatal assault. Note the imprint of the facial surface of the anterior teeth on the mucosa of the upper lip, indicating excessive pressure from a hand or gag to the child's mouth.

ii. Frena injuries, while thought to pathognomonically represent forced feeding or abuse injuries in young infants, have been identified as having additional non-abusive causes. They have been found in fatal abuse cases, particularly for children under 5 years of age and a direct blow to the face has been substantiated as a mechanism of injury.[1] In non-fatal cases, accidental falls of mobile children can result in more superficial tears and injuries. In isolation, a superficially torn frenum does not prove a diagnosis of physical abuse. In this case, however, the frenal injury is deep and severe and is only part of a constellation of physical findings indicating fatal abuse.

1. Maguire S, Hunter B, Hunter L, Sibert JR, Mann M, Kemp AM. Diagnosing abuse: A systematic review of torn frenum and other intra-oral injuries. *Arch Dis Child.* 2007;92(12):1113–1117.

CASE 8

Carl J. Schmidt

This 4-month-old boy was found unresponsive in a car seat. The parent rushed him to the emergency room where immediate resuscitation was attempted. When questioned, the parent was unsure of when she had last seen the child alive but was sure he was awake and alert when placed in the car seat. When asked to describe how she had fastened the straps, she said that they were twisted in the same way that they were found when the child was removed from the car seat. She found it difficult to adjust the straps, so twisting them allowed for a tighter fit. She also claimed the child was normally 'fussy' and moved a lot when placed in the car seat. It became apparent after questioning the parent that the car seat was used within the home as a place for the child to sleep instead of a crib. The car seat was obtained from another family member and the parent had not been given formal instruction in its use. Written instructions were also not given to the parent along with the car seat. Image 8a is a reenactment showing how the child was found. Image 8b shows the imprint of the car seat strap along the anterior surface of the neck.

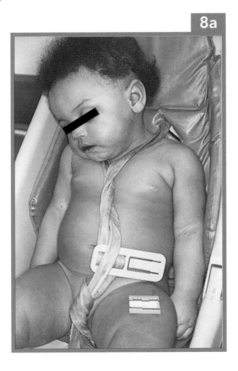
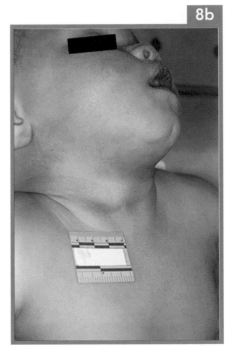

i. What else would you ask the caretaker?
ii. You find out the mother is pregnant and there are other children in the home. What else would you do?

i. This child was in the car seat a sufficiently long time for the pressure of the strap to cause an imprint on the child's neck. This imprint indicates subcutaneous haemorrhage. You would like to know where the car seat was being used — at home or in the car — when the child was placed in it. An important fact to establish is how long the child was in the car seat before he became unresponsive. This helps to address the problem of negligence. If the infant was in the car seat a short time before he became unresponsive, it is less likely that negligence is involved. If the child was in the car seat for a long time before someone noticed he was unresponsive, then it is much more likely that negligence was involved.[1] Another factor to consider is whether padding and attachments to prevent twisting of the car seat straps may have been available but were not used because the parent was unaware they were important, or had been discarded because the parent found it easier not to use them.

ii. In cases like these, the physician must attempt to find out as much as possible because, although product liability may also be a significant causal factor in this infant's death, neglect by leaving a child unattended in a car seat means that Child Protective Services may also have to intervene and investigate the condition of other children in the family.[2] This mother is pregnant and had this incident not occurred, it is likely she would have used the same car seat for the next infant. You also need to find out what kind of education was given to the parent regarding the use of car seats when discharged from the hospital after this infant's birth. Although economic circumstances may be difficult, infant car seat design has continued to evolve and car seats are now much safer, and the most modern car seat available should be the one used. Some are even provided free of charge to new parents when their newborn leaves the hospital. The transfer of car seats from friends and family, regardless of good intentions, may mean that outdated equipment, perhaps even those that have been subject to recall by the manufacturer, may be used, placing subsequent infants at risk.

1. Spitz WU, Spitz DJ, Fisher RS. *Spitz and Fisher's Medicolegal Investigation of Death: Guidelines for the Application of Pathology to Crime Investigation.* 4th ed. Springfield, IL: Charles C. Thomas; 2006.
2. Pasquale-Styles MA, Tackitt PL, Schmidt CJ. Infant death scene investigation and the assessment of potential risk factors for asphyxia: A review of 209 sudden unexpected infant deaths. *J Forensic Sci.* 2007;52(4):924–929.

CASE 9

Tor Shwayder

This 6-year-old girl presented with an area of decreased hair length in the middle of her scalp. It was a square-shaped area with hairs of various lengths but none greater than a few centimetres long, as shown in Image 9a. Her scalp underlying that area was normal with no pustules, scales, bald spots or tender areas. Her remaining hair reached below her collar line in length and appeared healthy. On further exam, her upper eyelashes looked 'gone'. Under magnification, lashes that measured 1–2 mm in length were seen remaining at the orifice of each follicle.

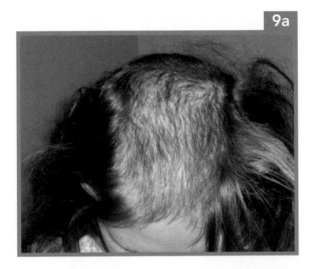

9a

   i. What is the diagnosis?
  ii. What are the key clinical features that assist you in making this diagnosis?
 iii. Can blood or skin biopsies support the diagnosis?
  iv. What is the treatment?

i. This child suffers from trichotillomania. Trichotillomania is an impulse disorder characterized by the manual pulling, plucking, twirling or twisting of the hair causing breakage and shortening of the hair from the scalp and/or other sites.[1] It can be done consciously or unconsciously. Most of these children deny they are pulling their hair either because they are defensive or because the action is done subconsciously. It is important to consider child abuse and abusive hair pulling as a cause of localized hair loss in children especially if a mechanical alopecia – trichotillomania or traction alopecia – is being considered.[2]

ii. The key clinical feature is that the hairs are of various lengths in the area but none are longer than a few centimetres. This is because there needs to be a given length of hair that the patients can physically grasp with their fingers or fingernails. Hair shorter than a few centimetres cannot be pulled or removed. In addition, the area involved is almost always irregular in shape (e.g. rectangular or star shaped) and usually on the side of the dominant hand (e.g. more on the right side of the scalp than the left). Careful examination is important as it may involve less visible areas of the scalp, as shown in Image 9b.

iii. There are no blood tests, but a skin biopsy of the scalp can show fractured hairs within the hair shaft which is quite indicative. Also there are neither 'exclamation point hairs' nor 'black dot hairs' as seen in alopecia areata and tinea capitis, respectively. The scalp always has some hair and is never completely bald. There are no red pustules, scars or dyschromia.

iv. Young children have a good prognosis. However, the prognosis is more guarded in older children, adolescents and adults. Sometimes just gently suggesting where the behaviour is coming from and offering some simple distracting actions to keep the hands busy may be of benefit. Behaviour modification and help from a trained psychiatric professional are often needed.

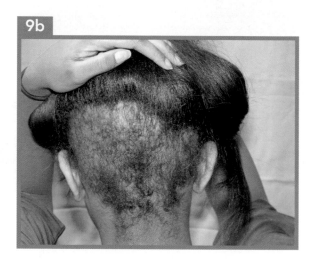

9b

1. Walsh KH, McDougle CJ. Trichotillomania. Presentation, etiology, diagnosis and therapy. *Am J Clin Dermatol.* 2001;2(5):327–333.
2. Saraswat A. Child abuse and trichotillomania. *BMJ.* 2005;330(7482):83–84.

CASE 10

Nicholas Bishop

A 1-month-old boy presented to the emergency department. His parents said he was not moving his left leg. This was confirmed on clinical examination, which also showed that he had blue sclerae. His clinical examination was otherwise essentially normal although he disliked being lifted up. A skeletal survey showed multiple fractures, including rib fractures and bilateral clavicle fractures. There was no evidence of altered bone shape or texture; the vertebrae looked normal. The skull x-ray showed small (<0.5 cm diameter) wormian bones. While there was no reported family history of bone disease, his parents insisted that he must have osteogenesis imperfecta because he had blue sclerae.

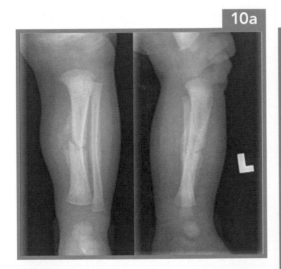

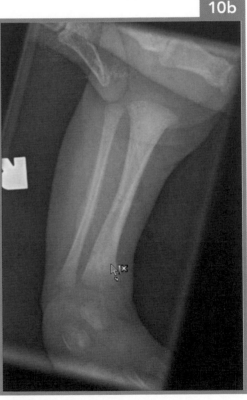

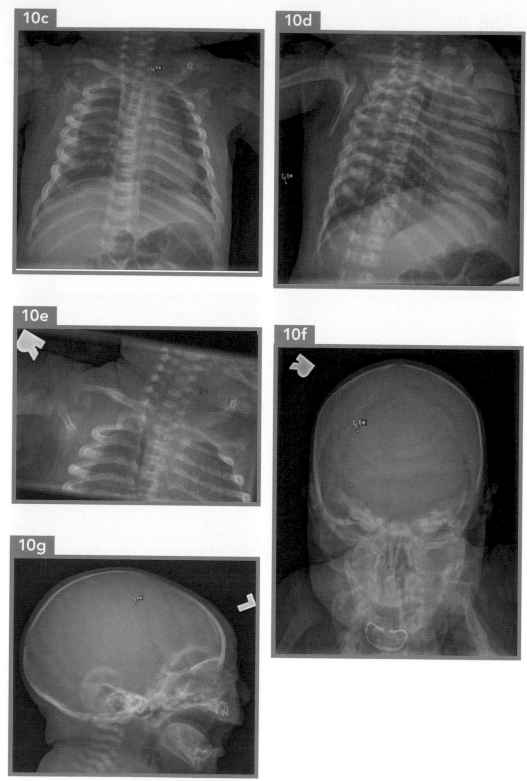

i. What is the aetiology of this patient's multiple fractures?

i. The types of fractures on this infant's skeletal survey are consistent with non–accidental injury rather than with bone disease. The left leg fracture is healing (Image 10a) and there are additional changes on the right side concerning for fractures (Image 10b). There are several rib fractures (Images 10c and 10d), which are vanishingly rare in osteogenesis imperfecta (OI) presenting at this age.[1] This number of fractures with an underlying diagnosis of OI would mean that the OI was severe in which case vertebral changes should also be expected. Clavicle fractures are possible in OI but are likely related to birth (Image 10e). Blue sclerae are perfectly normal up to age 6 months; Wormian bones (Images 10f and 10g) are commonly seen and of no significance. In view of the number, type and sites of fractures, the clinical signs in this case make non–accidental injury highly likely. While an extensive workup for underlying bone disease is indicated (including testing for OI), steps should be taken to report this case to Child Protective Services and to ensure the child's safety pending further medical investigation.[2]

1. Greeley CS, Donaruma-Kwoh M, Vettimattam M, Lobo C, Williard C, Mazur L. Fractures at diagnosis in infants and children with osteogenesis imperfecta. *J Pediatr Orthop*. 2013;33(1):32–36.
2. Flaherty EG, Perez-Rossello JM, Levine MA, Hennrikus WL. Evaluating children with fractures for child physical abuse. *Pediatrics*. 2014;133(2):e477–e489.

CASE 11

Vincent J. Palusci

You were asked to review x-rays for a 4-month-old girl who had a healing fracture of her right femur (Images 11a and 11b). She was wearing a Pavlik harness. The infant was brought to the emergency room 3 weeks ago on the day after she reportedly fell sideways from a 'futon'. She was unable to sit without support but was able to roll. Her mother had placed her down briefly to answer her cell phone. Her mother had turned away to answer the phone and she heard the infant hit the carpeted floor and begin to cry. She picked her up and she stopped crying. She did not notice any injury. She fed her a bottle of her regular formula, placed her in her bed, and she fell asleep. She slept well overnight, and the next day she was 'cranky' and had trouble feeding. Her mother later brought her to the emergency department when she noticed that her leg appeared swollen. A report to Child Protective Services had not been made.

    i. What do the images show?
    ii. What evaluation should be done to assess a differential diagnosis?
   iii. How do you assess whether this injury is abuse or accidental?

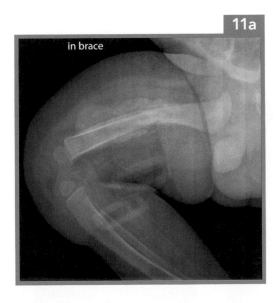

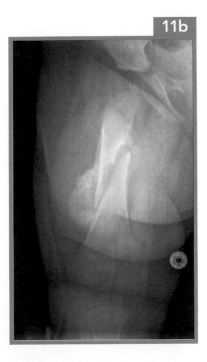

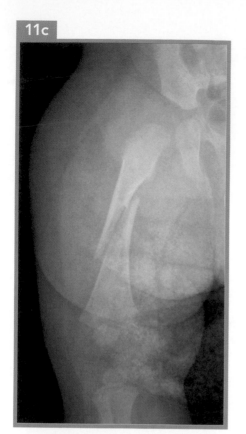

11c

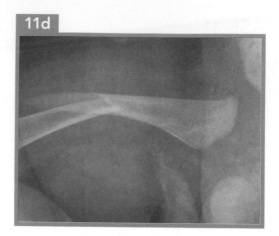

11d

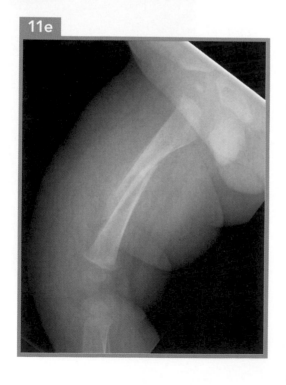

11e

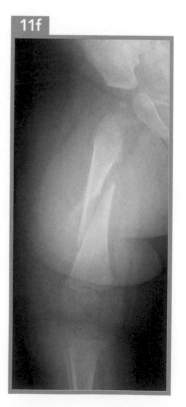

11f

i. Images 11a and 11b show a healing, complete fracture of the right femur diaphysis, with marked periosteal reaction, periosteal new bone formation, exophytic callus, blurring of the fragment edges and callus joining the bone fragments. This type of healing occurs more frequently when the leg is kept in a harness rather than immobilized in a cast.

ii. Prior x-rays should have been reviewed to understand the initial injury pattern and subsequent healing. Compared with prior images, the fracture has stable medial displacement and mild anteromedial angulation of the fracture fragments with significant increase in periosteal reaction and callus formation along the fracture plane. The initial x-rays demonstrate an acute spiral oblique fracture pattern with no evidence of healing (Images 11c and 11d). One week later, early periosteal new-bone formation and early callus formation are visible (Images 11e and 11f). Given the possibility of inflicted trauma in this presentation, initial and follow-up full imaging of the axial skeleton using a skeletal survey are indicated to identify additional fractures or bone disease.[1] Serum chemistries for calcium, phosphate, alkaline phosphatase, vitamin D and parathyroid hormone levels can help identify and categorize metabolic bone disease.

iii. To understand the mechanism of injury, you need additional information about the height of the futon, the surface the child landed on, how the child fell and the position she landed in. Did she land on her knee? Why did her mother wait to seek medical care given the complete fracture? Were other adults present when the reported accident occurred? Is there any family history of bone disease or dysplasia? These questions will require additional information from the mother, scene investigation, and involvement of Child Protective Services and possibly law enforcement.

1. Flaherty EG, Perez-Rossello JM, Levine MA, Hennrikus WL. Evaluating children with fractures for child physical abuse. *Pediatrics*. 2014;133(2):e477–e489.

CASE 12

Patricia O. Brennan

A 21-month-old girl was brought by ambulance to the emergency department in a collapsed state. She was very pale. Her pulse was 120 bpm and she was apyrexial. It was noted that she was unkempt. She had an infestation of head lice with matted hair (Image 12) and an excoriated scalp and an eczematous rash around her hairline at the nape of her neck and down her back between her shoulder blades. Investigations revealed haemoglobin of 2.9 g/dL with an iron deficiency picture. There were no other significant abnormalities on examination or investigation. She and her 4-year-old sister were primarily looked after by their father as their mother worked full time.

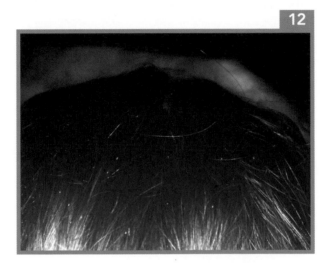

i. What are the possible causes of her profound anaemia?
ii. How would you manage the case?

i. Iron deficiency is a well-recognized cause of childhood anaemia. It can be due to blood loss, especially from the gut, but in early childhood, nutritional causes are more common, especially between the ages of 1 and 3 years. Around these ages, iron-fortified infant formulae and cereals are replaced by cow's milk and family foods. Often cow's milk intake is excessive at over 2 pints per day.

   In addition, this child had a prolonged infestation of untreated head lice. These feed on the blood of their host. Although each individual louse ingests only a minute amount of blood each day, the accumulated effect in a patient with iron deficient anaemia can be particularly profound, was true for this patient.[1,2]

ii. The patient was given a blood transfusion and then treated for the head lice infestation, a particularly difficult task due to the matted hair and excoriated scalp. She was also started on a balanced diet with iron supplements. The child's parents knew that she had head lice and failed to treat them and had also failed to give her a balanced diet rich in iron. A child protection investigation was initiated into the neglect of the child and her sister and they were placed together in foster care. Their parents accepted instruction into appropriate parenting and with support and supervision regained the care of their daughters.

1. Guss DA, Koenig M, Castillo EM. Severe iron deficiency anemia and lice infestation. *J Emerg Med.* 2011;41(4):362–365.
2. Speare R, Canyon DV, Melrose W. Quantification of blood intake of the head louse: Pediculus humanus capitis. *Int J Dermatol.* 2006;45(5):543–546.

CASE 13

Carl J. Schmidt

This was a 13-month-old child who was brought to the emergency room unconscious and with seizures. Despite resuscitative efforts, this girl died within a few hours of admission. Height and weight were within the expected values for her age. Interviews with family disclosed that this was a child who was otherwise thriving until the moment she became unresponsive. The only complaint was significant discomfort due to eruption of teeth, for which medication was prescribed.

Blood testing done in the hospital did not show any significant abnormalities. The autopsy disclosed no abnormalities. The image is that of a normal female toddler. Post-mortem toxicology results were normal for sodium and chlorine, but positive for lorazepam (51 ng/mL), naloxone, lidocaine/lignocaine (6.4 mcg/mL) and monoethylglycinexylidide, MEGX (4.1 mcg/mL). Examination of the child was unremarkable (Image 13).

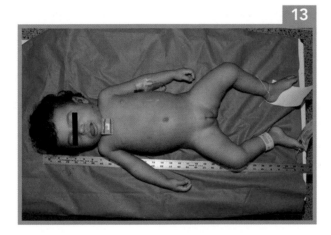

i. What is significant about the toxicology results?
ii. What is the source of the lidocaine?
iii. What are the cause and manner of death? What is the mechanism of death?
iv. What else may be inferred from this case?

i. The lidocaine is significantly elevated, as is MEGX, an active metabolite of lidocaine. The combined concentrations of both of these compounds place the lidocaine well within the range for toxicity, even after accounting for post-mortem redistribution. The initial presentation was that of seizures and loss of consciousness, and lidocaine was not used in resuscitation of this child.

ii. There was a prescription for 2% lidocaine solution in the home and the bottle was almost empty. Topical lidocaine was prescribed by the primary care provider to be placed on the gingivae to treat the pain of teething. The toddler was left with a teenage babysitter one afternoon who misunderstood the instruction for the application of the lidocaine and she administered it much more frequently than originally indicated. The child was unconscious for a short time before the seizures, but it was interpreted as napping, even though the child was not aroused when stimulated.

iii. The cause of death is acute lidocaine intoxication. The manner of death was determined to be accident, and it became clear that the excess administration of lidocaine was the result of linguistic and cultural impediments to understanding the instructions.[1] The babysitter also had no experience in taking care of children. Although the pathophysiologic reasons are not well understood, lidocaine can induce seizures and hypotension at high concentrations.[2]

iv. It is dangerous to leave children unattended with inexperienced caretakers, especially when they have to administer potentially hazardous medication. There is often the misconception that topical applications are harmless. The lidocaine was prescribed by a primary care provider who also did not anticipate the hazards of these kinds of drugs on small children.

1. Levine B. *Principles of Forensic Toxicology*. 3rd ed. Washington, DC: American Association for Clinical Chemistry; 2010.
2. Balit CR, Lynch AM, Gilmore SP, Murray L, Isbister GK. Lignocaine and chlorhexidine toxicity in children resulting from mouth paint ingestion: A bottling problem. *J Paediatr Child Health*. 2006;42(6):350–353.

CASE 14

Dena Nazer

A 10-year-old boy is referred to the gastroenterology clinic due to poor appetite and poor weight gain. In addition to failure to thrive, his physical examination reveals an almost circumferential hyperpigmented mark around his neck as shown in Image 14a. He states his father had a family friend 'burn' him due to his poor appetite.

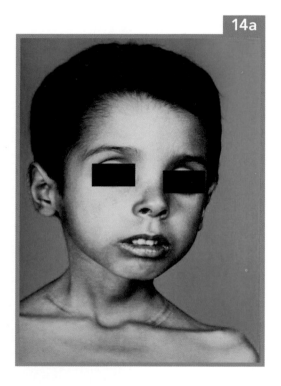

14a

i. What is your diagnosis?
ii. How would you further approach this case?

i. The diagnosis is maqua, which is a therapeutic burn. Maquas are small deep burns inflicted to the skin near diseased organs as part of a therapeutic process.[1] They are most often seen in the Arabic culture. A hot piece of metal or coal is usually used at the area of pain or illness.[2] In this case, the child had a poor appetite so the metal rod was heated and placed around his neck as it was thought to be the part of the body related to appetite. When further evaluated, this child was diagnosed with celiac disease. Maquas are also seen in cases of abdominal distention and recurrent abdominal pain where a hot rod is applied to the abdomen (Images 14b and 14c).

ii. Maquas are not intentionally abusive; however, caregivers should be respectfully discouraged from using them. They are painful and may cause complications. They may also result in delay in seeking medical care and delay in proper diagnosis of diseases such as celiac disease in this child.

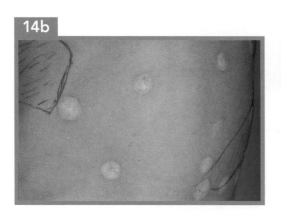

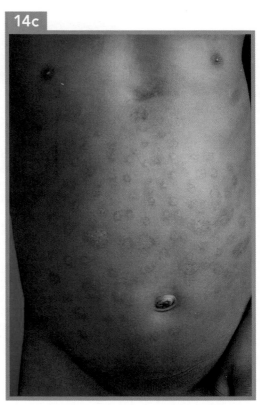

1. Rosenberg L, Sagi A, Stahl N, Greber B, Ben-Meir P. Maqua (therapeutic burn) as an indicator of underlying disease. *Plast Reconstr Surg.* 1988;82(2):277–280.
2. Nazer D, Smyth M. Cutaneous conditions mimicking child abuse. In: Palusci VJ, Fischer H, eds. *Child Abuse and Neglect: A Diagnostic Guide for Physicians, Surgeons, Pathologists, Dentists, Nurses and Social Workers.* London, England: Manson; 2011:69–90.

CASE 15

Dena Nazer

A 6-year-old girl was brought to your paediatric office for a medical evaluation for suspected sexual abuse. She disclosed her father put his 'private parts' in her private parts and 'bottom'. She disclosed it happened over 20 times. The last time it happened was 5 months ago. Her anogenital examination is shown (Images 15a and 15b).

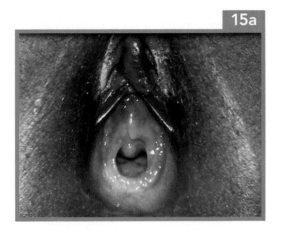

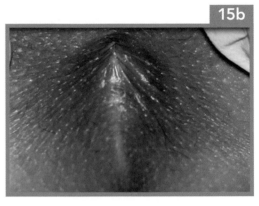

  i. What do the images depict?
 ii. Are the images consistent with her disclosure of sexual abuse? How would you explain that?

i. Children who disclose sexual abuse need a full multidisciplinary evaluation, which includes a medical examination. This child had an examination that showed normal labia majora, labia minora, urethra and clitoral hood. Her hymen was crescentic in shape with no transections or signs of trauma. She had no genital bleeding or discharge. Her anus showed normal tone, rugae and symmetry. She had no warts, fissures or lacerations. Her exam showed no signs of acute or chronic trauma. Due to her disclosure of penetration, she was tested for sexually transmitted infections; none were found.

ii. Her examination showed no signs of acute or chronic trauma and was normal. It was consistent with her disclosure of penetration. Most children who disclose sexual abuse have a normal examination due to the sexual abuse not causing any injury or injury healing (more than 5 months had passed in this case).[1,2]

1. Berkoff MC, Zolotor AJ, Makoroff KL, Thackeray JD, Shapiro RA, Runyan DK. Has this prepubertal girl been sexually abused? *JAMA*. 2008;300(23):2779–2792.
2. Nazer D, Palusci VJ. Child sexual abuse: Can anatomy explain the presentation? *Clin Pediatr (Phila)*. 2008;47(1):7–14.

CASE 16

Mary Lu Angelilli with Natalja Stanski

A 2-month-old baby girl was brought to the emergency department by her father. He stated he witnessed her gasp for air, vomit and then go limp. On arrival, she was stable and appeared 'back to baseline' according to her father. However, bruising was noted under her right eye and lateral to the left eye as shown in Image 16. Her parents then reported that her 13-month-old sister was jumping on the bed and hit her in the face with her bottle. There was no other reported trauma.

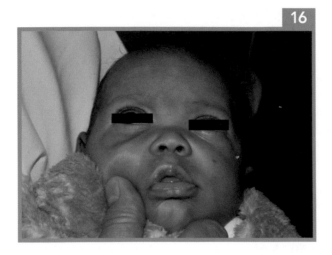

    i. What is your diagnosis?
   ii. How would you further evaluate this child?

i. Other than facial bruising, this baby's physical examination was completely normal. However, the history of trauma provided by the parents did not seem sufficient to explain the injuries present. Bruising in young infants who are non-ambulatory is extremely rare. In their landmark study, Sugar et al. identified bruising in only 0.6% of infants younger than 6 months of age presenting for well-child care.[1] Furthermore, facial bruising (excluding the forehead), even in ambulatory toddlers, was exceedingly rare. As a result, it is important for clinicians to have a high index of suspicion for child abuse when a young, pre-ambulatory infant presents with unexplained or poorly explained bruising, particularly to the face. The diagnosis in this child was physical abuse.

ii. Current recommendations suggest that for infants with facial bruising, the workup should include a skeletal survey, head imaging, trauma screening, laboratory studies, and a retinal examination.[2] As a result, the hospital child protection team recommended these studies and a referral to Child Protective Services for this infant. The baby's skeletal survey was negative for any acute or healing fractures. However, unilateral retinal haemorrhages were identified and a head CT scan revealed bilateral subdural haematomas. A diagnosis of child physical abuse was made and the child ultimately was discharged to a foster home. This case highlights the importance of thoroughly evaluating all bruising in young infants. While this baby had already suffered abusive head trauma when the bruise was noted, bruising has been reported as a frequent sentinel event in infants presenting with confirmed child physical abuse. In a study by Sheets et al., 27.5% of abused infants were found to have had a previous sentinel injury, of which bruising accounted for 80%.[3] It is clear that for many patients, early detection of bruising as an indication of abuse plays an important role in the prevention of abuse escalation.

1. Sugar NF, Taylor JA, Feldman KW. Bruises in infants and toddlers: Those who don't cruise rarely bruise. Puget Sound Pediatric Research Network. *Arch Pediatr Adolesc Med.* 1999;153(4):399–403.
2. Pierce MC, Smith S, Kaczor K. Bruising in infants: Those with a bruise may be abused. *Pediatr Emerg Care.* 2009;25(12):845–847.
3. Sheets LK, Leach ME, Koszewski IJ, Lessmeier AM, Nugent M, Simpson P. Sentinel injuries in infants evaluated for child physical abuse. *Pediatrics.* 2013;131(4):701–707.

CASE 17

Tor Shwayder

A 6-year-old boy presented with a recent onset of an itchy, red and uncomfortable rash in his perianal area. Pain had been increasing in severity especially when passing a bowel movement. This resulted in stool withholding and constipation. When his perianal area was examined, the doctor noticed the rash shown in Image 17.

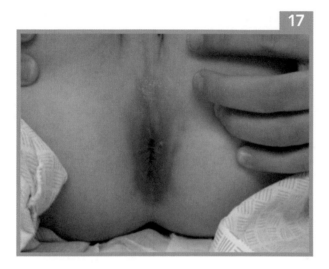

   i. What is the diagnosis?
  ii. What would confirm your diagnosis?
 iii. How is this condition treated?

i. This child has perianal streptococcal dermatitis. It usually presents as a bright red, sharply demarcated rash involving the perianal mucosa that is caused by group A beta-haemolytic streptococci. Typically the rash starts at the anus and spreads centrifugally and sometimes upward to the vulva or to the scrotum and penis as well.[1] Most children present with rectal itching or rectal pain as their chief complaint. Children may also present with blood-streaked stools.[2]

ii. A culture by swabbing the affected skin would confirm the diagnosis. However, you need to alert the laboratory to the site of the culture since the culture would overgrow with coliforms from the stool. It should not be labelled as a stool culture but rather as a bacterial wound culture for group A streptococcus.[1] The laboratory technician can subsequently re-culture those colonies that resemble streptococcus.

iii. The treatment is the same as for streptococcal pharyngitis – usually penicillins and their derivatives. As the inflammation calms down, the child should be able to pass his or her bowel movements and pain should resolve. Glycerin suppositories and stool laxatives do help.

1. Block SL. Perianal dermatitis: Much more than just a diaper rash. *Pediatr Ann.* 2013;42(1):12–14.
2. Brilliant LC. Perianal streptococcal dermatitis. *Am Fam Physician.* 2000;61(2):391–393, 397.

CASE 18

Mary E. Smyth

Two siblings were referred to a hospital's child protection team for evaluation. They were placed in emergency foster care after their 2-month-old sibling had died suddenly and unexpectedly. Images 18a and 18b show a 14-month-old boy weighing 6.83 kg (less than the third percentile).

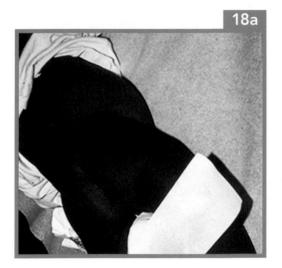

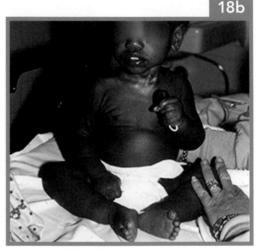

    i. Based on these images, why do you suspect these children were placed in foster care?
  ii. Which findings depicted in these images are indicative of abuse or neglect?

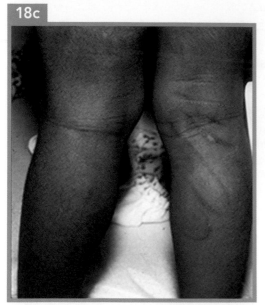

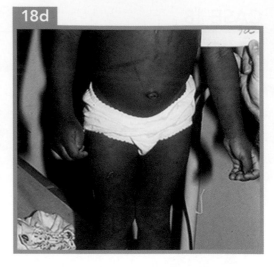

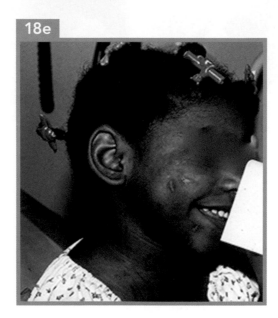

i. Abuse of multiple children within a family is well described. When one child dies and the circumstances of the death are suspicious, it is prudent to make a safety plan for other children living in the household.[1,2]

ii. The male child in the first two photos showed signs of profound malnutrition. His weight was well below the third percentile for his age. His arms and legs showed signs of loss of subcutaneous fat. His sister (Images 18c, 18d and 18e) had healed linear and loop-shaped scars, evidence of beating with a looped cord. These represent patterned injuries which mimic the shape of the implement used to inflict them.[3,4]

1. Christoffel KK, Zieserl EJ, Chiaramonte J. Should child abuse and neglect be considered when a child dies unexpectedly? *Am J Dis. Children*. 1985;139(9):876–880.

2. Lowen DE. Failure to thrive. In: Jenny C. ed. *Child Abuse and Neglect: Diagnosis, Treatment and Evidence*. St. Louis, MO: Elsevier Saunders; 2011:547–562.

3. Brodcur AE, Montelione JA. Trauma. In: Montelione JA, ed. *Child Maltreatment: A Comprehensive Photographic Reference Identifying Potential Child Abuse*. St. Louis, MO: GW Medical; 1994:4.

4. Brodeur AE, Montelione JA. Identifying, interpreting, and reporting injuries. In: Brodeur AE, Montelione JA, eds. *Child Maltreatment: A Clinical Guide and Reference*. St. Louis, MO: GW Medical; 1994:8, 44, 78.

CASE 19

Margaret T. McHugh with Anastasia Feifer and Lori A. Legano

An 11-year-old female recently disclosed to her older sister of 19 years that a family member had 'touched her' in the bathroom during a family event. The girl came from a large extended family who hosted frequent large gatherings in their home. She was too afraid to tell her sister who had abused her and she did not know exactly when this occurred, but said that it may have happened 'a few times'. She would not disclose any more information. Her sister brought the child to the emergency department for an evaluation, and findings of the genital exam are shown in Image 19.

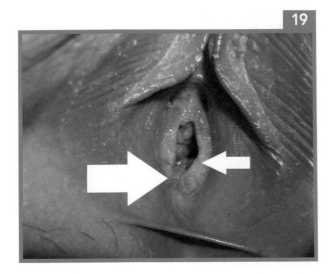

i. What does the examination show?
ii. Is the physical examination diagnostic of an acute rape?

i. Image 19 shows a hymenal transection at the 6:30 o'clock position (large arrow). The hymenal tissue can be followed clockwise from the 1 o'clock position until it becomes completely effaced at 6 o'clock, revealing the posterior rim of the vaginal opening. The tissue then resumes at the 7:00 position and extends anteriorly, where it can be followed until approximately 11 o'clock. There is also a mound or bump at the 4 o'clock position (small arrow) which is a solid elevation of tissue at the site of an attachment to an intravaginal column and is a normal finding.[1]

ii. A transection of the hymen is one of the few physical findings with high specificity for abuse; it is diagnostic for blunt force penetration of the vagina.[2] The specific sexual contact, however (e.g. insertion of penis, fingers or foreign body) cannot be ascertained based on physical findings alone. In addition, hymenal tissue is highly vascular and heals quickly (about 3 weeks, some research shows[3]), so timing of the abuse cannot be ascertained precisely unless the patient presents acutely with bleeding. It is important to remember that the vast majority of children who report sexual abuse have a normal anogenital exam. This occurs because tissues heal very quickly and sexual abuse (even, in some cases, penetration) may not cause damage sufficient to be evident on examination.[2] Any child with a disclosure of sexual abuse should be interviewed by a trained professional and given a complete physical and anogenital examination while reducing the number of interviews to prevent re-traumatization and imprecisions in history.

1. Adams J and the Terminology Subcommittee of the APSAC Task Force on Medical Evaluation of Suspected Child Abuse. *Practice Guidelines: Descriptive Terminology in Child Sexual Abuse Medical Evaluations.* American Professional Society on the Abuse of Children, 1995. www.apsac.org
2. Adams J. Medical evaluation of child sexual abuse. *J Pediatr Adolesc Gynecol.* 2004;17:191.
3. Stewart D. Physical findings in children and adolescents experiencing sexual abuse or assault. In: Jenny, C., ed. *Child Abuse and Neglect: Diagnosis, Treatment, and Evidence.* St. Louis, MO: Elsevier Saunders; 2011:69–81.

CASE 20

Patricia O. Brennan

This 4-year-old boy attended the emergency department after he had cut his knee. The laceration required suturing but during the procedure, the doctor noticed these marks on the boy's skin (Image 20). He was concerned that they were bruises. The mother said the boy had not injured himself but he was under the care of a paediatrician for the rash.

    i. What examination would you perform?
   ii. What is the condition?
  iii. What is the differential diagnosis?

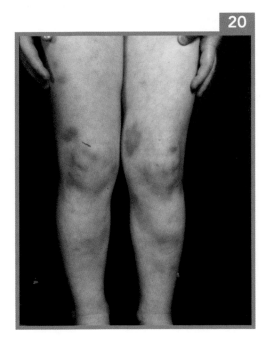

i. A full external examination was necessary in this boy as the doctor was concerned that the boy had bruises without any explanation of a consistent incident to cause bruising. The doctor was looking for signs which might be associated with conditions causing easy bruising.

ii. The bruise-like lesions were not actually bruises, but mastocytomas, caused by aggregates of mast cells in the dermis. When the doctor gently rubbed the boy's skin, a wheal appeared (Darier sign). This is highly specific for cutaneous mastocytosis, in which there is a spectrum of presentations from single or multiple mastocytomas to urticarial pigmentosa to diffuse cutaneous mastocytosis. Generalized flushing and localized blistering can occur but pruritus is rare in infants and children.

   This boy had multiple mastocytomas. These most commonly occur on the trunk or buttocks and less frequently on the limbs, head and neck. They only rarely occur on palms and soles. The condition affects infants and children more frequently than adults, and in the young there is a tendency to spontaneous resolution before puberty. Where the condition persists into adulthood, 15%–30% will develop internal organ involvement. Familial cases have been reported but are rare.[1,2]

iii. When the mastomas present as yellow-brown or red-brown macules, child abuse is sometimes suspected. Other misdiagnoses include café-au-lait spots, naevi and meningococcal disease. Cutaneous mastocytosis with extensive blistering has been confused with staphylococcal scalded-skin syndrome.

1. Hannaford R, Rogers M. Presentation of cutaneous mastocytosis in 173 children. *Australas J Dermatol.* 2001;42(1):15–21.
2. Kiszewski AE, Duran-Mckinster C, Orozco-Covarrubias L, Gutierrez-Castrellon P, Ruiz-Maldonado R. Cutaneous mastocytosis in children: A clinical analysis of 71 cases. *J Eur Acad Dermatol Venereol.* 2004;18(3):285–290.

CASE 21

Vincent J. Palusci

This 8-month-old African female infant was found in a house with his 3-year-old sibling. No adults were present. The sibling appeared malnourished. The infant appeared well hydrated and well nourished but had severe diaper dermatitis. The children were taken to foster care where they were cleaned and fed. Developmentally, she was able to sit, crawl and babble. Upon changing her diaper, the foster mother noted some blood mixed in the stool, and the stools were large and hard. The infant appeared to have pain with defaecation but was otherwise happy. The foster mother brought her to a physician for routine medical care and immunizations, and the perianal lesion shown (Image 21) was found.

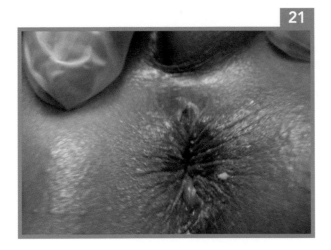

i. What does the image show?
ii. What are the possible causes for this finding?

i. The infant had an superficial laceration (also called a fissure) in the anterior anal mucosa. There were mucosal flaps of tissue overlying red granulation tissue, suggesting this had been present for at least a few days. Additionally, there was a posterior mound of tissue which could represent a healed fissure, tag or musical fold. There was also faecal matter and small fiber-like foreign body material suggestive of a nappy or toilet paper. There was normal perianal hyperpigmentation which is seen in dark-skinned children. The visualized anal rugae were normal and no scars or other trauma were seen.

ii. Given the lack of supervision and signs of other neglect (malnutrition, poor hygiene), there were concerns that these children could have also been physically and sexually abused.[1] Anal fissures are often seen as a result of infant constipation, which in this case could have resulted from poor diet and decreased fluid intake.[2] The lack of adequate diaper changing would have contributed to the size and lack of healing. However, anal sodomy and sexual abuse could have also caused the fissure and a more thorough physical examination and investigation was needed. Although the time frame is unclear, consideration should have been given to the collection of forensic trace specimens and DNA as well as tests for sexually transmitted infections. Imaging of the axial skeleton and brain should also be considered, as should further examination of the anus to the internal sphincter.

1. Myhre AK, Adams JA, Kaufhold M, Davis JL, Suresh P, Kuelbs CL. Anal findings in children with and without probable anal penetration: A retrospective study of 1115 children referred for suspected sexual abuse. *Child Abuse Negl.* 2013;37(7):465–474.
2. Palusci VJ. Anogenital findings and sexual abuse. In: Palusci VJ, Fischer H, eds. *Child Abuse and Neglect: A Diagnostic Guide for Physicians, Surgeons, Pathologists, Dentists, Nurses and Social Workers.* London, England: Manson Publishing Ltd; 2011:163–191.

CASE 22

Carl J. Schmidt

This 11-month-old child was brought to the emergency department by his parents. They stated they had put the child to sleep 12 hours before he was found unresponsive. They brought him to the emergency department by private car. No resuscitation was attempted. His birth weight was 3.8 kg and weight at death was 6.75 kg. Bruises were seen on the face, and rigor was absent. His skin appeared as in the images.

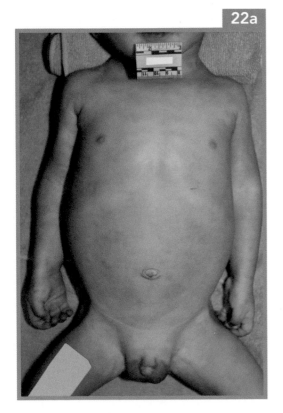

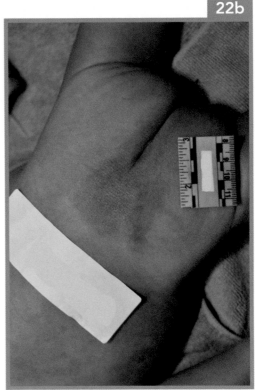

i. What does Image 22a show? Is the timeline given by the parents plausible?
ii. What other observations can the autopsy show to support malnutrition and neglect?
iii. What does Image 22b show?

i. The discoloured appearance of this child's abdomen is due to decomposition. The green colouring of the abdomen is diffuse and apparent because of the thinness of the abdominal wall due to an almost absent panniculus due to malnutrition. Green discolouration is due largely to the decomposition of haemoglobin into biliverdin. These changes tend to occur faster in small children, but changes like those seen here indicate the child had been dead much longer than 12 hours. Rigor had also passed.

ii. This child's height and weight were below the third percentile for his age consistent with malnutrition.[1] Other findings on post-mortem examination to support prolonged malnutrition included a thin abdominal fat pad, absent periadrenal fat, almost absent mesenteric adipose tissue, atrophy of the thymus and depletion of the lymphoid follicles in the spleen. This child suffered from malnutrition and neglect.

iii. This image shows a Mongolian spot, an area of congenital hyperpigmentation often confused with an ecchymosis due to blunt trauma. In this case, there was also blunt trauma because this child was beaten occasionally with a paddle as told by a witness. An incision into the Mongolian spot showed there was haemorrhage within its subcutaneous tissue obscured by the hyperpigmentation. The cause of death in this case was malnutrition and neglect.[2] Because of the pattern of neglect, the manner of death is homicide.

1. Bays J. Conditions mistaken for child physical abuse. In: Reece RM, Ludwig S, eds. *Child Abuse and Neglect: Medical Diagnosis and Management*. 2nd edn. Philadelphia, PA: Lippincott Williams & Wilkins; 2001:177–206.
2. Knight LD, Collins KA. A 25-year retrospective review of deaths due to pediatric neglect. *Am J Forensic Med Pathol*. 2005;26(3):221–228.

CASE 23

Dena Nazer

A 2-month-old baby girl presented to the emergency department with a 3-day history of swelling of her left leg. Her mother denied any history of trauma. The baby cried when her left leg was moved but otherwise was doing well, so the mother thought to wait before bringing her in. When the grandmother saw the baby's swollen leg, she brought her to the emergency department immediately. On physical examination, her left leg appeared swollen (Images 23a and 23b). X-rays are shown (Images 23c and 23d).

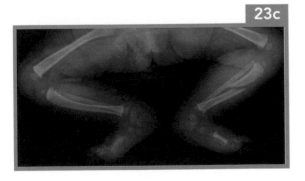

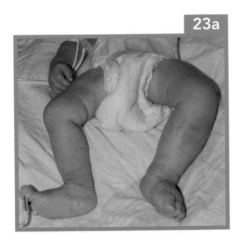

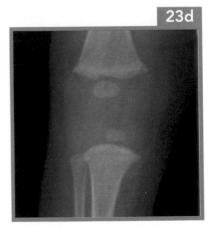

  i. What do the images show?
 ii. What imaging studies are important to further evaluate this baby?

i. The left leg is swollen as compared to the right side and the skin is taut from the swelling. A close-up photo shows bruises of the left leg. A fracture was suspected and thus x-rays of the legs were obtained. They show an acute oblique displaced fracture of the left tibia. There is also a metaphyseal corner fracture or classic metaphyseal lesion (CML) of the distal left tibia.

ii. In children less than 2 years old, a skeletal survey needs to be obtained when physical abuse is suspected. The skeletal survey for this infant showed a total of 30 fractures at different stages of healing that included multiple CMLs and posterior rib fractures, both of which are highly specific for child abuse.[1] A magnified x-ray of her distal right femur and proximal right tibia showed a CML of the distal right femur and a CML of the proximal right tibia. Diaphyseal fractures such as the tibia fracture in this infant occur four times more commonly than CMLs, but the CML has a greater specificity for abuse. The CMLs occur most often in infants less than 6 months old. They result from the flailing of the extremities during violent shaking. They could also result when a child's extremity is grabbed and yanked forcefully or twisted. The distal femur as in this child is a common site for CML, which is a strong indicator for abuse. Thus this region should be carefully evaluated with high-detail skeletal radiographs in all cases of suspected infant abuse.[2]

1. Flaherty EG, Perez-Rossello JM, Levine MA, Hennrikus WL. Evaluating children with fractures for child physical abuse. *Pediatrics*. 2014;133(2):e477–e489.
2. Kleinman PK, Marks SC, Jr. A regional approach to the classic metaphyseal lesion in abused infants: The distal femur. *AJR*. 1998;170(1):43–47.

CASE 24

Nicholas Bishop

A 2-year-old child was admitted to the hospital with a chest infection. On clinical examination, the child was well kept, thriving and socially normal. There were no dysmorphic features, and the sclerae were white. The fontanels were normally sized. The chest x-ray showed a single healing rib fracture. Skeletal survey showed wormian bones (Images 24a and 24b) and there was evidence of systemic bone disease in terms of abnormalities of bone shape and radiological density. There was a fracture of the humeral condyle (Image 24c). Biochemical testing showed a normal vitamin D level and an elevated alkaline phosphatase consistent with a healing fracture. The parents were adamant that they had not injured their child.

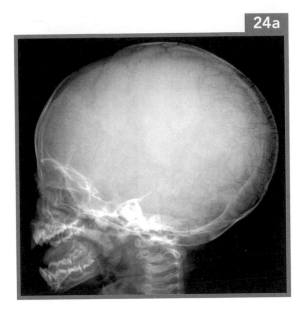

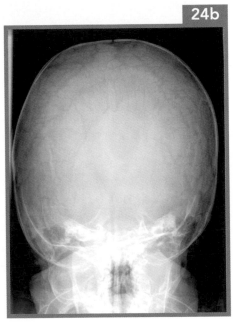

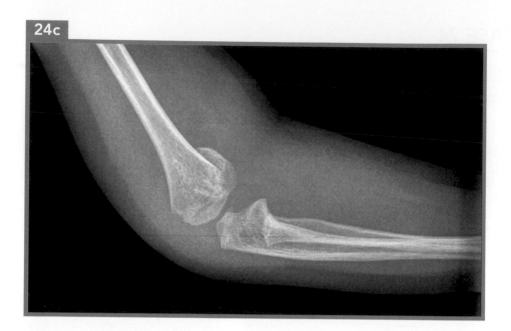

i. What would you do next?

ii. Does the injury type or signs of systemic bone disease exclude abuse as a cause of the fractures?

i. A full family history should be taken. On detailed questioning the mother said that she had a number of fractures as a child and that she has always been 'double-jointed'; she had suffered from back pain that had limited her daily activities and had been seeing a chiropractor. You should consider requesting an x-ray of the mother's back and advise her not to visit the chiropractor until this has been reported. You should also think about genetic testing for type I collagen defects. Osteogenesis imperfecta (OI) not infrequently presents in mild cases like this and many cases are initially suspected of being cases of non-accidental injury. Many families remain angry about these suspicions for a long time.

ii. There were signs of radiological osteopenia in this case but the fracture type is common after accidental falls in normal children. Radiological osteopenia requires substantial loss of mineralized bone tissue (likely >30%) and bone density measured quantitatively by dual energy x-ray absorptiometry is often in the normal range in older children with mild OI. However, despite this, some of such patients go on to develop vertebral crush fractures. Genetic testing for OI is indicated as there are several loci which have been implicated in classic OI types.[1] Child abuse has been implicated as a cause of fracture in children with OI, although the presence of an underlying bone disease can alter the amount or types of force required.

1. Renaud A, Aucourt J, Weill J et al. Radiographic features of osteogenesis imperfecta. *Insights Imaging.* 2013;4(4):417–429.

CASE 25

Mary Lu Angelilli with Ali Saaleem

A 5-week-old baby girl presented with irritability for approximately 6 hours prior to presentation. Her parents also noted swelling of her right thigh within the previous hour. Her parents denied any history of trauma and she was otherwise asymptomatic and feeding well. On her initial physical examination, the infant was noted to have a swollen and tender right thigh. She also had bruises on her forearms bilaterally (Image 25a). A chest x-ray was also obtained (Image 25b).

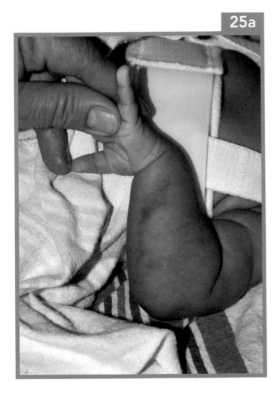

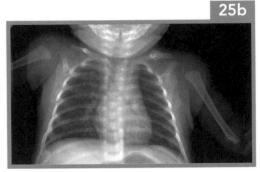

   i. What findings do you see on her first x-ray?
  ii. Would additional imaging help?
 iii. How would you further evaluate this infant?

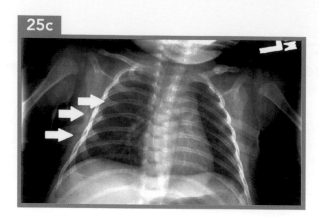

25c

i. An x-ray of the right thigh showed a spiral fracture of the midshaft of the right femur. There was also a healing fracture with callus formation of the mid-left clavicle seen on the initial bone survey. No other fractures were seen.

ii. Oblique or 'rib' views can be better at showing posterolateral lesions, particularly on the right (arrows, Image 25c). These views should be considered as a routine part of a skeletal survey to evaluate for occult child abuse.

iii. This infant should be evaluated for child abuse. She had an initial skeletal survey in addition to head imaging and a dilated retinal exam. She also had a complete blood count and liver enzymes drawn. As a follow-up, she had a bone survey obtained approximately 2 weeks after the initial bone survey. It showed six additional fractures (arrows point to three of these). It demonstrated the healing displaced fracture of the midshaft of the right femur and the healing fracture of the left mid-clavicle. In addition it showed healing fractures of the anterolateral aspect of the right fourth and fifth ribs, healing fractures of the bilateral distal tibiae and healing fractures of the bilateral distal humeri. This case stresses the importance of a follow-up bone survey in suspected cases of child abuse, especially in children under the age of 2 years.[1] Fractures can be difficult to identify on an initial physical examination, prompting the need for skeletal surveys in younger, particularly preverbal, children.[2] The American Academy of Pediatrics (AAP) recommends that a skeletal survey be completed for any child aged 2 years or younger who is suspected of being a victim of physical abuse. However, initial surveys may not reveal all fractures. Therefore, a follow-up survey is recommended approximately 2 weeks following the initial survey.

1. Harper NS, Eddleman S, Lindberg DM. The utility of follow-up skeletal surveys in child abuse. *Pediatrics*. 2013;131(3):e672–e678.
2. Offiah A, van Rijn RR, Perez-Rossello JM, Kleinman PK. Skeletal imaging of child abuse (non-accidental injury). *Pediatr Radiol*. 2009;39(5):461–470.

CASE 26

Tor Shwayder

A 2-year-old girl presented with this patchy area of hypopigmentation involving her vulva and rectal area (Image 26a). Her parents were very distraught and brought the child to the emergency department.

i. What is the diagnosis?
ii. Where else should you examine to confirm your diagnosis?
iii. What tests (blood or skin) would be helpful?
iv. What treatment options are there?

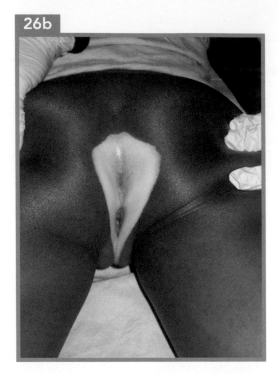

26b

i. This child has vitiligo. In Image 26a there is an area of complete 'white' skin around the vaginal introitus and areas of patchy light brown and flesh-coloured skin on the buttocks and inner thighs. These latter areas were originally white and have filled in on their own.

ii. Vitiligo comes in various distributions, one of which is 'lip-tip' syndrome. The vitiligo affects the perioral tissues, eyelids, vulvar and perianal areas, fingers and toe tips. A full medical examination with special attention to these areas is needed. Image 26b shows a child with vitiligo of the vulvar and perianal area.

iii. A biopsy of the skin would show lack of melanocytes. Blood tests are not needed to confirm the diagnosis. Some experts would suggest checking for auto-antibodies or other conditions such as thyroid disease. This is controversial as the entities are found in parallel and not linked in a causative manner.

iv. One of the most important concerns in vitiligo is cosmetic, which is a main concern for children and their parents. Treatment options include observation, ultraviolet light and vitiligo grafting surgeries. Topical steroids and topical immune modulators may have benefit.[1] Vitiligo in children causes marked psychosocial and long-lasting effects on the self-esteem of both the affected children and their parents.[2]

1. Palit A, Inamadar AC. Childhood vitiligo. *Indian J Dermatol Venereol Leprol*. 2012;78(1):30–41.
2. Kanwar AJ, Kumaran MS. Childhood vitiligo: Treatment paradigms. *Indian J Dermatol*. 2012;57(6): 466–474.

CASE 27

Pamela Wallace Hammel

This toddler was brought by his parents to the paediatrician with several foot lesions (Images 27a and 27b). They reported he was playing with his older brother when these cuts occurred and they were concerned they might become infected. On examination, there are several superficial cuts both above and below the foot, although none appear to be infected.

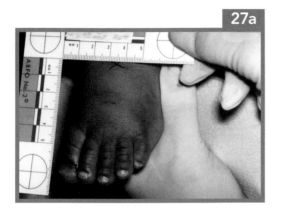

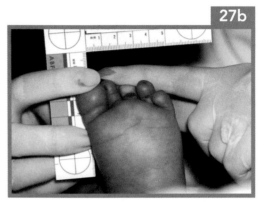

   i. What do the images show?

  ii. What is the possible aetiology of these injuries?

i. The images show lesions resulting from human bites to the toes. Notice there are symmetrical lesions both above and below a number of toes. There is a series of four distinct bites to this foot; beginning higher on the foot and progressing to the toe. The hands and feet of a child easily fit into the adult abuser's mouth, and often several bites will occur before the adult lets go.

ii. When bite marks are suspected to the hands and feet; the easiest way to determine if they are bites is to examine the ventral surface. With such intense pressure, usually the lower teeth will result in deeper marks on the toes/feet. Sequential biting of hands and feet is a frequent finding in child abuse.[1] These lesions have been noted in many assaults of children from infants to toddlers, when the hands and feet easily fit into the mouth of the assailant, and they are often bitten sequentially as the hand/foot is withdrawn. These lesions are often noted as only incidental injuries, but bite marks actually rarely occur accidentally and are good indicators of inflicted abuse.

1. Fischer H, Hammel P, Allasio D, Tunnessen W W Jr. Picture of the month. Human bite marks. *Arch Pediatr Adolesc Med*. 1996;150(4):429–430.

CASE 28

Vincent J. Palusci

A 12-year-old girl was brought to your office with concerns from her mother that 'her opening is too big'. The mother reported that she and the father had separated, contemplating divorce, and the girl stayed with her father on alternative weekends. The child denied that he has 'done anything' to her and she also denied any other sexual contact with anyone else. She had complained of vaginal discharge and her mother 'checked her down there' to see if she was having her first period. As a primary care physician, you explain you are not a paediatric gynaecologist but offer to do an examination as she was due for her routine well-child exam for sports in school. She was Tanner stage III. With her lying on the examination table on her back and her mother at her side, you see the image as presented (Image 28).

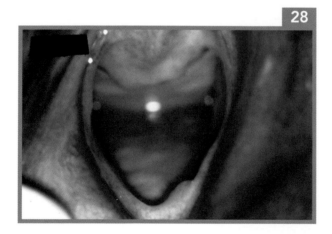

i. What does the image show?
ii. Do these findings indicate sexual abuse and/or trauma?

i. The image depicts a view of the hymen and vagina without much estrogenization. The hymen is crescentic in shape and does not extend completely around the genital opening. The posterior fourchette and fossa navicularis are not visible. The depicted labia minora has increased vascularity and mucus membranes are erythematous, but this may be non-specific and artefactual from the lighting. There is no visualized vaginal foreign body, discharge or trauma. The posterior rim of the hymen is thin and there appears to be a bump at the insertion of an intravaginal ridge in the inferior half at 5 o'clock with her in the supine position. Based on the size of the examiner's fingers, the rim appears to be at least 1 mm in thickness in all locations on the posterior half of the hymen.[1]

ii. These findings should be interpreted with caution. Historically, expert opinion has suggested that the thinness of the hymen rim was indicative of sexual abuse and/or trauma to this area; however, the paucity of research evidence in this area has more recently made this finding more indeterminant.[2] Girls with complete transections of the hymen or bruises and lacerations are more easily found to have been abused, but the smoothness and otherwise normal appearance of the hymenal tissues in this image suggest that this finding is a normal variant. The bump is an accepted normal finding when associated with an intravaginal ridge. In the absence of disclosure or other evidence, these physical findings do not currently indicate sexual abuse or trauma.

1. Palusci VJ. Anogenital findings and sexual abuse. In: Palusci VJ, Fischer H, eds. *Child Abuse and Neglect: A Diagnostic Guide for Physicians, Surgeons, Pathologists, Dentists, Nurses and Social Workers.* London, England: Manson Publishing Ltd; 2011:163–191.
2. Adams JA. Medical evaluation of suspected child sexual abuse: 2011 update. *J Child Sex Abus.* 2011;20(5):588–605.

CASE 29

Dena Nazer

A 5-year-old boy was brought to the emergency department by the police. They were notified by one of the neighbours, who heard him crying. The child stated he wet his pants and his mother asked her boyfriend to 'pop' him on his hands with a comb. The boyfriend also had him stand in the corner without changing his wet pants for hours. His hands are shown in Image 29a. Images 29b, 29c and 29d show additional skin findings.

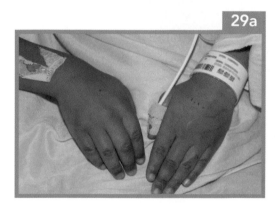

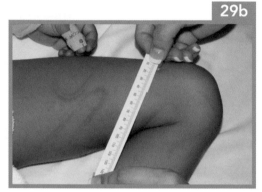

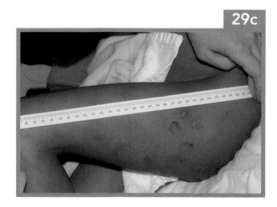

29d

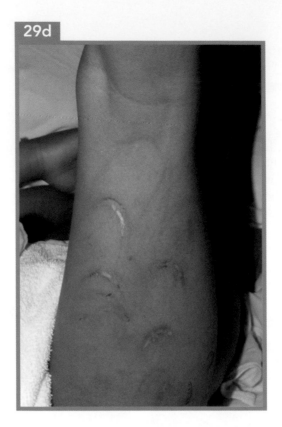

i. What do the images show?

ii. What is your diagnosis?

i. There is bilateral swelling of the child's hands (Image 29a). There are also multiple pinpoint abrasions on the dorsa of both hands, especially the left. The child stated those were from being hit hard with the comb, which he referred to as 'popping'. The distance between the abrasions matched the comb that the child described which was found in the home. The child had a full physical examination with a detailed exam of his skin. He had multiple patterned marks on the lateral, medial and posterior aspects of his left leg as shown in the photos. He disclosed he was whipped with a belt as well as with a cord. The patterned marks and loop marks were consistent with his disclosure. Physical discipline involves usually concealed areas of the body such as the buttocks, thus the skin should be examined in detail. This case needs to be properly recognized by the physician and reported to Child Protective Services to prevent further injury and possible death.

ii. Children usually sustain abuse at the hands of a caregiver who misinterprets the child's behaviour as naughty and responds inappropriately as in this case when the child wet his pants. The American Academy of Pediatrics has proposed that 'striking a child with an object' is a type of physical punishment that 'should never be used'.[1] Corporal punishment has deleterious side effects as in this case and is of limited effectiveness. It is very important in this case to document all the disclosures made by the child and obtain a thorough history from the child as well as the parent. Physical examination in this child has to be thorough and include a careful skin examination. The physical examination has to accomplish three main objectives: (1) medical – to assess the physical injury and develop an appropriate treatment plan; (2) psychological – to afford the child a sense of safety; and (3) legal – to provide documentation that may be used as evidence of child maltreatment.[2]

1. American Academy of Pediatrics. Committee on Psychosocial Aspects of Child and Family Health. Guidance for effective discipline. *Pediatrics*. 1998;101(4 Pt 1):723–728.
2. Legano L, McHugh MT, Palusci VJ. Child abuse and neglect. *Curr Probl Pediatr Adolesc Health Care*. 2009;39(2):31.e1–31.e26.

CASE 30

Margaret T. McHugh with Anastasia Feifer and Lori A. Legano

A 9-year-old girl with autism who resided in a group facility was brought to the emergency department for evaluation. A nurse had examined her after she pointed to her buttocks and said 'Ow'. The nurse noted these marks on the child (Image 30) and was concerned that another child had sexually abused her on the playground on the day before as children of mixed ages were playing together that day. The adult who was supervising on the playground stated that she did not see any unusual activity and the girl had been playing on the monkey bars alone. Her vital signs were normal. On physical examination, she had scattered bruises of varying colours on her anterior shins, but no other marks or lacerations. Her genital examination was normal for her age. She was cooperative with the examination, but did not speak or make eye contact with the examiner.

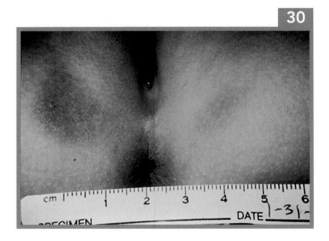

i. What are potential aetiologies for this injury?
ii. What further investigation would you consider for unexplained bruising in a child?

i. The presence of bilateral gluteal or perineal bruising in an active child should generate a short list of differential diagnoses, including inflicted trauma, straddle injury or coagulopathy. In this case, though this was a non-verbal child and it was possible that no disclosure of abuse could be elicited, it was likely that she sustained a straddle injury during the course of normal play, given the history and appearance of the bruising. The injuries were bilateral and symmetric, in a single plane and sparing the anus and genitals – consistent with the pelvis making contact with a hard surface. Straddle injuries are about 3% of total playground injuries.[1] In girls, they can cause labial haematoma and/or laceration and urethral injury. In boys, they can lead to scrotal laceration, penile laceration or contusion and even urethral rupture. Perineal injury can be found in both males and females. About 10%–15% of these injuries require surgical repair.[1]

ii. The most important initial step for a bruised child without a clear account of injury is to take a very careful history. Depending on the age and development of the child, abuse may be higher or lower on the short list of differential diagnoses, including inflicted trauma, accidental trauma, and/or coagulopathy. A non-mobile infant with unexplained bruising should make the provider think of coagulopathy or abuse.[2] Bruising in a toddler or older child is very common, though location of the bruises may prompt suspicion. Marks on the ears, neck/face (excluding forehead), trunk, buttocks or genitalia are not pathognomonic for abuse, but should arouse more suspicion for inflicted injury.[2] Additionally, patterned bruises without a supporting history (loop shaped or linear, for example) merit consideration for abuse. Patient and family history should focus on coagulopathy (epistaxis, mucosal bleeding, bleeding from circumcision) and genetic anomalies (such as collagen vascular disease).[3] Extensive unexplained bruising in which the aetiology is *not* abuse includes haemophilia, von Willebrand disease, disorders of fibrinogen, vitamin K deficiency, factor XIII and other factor deficiencies, thrombocytopenia, leukaemia, aplastic anaemia and other bone marrow infiltrative or failure syndromes, platelet function abnormalities, collagen disorders, corticosteroid use and others.[3] A child with concerns for abuse based on bruising should also undergo basic laboratory screening tests, including complete blood count (CBC), coagulation panel (prothrombin time [PT]/activated partial thromboplastin time [aPTT]), testing for Factor VIII/Factor IX levels, and testing for von Willebrand's disease. A consultation with a haematologist should also be considered, or with medical genetics, depending on history and physical findings.[3]

1. Dowd MD, Fitzmaurice L, Knapp JF, Mooney D. The interpretation of urogenital findings in children with straddle injuries. *J Pediatr Surg.* 1994;29(1):7–10.
2. Jenny C, Reese RM. Cutaneous manifestations of child abuse. In: Reese RM, Christian CW, eds. *Child Abuse: Medical Diagnosis and Management.* Chicago, IL: American Academy of Pediatrics; 2009:19–51.
3. Carpenter SL, Abshire TC, Anderst JD. Evaluating for suspected child abuse: Conditions that predispose to bleeding. *Pediatrics.* 2013;131(4):e1357–e1373.

CASE 31

Mary E. Smyth

This 6-year-old boy was engaged in a physical altercation with a same-age neighbour. He was brought to the child protection clinic for evaluation of his injuries. He had been in good health with no significant medical history. He was verbal and cooperative and described what had happened in great detail. Image 31 shows two of the injuries sustained by this child.

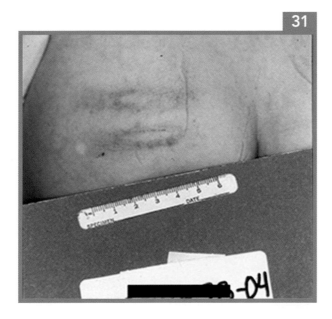

i. How are the bruises seen on this child characterized?
ii. What are clues that help to verify the cause of these injuries?
iii. Can these marks be used to identify who inflicted them?

i. These injuries represent patterned bruises, elliptical in shape. Close inspection shows that the bruises are composed of tiny petechial haemorrhages.

ii. The elliptical shape of these bruises indicates that the child was struck with a rod–shaped implement.[1] The petechial nature is consistent with rupture of tiny capillaries near the surface of the skin from rapid contact with the object. The boy stated that he was hit many times with a souvenir pencil (approximately 12 inches [4.5 inches] long and 4.4 cm [1.75 inches] in circumference). A flat object such as a ruler would produce parallel linear injuries rather than the elliptical bruises seen here.

iii. While the marks confirm the object, the exact amount of force and strength with which the object was applied to the skin cannot be precisely estimated. Given the age and strength of a normal child, it is possible that these injuries were inflicted by another child and not an adult or parent. In this case, the disclosures made by the child and other historical information are key to determining the events that occurred.

1. Trott A. Mechanisms of surface soft tissue trauma. *Ann Emerg Med.* 1988;17(12):1279–1283.

CASE 32

Tor Shwayder

A 2-year-old girl presented with linear abrasions noticed on her back. She was initially seen by the physician assistant who was concerned about child abuse. The child's back had linear bruises and healed abrasions as shown in Image 32a. Her physical examination was otherwise normal, including growth parameters.

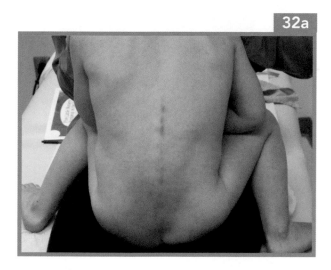

i. What is the likely aetiology of these marks?

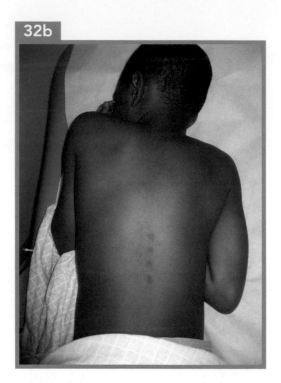

32b

i. These marks appear to be accidental. They occur when a child bumps down a staircase on his/her buttocks catching the spinous processes of his/her mid to lower spine on the stair edge. The longitudinal abrasions just over the spinous processes in this area are the key feature. The question to ask the parents is: 'Has your child been playing up and down the staircase as if it were a slide?' In some children these abrasions and bruises heal and result in hyperpigmentation of the skin as shown in Image 32b. Any mark or bruise on a child may raise the concern of child abuse and it is essential to distinguish between accidental and abusive injuries especially in children too young to make a disclosure. In children who are mobile and active like this child, bruises from play and accidents tend to occur on bony prominences.[1]

1. Kos L, Shwayder T. Cutaneous manifestations of child abuse. *Pediatr Dermatol.* 2006;23(4):311–320.

CASE 33

Alan Sprigg

A 2-month-old infant who had been delivered by a forceps delivery had presented to the family physician with ill-defined scalp swelling noticed 4 days previously. There was no history of recent injury. He was very irritable. A rash over his chest had appeared that day. He was referred to paediatrics for assessment and the 'rash' over the chest looked like fingertip bruising. The infant's skull x-ray is shown (Image 33).

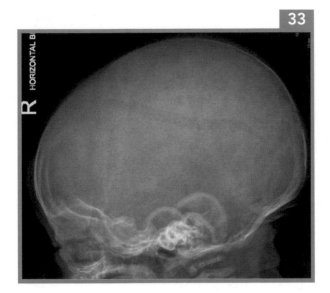

i. What do you notice on the skull x-ray (Image 33)?
ii. What would you do?
iii. Is any further imaging needed? If so, what would you request and in view of the irritability what might you find? What is the significance of the findings?

i. The x-ray showed a widened skull fracture in the right parietal bone extending from the coronal suture to the lambdoid suture. While any unexplained skull fracture is suspicious for non-accidental injury, a widened skull fracture has a higher association, implying more force at impact.[1] A skull fracture implies forceful hard impact which may be accidental or not. It may be associated with shaking injury (shake and throw injury). Finding scalp swelling over this means it is a recent injury (possibly up to 7 days old).

ii. A thorough clinical evaluation is essential, in case the 'rash' is related to sepsis and appropriate treatment should be started as necessary. In addition, further assessment for trauma should be considered. Coagulation tests, bone biochemistry, ophthalmic assessment and a full skeletal survey were normal in this case. However, the clinical history of unexplained scalp swelling is suspicious for trauma.

iii. Logically it would have been more appropriate to request a CT scan initially to look for intracranial complication of trauma. The CT involves radiation but is available in most hospitals without the need for starvation in a 2-month-old. MRI saves radiation, but is less widely available and is intolerant of patient movement without sedation or anaesthesia. Acute blood on MRI is much more difficult to identify than on CT for a non-specialist. Cranial ultrasound has almost no general application in suspect trauma. A neuroradiological opinion revealed no intracranial complications. Ophthalmology, skeletal survey and bone biochemistry were normal. The issue of how a complex skull fracture occurred remains, without any revealed history of trauma on serial questioning. A carer may conceal an accidental injury or a carer may know about a non-accidental injury but decline to reveal it for fear of consequences. If there is no admission, it may be difficult to exclude either the mother or father as perpetrators. The presence of recent 'fingertip bruising' caused additional concern about non-accidental injury and a full child protection investigation was initiated.

1. *Child Protection Companion 2013.* Royal College of Paediatrics and Child Health, London; 2013.

CASE 34

Patricia O. Brennan

This 14-year-old boy told his teacher he had been hit on his back with a cane 2 days previously when his father became angry. He said he was frightened of his father as he had been hit on several occasions previously. On examination, the doctor found tenderness and linear purple marks horizontally, which he thought were scars, across the boy's lower back as shown in Image 34. The boy had no other signs of injury.

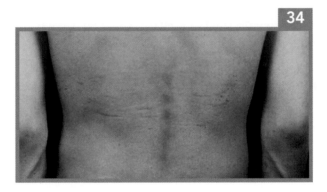

    i. What is the nature of the marks?
   ii. What are the possible causes?
  iii. How should you manage the case?

i. The boy has striae across his lower back. These are not scars from previous injury. Striae are caused by thinning and flattening of the epidermis with associated dermal thinning and dilatation of blood vessels. Collagen bundles are frayed or ruptured and elastic fibres may be absent or, if present, damaged. They are often violaceous or reddish-pink at first, becoming white and depressed and less noticeable later.[1]

ii. There are several possible causes, but the most common is in a significant percentage of the adolescent population between the ages of 10 and 16 years of age. Striae occur over the thighs, gluteal region and breasts in up to 70% of girls and in the lumbosacral region in 40% of boys. They have been associated with a growth spurt, increased adipose tissue and increased adrenocortical hyperactivity in adolescence.[2] Striae also occur in pregnancy, Cushing's syndrome, exogenous administration of cortisol and pituitary hyperactivity and also in acute infections. They often resemble whip or belt markings and have been known to prompt investigations into possible child abuse.

iii. The boy was well and on no medication and the striae were due to adolescence. However, he had made a clear allegation that he had been hit by his father on more than one occasion and he needed referral to the child care agencies for a full child protection investigation.

1. Ammar NM, Rao B, Schwartz RA, Janniger CK. Adolescent striae. *Cutis*. 2000;65(2):69–70.
2. Sisson WR. Colored striae in adolescent children. *J Pediatr*. 1954;45(5):520–530.

CASE 35

Dena Nazer

A 2-year-old girl was brought to the emergency department by her parents who noticed many bruises on her face. Her father said he was holding her last night and accidently dropped her on gravel when he was walking across the street. Both parents said they noticed no bruises last night but noticed the swelling this morning (Images 35a and 35b).

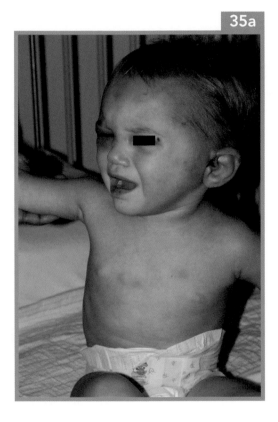

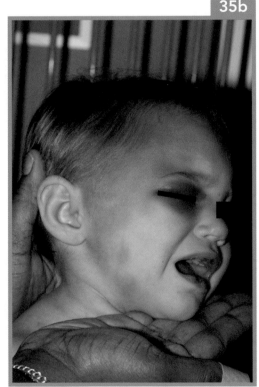

i. What do the images show?
ii. What tests and imaging are important to determine the aetiology for this patient's presentation?

i. Images 35a and 35b show the child's face with multiple bruises involving her forehead, cheeks and the entire right side of her face. She had a right black eye that was swollen and bruises involving her left ear. She also had bruises on her chest. The location and the severity of bruises were not consistent with the story provided by her father. The child was mobile and active, however accidental bruises typically involve bony prominences like the knees and not the face, ears or chest. The bruises of this child do not have a specific pattern to them, so it would be hard to distinguish whether they were caused by a hand or an object. It was also not possible to accurately estimate when the bruises occurred by physical examination alone, so we were not able to tell whether they all occurred in the same setting or over days.[1]

ii. This child needed a complete workup for suspected physical abuse.[2] She had a skeletal survey done as well as head imaging due to the severity of the facial bruising. She also had blood work for liver enzymes to screen for abdominal trauma. Child Protective Services were notified.

1. Bariciak ED, Plint AC, Gaboury I, Bennett S. Dating of bruises in children: An assessment of physician accuracy. *Pediatrics*. 2003;112(4):804–807.
2. Kellogg ND. Evaluation of suspected child physical abuse. *Pediatrics*. 2007;119(6):1232–1241.

CASE 36

Patricia O. Brennan

This small boy attended the emergency department with a burn on the back of his hand as shown in Image 36a. He was too young to give an explanation, but his mother said he touched the hot front of a cooker (Image 36b). The doctor was concerned about non-accidental injury.

   i. What is the nature of the injury?
   ii. Why was the doctor worried about its origin?

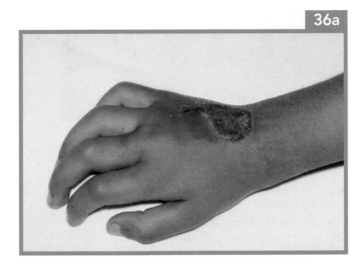

36a

81

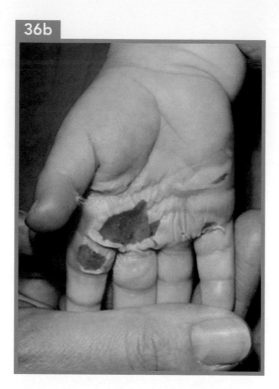

36b

i. The boy has sustained a burn to the dorsum of his right hand. It is most probably a contact burn.

ii. Many emergency department attendances are for burns in infants and young children. They usually occur from one of three causes, fleeting inattention of the parents, more prolonged inattention at the level of neglect and deliberate infliction of the burn.[1] There are various types of burns, including scalding, the most frequent type in infants and young children, contact burns and flame burns. Non-accidental burns are most commonly scalds or contact with hot objects. Children of single parents or whose parents have a low income are more at risk.[1,2] The doctor was worried about the origin of this burn as the history given does not fit with the injury. A young infant explores the world with the palms of the hands, not the back of the hands, and this injury (Image 36a) is on the dorsum of the hand, making accidental injury less likely. In addition, there was no history consistent with the injury and there was delay in presentation, as the injury occurred more than 24 hours before presentation and the parent did not appear to be concerned about the injury. All these factors led to the increasing suspicion that the burn had been inflicted on the child. In contrast, the burn to the hand shown here (Image 36b) had a history of how it occurred which was consistent with the injury in addition, the burn was on the palm of the hand, an area which the child uses to reach out and grab things.

1. Greenbaum AR, Donne J, Wilson D, Dunn KW. Intentional burn injury: An evidence-based, clinical and forensic review. *Burns.* 2004;30(7):628–642.
2. Hobbs CJ. When are burns not accidental? *Arch Dis Child.* 1986;61(4):357–361.

CASE 37

Dena Nazer

A 6-month-old baby girl was noted to have a bruise on her left forearm. She was previously healthy and was asymptomatic. She had a good appetite and had not been noted to be fussy or in pain. Her physical examination was otherwise normal and revealed no additional bruises or injuries. Her forearm is shown in Image 37.

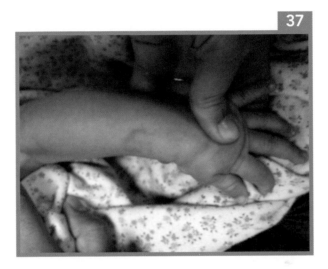

i. What is your diagnosis?
ii. How would you further evaluate this infant?

i. The image shows a bruise on the child's dorsal left forearm. The mother noticed the baby had been teething for the past week and had been sucking on her forearm. The location of the suction mark fit perfectly with the shape of her mouth and the location where the baby can reach and suck. She was also witnessed sucking on her forearm during the medical visit. This suction mark is similar to the associated ecchymosis seen in bite marks and results from the negative pressure caused by suction and tongue thrusting.[1,2] It may also result from positive pressure from teeth that disrupt the small blood vessels.[2]

ii. The suction mark is consistent with the provided explanation. In the absence of additional concerns after obtaining a full history and physical examination, there is no need for further testing. The mother was advised to provide her baby with something to chew on such as a firm rubber teething ring and to try to distract the baby so she cannot cause additional marks.

1. Brogdon BG, Shwayder T, Elifritz J. Dermatological signs of physical abuse. In: Brogdon BG, Shwayder T, Elifritz J, eds. *Child Abuse and Its Mimics in Skin and Bone*. Boca Raton, FL: CRC Press/Taylor & Francis; 2013:141–163.
2. Kellogg N. Oral and dental aspects of child abuse and neglect. *Pediatrics*. 2005;116(6):1565–1568.

CASE 38

Vincent J. Palusci

This 3-year-old child was known to have a genetic syndrome resulting in severe developmental delays, inability to move, hypotonia and wasting. You had been asked to review the child's fractures to help determine whether they had been caused by abuse or underlying medical disease. On chest CT scan, a fracture was noted which was not visible on plain x-ray (Images 38a and 38b). A skeletal survey was ordered which shows multiple bones with decreased density and increased density in the metaphyses (Images 38c, 38d and 38e).

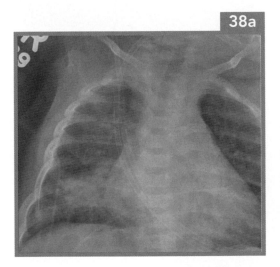

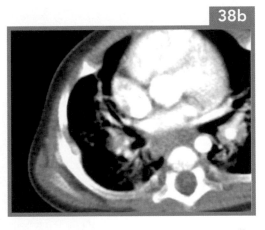

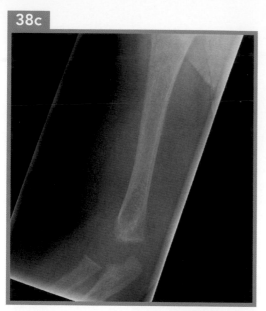

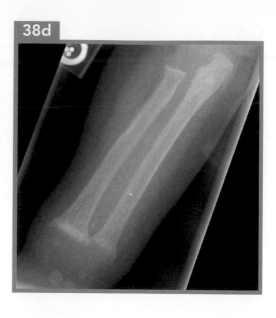

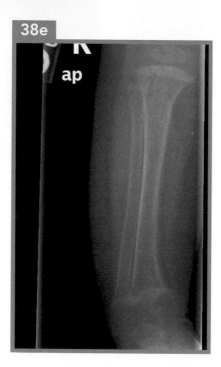

i. Can you identify the rib fracture on the chest CT? Can you correlate the plain x-ray findings with the CT findings?
ii. Given the child's genetic condition and disabilities, how would you evaluate the fracture identified? Is it abuse? Are there other potential reasons for the injuries depicted?

i. The chest CT depicts a fracture of the posterior lateral rib with periosteal new bone formation. The chest x-ray does not demonstrate the lesion, likely because the lung findings obscure the proper visualization. This fracture is concerning as there is no history as to why it occurred and the imaging does not demonstrate obvious bone disease.

ii. The long bone findings identified in the skeletal survey suggest metabolic bone disease resulting from the child's underlying genetic condition and immobility.[1,2] Given the child's disabilities, there is increased likelihood that the rib fracture may have been caused by routine care and/or chest physical therapy. The child should be evaluated with serum chemistries to identify abnormalities in calcium, phosphorus or other bone metabolic abnormalities to further identify treatable causes of bone fragility. Steps should be taken to notify medical caregivers about the child's increased risk of fracture given these concerns.

1. Brill PW, Winchester P, Kleinman PK. Differential diagnosis I: Diseases simulating abuse. In: Kleinman PK, ed. *Diagnostic Imaging of Child Abuse*. 2nd ed. St. Louis, MO: Mosby; 1998:178–196.
2. Joshi N, Slovis TL. Imaging child abuse. In: Palusci VJ, Fischer H, eds. *Child Abuse and Neglect: A Diagnostic Guide for Physicians, Surgeons, Pathologists, Dentists, Nurses and Social Workers*. London, England: Manson Publishing Ltd; 2011:91–120.

CASE 39

Carl J. Schmidt

This 18-month-old girl was found dead in bed in the morning. The toddler lived with her bio-logical mother and the latter's boyfriend, not her father. The child was in the care of the boyfriend since her mother worked at night. He claimed to be unaware of anything amiss when the mother came in from work in the morning. Emergency medical services was called when she did not awake in the morning, but it was apparent that there was some rigidity and lividity. No prolonged resuscitation was attempted. Weight was 9.2 kg (less than fifth percentile) and height was 73 cm (less than third percentile). During autopsy, there was no evidence of injury externally or inter-nally. No pathologic evidence of disease was identified (Images 39a and 39b). Toxicology testing from peripheral blood revealed morphine (130 ng/mL) and was also positive for quinine, nicotine and caffeine.

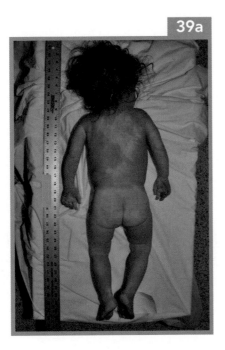
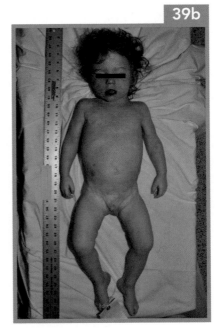

  i. What is significant about the toxicology results?
 ii. What is the source of the morphine?
iii. What are the cause and manner of death? What is the mechanism of death?
 iv. What else may be inferred from the data presented here?

i. The most significant finding is the confirmed blood concentration of morphine. It is rare for children of this age to receive morphine for medical reasons. This is a high morphine concentration even when considering post-mortem redistribution (the main cause of the change on a drug concentration post-mortem, often causing drug concentrations to rise) since the specimen was from peripheral blood. There was no documented prescription for morphine and it is safe to assume the child was not previously exposed to opiates. It is also rare to find positive results for caffeine, nicotine and quinine. There was no medical indication for quinine in this child, and the source must have an explanation.

ii. The most likely source of the morphine in the toxicology result is from a by-product of heroin metabolism until proven otherwise. Quinine is an antimalarial agent often used to cut heroin and when found with morphine, this points to heroin as its source. Heroin and its immediate metabolite, 6-acetylmorphine, have very short half-lives but are highly lipid soluble and readily penetrate the blood-brain barrier. The active metabolite of heroin is morphine. It is common to find only morphine in post-mortem toxicology analysis after heroin use and the source can be further confirmed by looking for cutting agents.

iii. The cause of death is acute opiate intoxication. Because this child must have had heroin administered to her, the manner of death was certified as homicide in the absence of any definitive evidence of accidental ingestion. Questioning of the adults in the home disclosed the male had a history of heroin abuse, but he denied having any in his possession on the night this toddler died. The mechanism of death is suppression of respiration by morphine. The effect is probably more intense in naïve users of narcotic analgesics, such as this child.

iv. This toddler was also the victim of neglect. Her height and weight were low, but her parents were adults of average size and weight. The nicotine in the blood most likely originated from indirect exposure to tobacco smoke. The use of drugs to control children has been documented in the literature.[1]

1. Yin S. Malicious use of pharmaceuticals in children. *J Pediatr.* 2010;157(5):832–836.

CASE 40

Mary Lu Angelilli with Julie Gleesing

A 5-month-old male infant was brought to the emergency department by his parents due to swelling of his head. They provided a history of falling from his bouncer seat which was placed on a kitchen table earlier that day. According to the parents, the infant landed head-first on a hardwood floor. He cried immediately and appeared fine thereafter. Later in the day, they noticed that his head was swollen. Three-dimensional (3D) computed tomography (CT) of the head was obtained after arrival to the emergency room (Image 40).

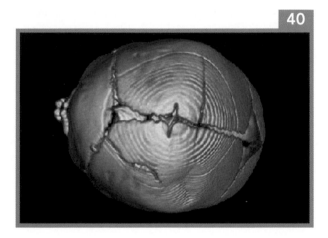

i. What is the diagnosis based on 3D CT head imaging? Is it likely accident or abuse?
ii. How should you further evaluate the infant?

i. This CT image shows one depressed impact zone, approximately triangular in shape, with three skull fractures originating from the depression. This can be seen at the bottom portion of the image. The first fracture is seen in the posterior right parietal bone and the second and third are seen in one plane in the right and left parietal bones, respectively. Although a single skull fracture can be a presentation of accidental trauma in children, this presentation with three skull fractures is unlikely to have occurred from a simple accidental trauma. Most short falls (<1.5 meters) result in only minor injuries, including bruising and even moderate falls, like those down a flight of stairs, are unlikely to produce severe head trauma. In one particular study of more than 4600 children who suffered short falls ($n = 1732$), only two children presented with a single linear skull fracture.[1] None of the children presented with multiple skull fractures. After the completion of the study, the authors concluded that serious injuries attributed to an accidental fall from a short height are unlikely and more often are a sign of serious child abuse.

ii. Further evaluation of this child should include a thorough physical examination paying careful attention to bruising, swelling or any pain on palpation.[2] The workup should also include a complete skeletal survey to identify any other osseous injury, an ophthalmological examination to visualize potential retinal haemorrhages and further head imaging including MRI to delineate any intracranial bleeding or other signs of trauma.[3] On further evaluation, this child was noted to have bruising on his physical examination and multiple healing rib fractures on his skeletal survey. Subsequently in court, the child's father admitted that he forcefully threw the baby down a flight of stairs.

1. Schunk JE, Schutzman SA. Pediatric head injury. *Pediatr Rev.* 2012;33(9):398–410; quiz 410–411.
2. Kellogg ND. Evaluation of suspected child physical abuse. *Pediatrics.* 2007;119(6):1232–1241.
3. Herman BE, Makoroff KL, Corneli HM. Abusive head trauma. *Pediatr Emerg Care.* 2011;27(1):65–69.

CASE 41

Mary E. Smyth

Child Protective Services received a referral for this infant who was noted to have bleeding from her mouth on multiple occasions. The parents were distraught and denied any intentional trauma to this child. The child was healthy and had an unremarkable neonatal and past medical history. Image 41 shows where the bleeding occurred on the child's lip.

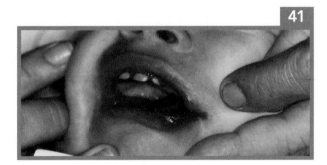

i. What condition is seen in this patient?
ii. What is the treatment and prognosis?

i. This child has an infantile haemangioma on her lower lip. Most of these lesions are seen shortly after birth as was the case for this patient. Infantile haemangiomas are composed of a proliferation of endothelial cells and typically grow during the first year of life and then regress over the next decade. No special treatment is indicated for small lesions, not located in vital areas of the body.

ii. Potential complications of these lesions are ulceration and bleeding, especially when they are located on areas that are easily traumatized such as the lips. The parents of this child were provided with pictures and a letter documenting the benign nature of this condition for daycare providers and other well-meaning parties who might be concerned about possible abuse.[1,2]

1. AlJasser M, Al-Khenaizan S. Cutaneous mimickers of child abuse: A primer for pediatricians. *Eur J Pediatr.* 2008;167:1221–1230.
2. Wheeler DM, Hobbs CJ. Mistakes in diagnosing nonaccidental injury: 10 years' experience. *Br Med J (Clin Res Ed).* 1988;296:1233–1236.

CASE 42

Vincent J. Palusci

A 2-month-old girl was brought to your office with a history of facial lesions shown which had become progressively worse over the day (Image 42). The infant was taking less formula from the bottle and was sleeping more than usual. No vomiting, diarrhoea or fever had been noted.

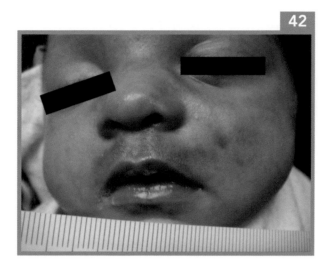

   i. What does the image show?
  ii. What tests are important to determine the aetiology for this patient's presentation?
 iii. What important information about the social history will help child protective authorities provide for a safe environment for the infant?

i. The child had bruises over the upper lip. There may have been additional lesions over the cheek that are not well depicted. Child abuse is strongly suspected.

ii. A complete physical examination should be done, including examination of the inside of the mouth to look for intraoral injuries such as torn frena, injuries to the palate or injuries to the inner cheeks or gums. A history of any bleeding, bruising or trauma should be asked. Weight, height and head circumference should be measured and information about the birth should also be sought, including whether the infant was given supplemental vitamin K at birth. No other skin findings were noted and there were no frena injuries.[1] Given the possibility of inflicted trauma in this presentation, head imaging and full imaging of the axial skeleton using a skeletal survey is indicated. Coagulation tests such as a complete blood count, prothrombin time and partial thromboplastin times are also indicated to determine if the child has an underlying coagulation disorder contributing to the bleeding.[2]

iii. A full psychosocial assessment was needed to determine the strengths and needs of the family to raise and protect this infant. It was important to review who had been caring for the infant and what findings, if any, there had been on well-baby medical visits since birth. It was critical to speak with the caretakers about the baby's ability to feed from the bottle, whether the baby had been crying or fussy, and whether solids had been introduced, and whether they had attempted to force the bottle or other objects into the infant's mouth to promote intake. Physical abuse, force feeding, facial trauma or underlying bleeding disorders are all possible explanations for these findings.

1. Maguire S, Hunter B, Hunter L, Sibert JR, Mann M, Kemp AM. Diagnosing abuse: A systematic review of torn frenum and other intra-oral injuries. *Arch Dis Child*. 2007;92(12):1113–1117.
2. Anderst JD, Carpenter SL, Abshire TC. Evaluation for bleeding disorders in suspected child abuse. *Pediatrics*. 2013;131(4):e1314–e1322.

CASE 43

Margaret T. McHugh

A 7-year-old girl was brought to the emergency department by the mother for evaluation of swelling 'down there'. She reported to her mother that she fell in the park. Her mother was concerned that she was sexually molested. During examination, these findings were noted (Image 43a). Child was not seen for follow-up to demonstrate diminution in the size of labia and clitoral hood with resolution of hematoma.

   i. Were the mother's concerns reasonable given the images provided?
  ii. Would additional history and information from prior medical exams have been helpful?
 iii. What other findings are noted?

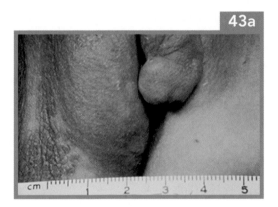

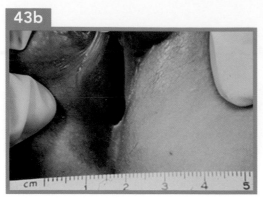

43b

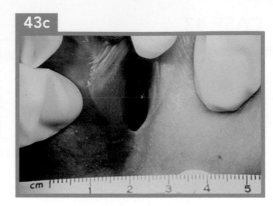

43c

i. The mother should be concerned about trauma from whatever cause. Image 43a shows a swelling of the right labia majorum and clitoral hood consistent with blunt trauma.

ii. Further evaluation (Images 43b and 43c) demonstrates a haemangioma that appeared to have been traumatized with subsequent bleeding into the haemangioma. The mother reported that she has noted a slight difference in the size of the child's labia from infancy. After the child complained of pain after a fall on the monkey bars, her mother saw a marked increase in the size and change in colour of the area.

iii. The images show asymmetry with one side having a mild labial adhesion with no apparent hymenal injury. Hymenal findings are uncommon after blunt accidental trauma to the genitals, although they can occur in association with severe external findings and can simulate child abuse.[1]

1. Levin AV, Selbst SM. Vulvar hemangioma simulating child abuse. *Clin Pediatr.* 1988;27:213–215.

CASE 44

Dena Nazer

A 3-month-old baby girl presents with a 2-day history of redness of her eyes. Her parents initially noticed redness of her right eye and then the next day noticed redness of her left eye. They denied any history of trauma. She has been acting normally and is otherwise asymptomatic. Image 44a reveals findings on the day of presentation.

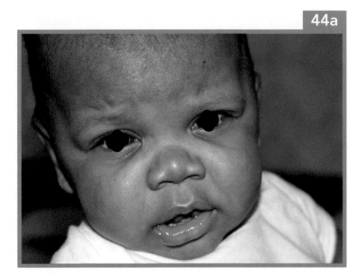

44a

   i. What is your diagnosis?
  ii. What is your differential diagnosis?
 iii. What are your next steps in evaluating this infant?

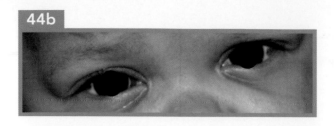

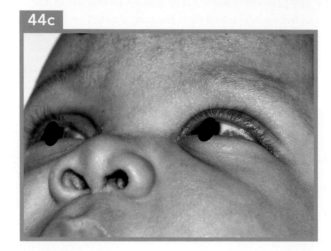

i. The image shows the face of an infant with bilateral subconjunctival haemorrhages. Image 44b is a close-up of her eyes. To better visualize the subconjunctival haemorrhage, sometimes it is helpful to rotate the head slightly so the baby looks to the side as shown in Image 44c.

ii. The differential diagnosis of subconjunctival haemorrhage includes traumatic (including child abuse), infectious, haematological and oncological aetiologies. It results from the rupture of the small vessels of the subconjunctiva and may result from direct trauma to the eye or from increases in intrathoracic pressure such as coughing, vomiting or constipation.[1] A subconjunctival haemorrhage is common in newborn infants.[1] It is thought to be due to pressure changes across the infant's body during childbirth.[1] The parents of this infant gave a history of the baby having subconjunctival haemorrhages at birth and resolving within 2 weeks.

iii. Child abuse and consultation with a child abuse paediatric specialist should be considered even in the absence of historical or clinical signs of physical abuse in children with subconjunctival haemorrhages beyond the newborn period.[2,3] In this baby, there was no history of trauma or any other symptoms provided. Her physical examination was otherwise normal with no signs suggestive of abuse or neglect. A social work assessment revealed no risk factors. The child protection team recommended an ophthalmology consultation, a head MRI scan to evaluate for head trauma and a skeletal survey to evaluate for acute or healing fractures. A paediatric ophthalmologist examined the eyes and documented no retinal haemorrhages or any other injuries or abnormalities apart from the subconjunctival haemorrhages. The head MRI was normal. The skeletal survey showed healing rib fractures of the left lateral second to fourth ribs. The combination of subconjunctival haemorrhages and unexplained rib fractures resulted in a diagnosis of child physical abuse.

1. Katzman GH. Pathophysiology of neonatal subconjunctival hemorrhage. *Clin Pediatr (Phila)*. 1992;31(3):149–152.
2. DeRidder CA, Berkowitz CD, Hicks RA, Laskey AL. Subconjunctival hemorrhages in infants and children: A sign of nonaccidental trauma. *Pediatr Emerg Care*. 2013;29(2):222–226.
3. Spitzer SG, Luorno J, Noel LP. Isolated subconjunctival hemorrhages in nonaccidental trauma. *J Aapos*. 2005;9(1):53–56.

CASE 45

Vincent J. Palusci

A 4-year-old obese boy was referred to your office for evaluation of sexual abuse. His mother was concerned that his penis 'has been rubbed off' after a court-ordered visit with his father. The parents were divorced and lived apart. The child reportedly stated to the mother that his father 'hurt my pee pee' and the mother noticed a change in his genitals (Image 45a).

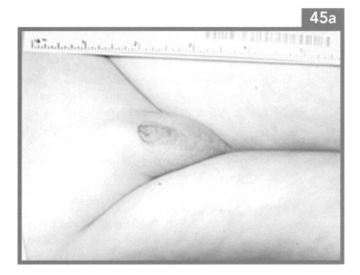

i. What does the image show?
ii. What are the possible causes for this finding?

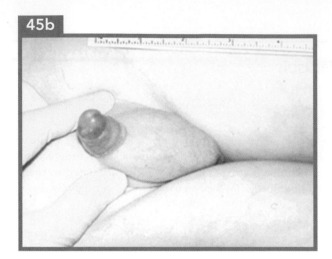

i. The penis is tethered by ligaments to the underlying bone and the accumulated fat over-lying the anterior pubic bone can surround and obscure the penile shaft and glans. With pressure applied laterally to the fat, the circumcised penis is revealed (Image 45b) with concomitant erythema of the glans and shaft secondary to chronic irritation within the fat pad.[1]

ii. The erythema depicted is nonspecific for sexual abuse and is likely related to chronic irrita-tion. This finding neither confirms nor disputes the child's disclosure. A variety of findings have been described as the result of sexual abuse of boys, including genital burns, bruises, incised wounds, lacerations or scars and other traumatic lesions. There can be accompa-nying physical abuse as well, with other findings including anal findings, non-anogenital bruises, fractures, burns, mouth injuries, brain and retinal haemorrhages and poor nour-ishment or underweight.[2]

1. Palusci VJ. Anogenital findings and sexual abuse. In: Palusci VJ, Fischer H, eds. *Child Abuse and Neglect: A Diagnostic Guide for Physicians, Surgeons, Pathologists, Dentists, Nurses and Social Workers.* London, England: Manson Publishing Ltd; 2011:163–191.
2. Hobbs CJ, Osman J. Genital injuries in boys and abuse. *Arch Dis Child.* 2007;92(4):328–331.

CASE 46

Dena Nazer

A 10-year-old boy was admitted to the paediatric intensive care unit after being hit by a car. He was riding his bike alone at 11 p.m. in the street. He had a closed head injury, but was conscious and able to answer questions. A full physical examination revealed several marks on his right thigh and left back as shown in Images 46a and 46b. When asked, he disclosed he was whipped with a cord by his mother's boyfriend.

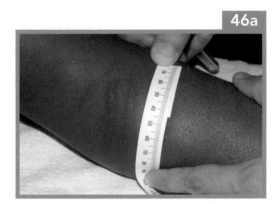

i. How would you further evaluate this patient?

i. There was concern for inadequate supervision and neglect of this child. This prompted the involvement of the hospital's child protection team which was able to obtain a thorough history and physical examination and to properly document the injuries. It is important for all patients to have a detailed physical examination especially when there are concerns of child maltreatment.[1] This child's physical examination revealed multiple loop marks that were consistent with his disclosure of being whipped with a cord. Patterned bruises and injuries in children should raise the suspicion of child abuse especially when they resemble certain objects that are used to inflict injuries (e.g. cords) as in this child. Inflicted injury also tends to occur in places away from bony prominences such as the buttocks, trunk, hands, upper arm, head and neck.[2] Child Protective Services were notified due to the physical abuse as well as the neglect. This child did not need any further laboratory testing or imaging specific for the abuse in addition to what he received due to the trauma related to being struck by the car. His evaluation did not reveal any further injuries.

1. Legano L, McHugh MT, Palusci VJ. Child abuse and neglect. *Curr Probl Pediatr Adolesc Health Care.* 2009;39(2):31.e1–e26.
2. Kellogg ND. Evaluation of suspected child physical abuse. *Pediatrics.* 2007;119(6):1232–1241.

CASE 47

Dena Nazer

A 10-month-old baby boy presented to the emergency department due to swelling of his head noticed by his mother. She noticed the swelling when she was getting the baby dressed in the morning. She denied any history of trauma. The mother's boyfriend then stated that the previous evening the baby fell and hit his head on the barbell in the living room. The baby was reaching to play with a dangling cord (Image 47a). The baby attempted to stand on the barbell's bar and hold the cord but lost his balance and hit his head on the barbell. He cried immediately. The boyfriend stated the mother was in the shower when that happened. The mother said she did recall him crying when she left him in the living room with her boyfriend, however she was not aware he fell. His physical examination was significant for extensive subgaleal haematoma on both sides of his head. Otherwise his examination did not show any further signs of trauma. His skull x-rays are shown in Images 47b, 47c and 47d.

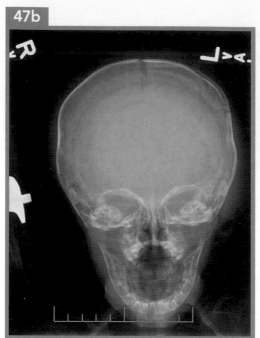

47b

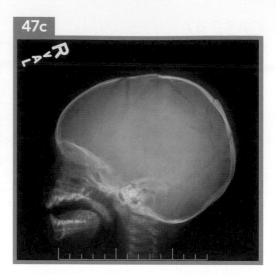

47c

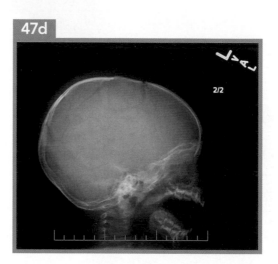

47d

2/2

i. What injury do you see in the radiology images?
ii. Is the injury consistent with an accidental injury?

i. The skull x-rays of this child show a depressed, comminuted fracture of the left frontal-parietal calvarium. A skull fracture is considered depressed when the skull has an inward displacement of the bone and the normal curvature is disrupted as in this child. It is also a comminuted fracture because the skull bone is broken into fragments.

ii. When assessing a fracture in a child, we need to consider the site and type of fracture as well as the development of the child.[1] No fracture on its own can distinguish abuse from non-abuse even in those with a lower probability for abuse.[1] In children under 2 years old with a skull fracture and a history of minor trauma, certain features raise the suspicion for abuse. These features include multiple or complex fracture, diastatic fracture (maximum fracture width more than 3 mm), depressed fracture, growing fracture, non-parietal fracture, involvement of more than one cranial bone and associated intracranial injury.[2] In a study on children less than 18 months of age presenting with isolated skull fractures, the skeletal survey revealed additional fractures in 6% of patients.[3] This child is developmentally able to reach to the cord shown in Image 47a and cruise on the furniture when holding with one hand. Falling on the bar of the barbell may have concentrated the impact to his left parietal area resulting in a depressed skull fracture. However we were concerned due to the short distance of fall and the severity of the fracture. A head CT scan was performed that re-demonstrated the fracture; however there was no intracranial bleeding. A skeletal survey was done which did not show any additional fractures. We suspected abuse due to the severity of the fracture as compared to the history of a short fall and a report was made to Child Protective Services.

1. Kemp AM, Dunstan F, Harrison S et al. Patterns of skeletal fractures in child abuse: Systematic review. *BMJ*. 2008;337:a1518.
2. Hobbs CJ. Skull fracture and the diagnosis of abuse. *Arch Dis Child*. 1984;59(3):246–252.
3. Laskey AL, Stump TE, Hicks RA, Smith JL. Yield of skeletal surveys in children ≤18 months of age presenting with isolated skull fractures. *J Pediatr*. 2013;162(1):86–89.

CASE 48

Vincent J. Palusci

A 17-year-old girl was brought to your office for a routine evaluation prior to attending school. She wished to continue playing tennis at school, but had experienced pain in her right upper extremity related to using her racquet. You noticed in her chart that there was an incident last year in which she had a fight with her boyfriend. As you examine her, you noticed several bruises as shown in Image 48. She stated they are bruises that occurred after she received some physical therapy for her arm pain last week.

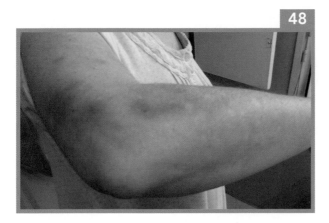

 i. Is the distribution of lesions in Image 48 concerning for abusive trauma?
ii. What non-abusive mechanisms can cause this pattern of bruising?

i. The teenager had multiple areas of discolouration over her arm and forearm which were consistent with bruises or contusions. They were located above the elbow posteriorly as well and laterally over the forearm. This location has been associated with defensive wounds after a fight. The lesions did not depict a specific pattern and were generally absent over bone prominences. No lacerations or scarring were noted. This could be concerning for inflicted trauma during physical altercation, but additional mechanisms should be explored. Furthermore, if an appropriate mechanism is not identified, studies to assess for a coagulation disorder should be considered.[1]

ii. Direct trauma to the skin over the areas of bruising and contusion could cause these lesions and a history of falls, sports or other blunt trauma should be sought. A bleeding diathesis with associated minor trauma can also cause these types of lesions. Additional information is needed to assess the physical therapy procedures which the child has reported caused the bruising. Upon contacting the therapist with the mother's consent, you find out that a particular type of deep massage was used. Using a plastic implement, the skin was squeezed and rubbed directly over muscles and tendons in an attempt to regenerate healthy soft tissues and to eliminate or reduce unwanted scar tissue that may be causing pain or movement restriction. The therapist tells you that bruising and swelling is a common effect of the treatment, and the procedure does produce unusual lesions which can persist for several weeks. The teenager says that the bruises appeared a few hours after the procedure, but her pain on movement has improved.

1. Carpenter SL, Abshire TC, Anderst JD. Evaluating for suspected child abuse: Conditions that predispose to bleeding. *Pediatrics*. 2013;131(4):e1357–e1373.

CASE 49

Margaret T. McHugh

This 6-year-old girl was referred to the endocrine service for evaluation of an 'enlarged clitoris'. The workup for a metabolic disorder was unremarkable. When a physician attempted to examine her genitalia, the child became hysterical and ran from the examination room. The endocrine team was alarmed by her behaviour and was concerned that she might have been sexually abused. Their concern was based on the child's obvious distress at the prospect of a genital examination. When questioned about her child's behaviour, the mother reported that the child has had this reaction to genital exams ever since she was examined by another physician who 'made her bleed there'. When she was examined, these findings were seen (Images 49a and 49b).

  i. How can a genital examination be facilitated in a frightened child?
 ii. What additional historical information is needed?
iii. What diagnosis can be made from these findings?

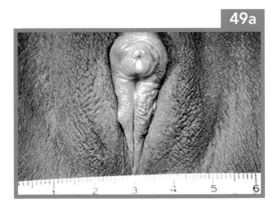

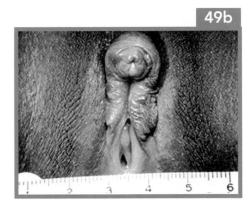

i. The child was able to cooperate for the genital examination after an extensive preparation by a child development specialist. The images were obtained during that exam after preparation. Image 49a demonstrates what appears to be an enlarged/prominent clitoris. Image 49b was obtained with mild downward traction and clearly demonstrates an adhesion of the superior/anterior aspect of the labia minora.

ii. On further questioning of the mother, she reported that the child had complained of burning on urination and was seen by a primary care provider. While the physician was examining the child, the mother observed that he 'pulled on her down there'. The child began to cry and subsequently the mother noted blood in the child's underwear.

iii. These findings are consistent with labial adhesions that were partially separated during the previous examination. The non-estrogenized genital tissue of a prepubertal girl can be traumatized with vigorous traction during an examination.[1]

1. Leung AK, Robson WL, Tay-Uyboco J. The incidence of labial fusion in children. *J Paediatr Child Health*. 1993;29(3):235–236.

CASE 50

Mary E. Smyth

This 5-year-old male was referred to the hospital child protection team because of circumferential bruising of his wrists and ankles, suspected of being ligature marks. He began complaining of knee pain and swelling, and bruising around his ankles 2 weeks after a viral illness. He then fell off a bunk bed ladder and was evaluated in the emergency centre where foot swelling and bruises on his scrotum, wrists and ankles were noted. The patient and all members of his family denied any abusive trauma. These pictures show the appearance of the patient's wrists and ankles (Images 50a and 50b).

   i. How should the cutaneous findings in this patient be described and what diagnosis does this suggest?
  ii. What laboratory studies, if any, will help make this diagnosis?
 iii. Why is the 'bruising' in this patient worse around the ankles and wrists? Should this case be reported to Child Protective Services?

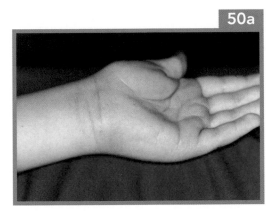

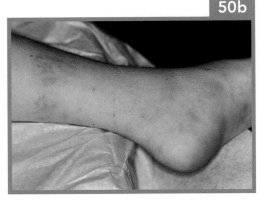

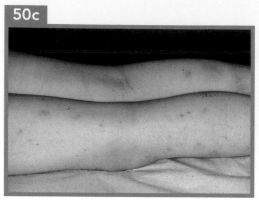

50c

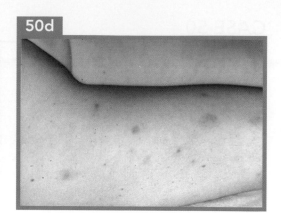

50d

i. These pictures (Images 50c and 50d) show the patient's legs and buttocks. The pictures show diffuse petechiae and purpura located mostly on the patient's lower extremities and buttocks. This is the classic appearance of the purpuric 'rash' seen in Henoch-Schönlein purpura (HSP). The rash may begin as urticarial wheals that evolve into macules and papules and finally petechiae and purpura which may be palpable. Typically the rash occurs in dependent areas but may also involve the upper extremities, face and trunk.

ii. The diagnosis of HSP is a clinical one, with a history spanning days to weeks. HSP is a small vessel vasculitis and as such may involve multiple organ systems including the joints, liver and kidneys.[1]

iii. The rash and bruised appearance may be accentuated over pressure points as in this case where underlying vascular fragility was exacerbated by the patient having worn clothing with elastic at the wrists and ankles. Differentiation from physical abuse is made primarily through history and clinical presentation and the associated multisystem involvement seen in HSP.[2,3]

1. Barron KS. Vasculitides. In: Rudolph CD, ed. *Rudolph's Pediatrics*. 22nd ed. New York, NY: McGraw-Hill Medical; 2011:810–811.
2. AlJasser M, Al-Khenaizan S. Cutaneous mimickers of child abuse: A primer for pediatricians. *Eur J Pediatr.* 2008;167(11):1221–1230.
3. Brown J, Melinkovich P. Schonlein-Henoch purpura misdiagnosed as suspected child abuse. A case report and literature review. *JAMA* 1986;256(5):617–618.

CASE 51

Pamela Wallace Hammel

This child was brought to the emergency department by her mother. Her mother stated she had been bitten by her sibling on both her cheeks and chest (Image 51a).

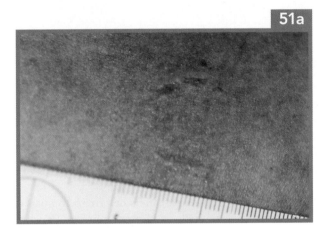

i. What does the image show?
ii. What can be done to identify the person who bit the child? How does this affect the case?

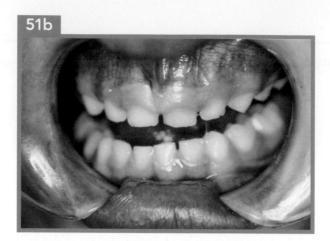

51b

i. Two impressions in the skin overlying an area of erythema were apparent. The impressions were not continuous or uniform, suggesting patterns left by small teeth. A paediatric bite is smaller overall and displays spacing between the teeth from diastemas present in the primary dentition. It is difficult to determine a paediatric from adult bite, especially in the mixed dentition. The upper arch is superior in the image. The size and number of teeth can be used to differentiate young children from adults.[1]

ii. When a potential biter can be identified, it can be helpful to compare images of the mouth/teeth with the bite. Differences in angle of photography can prevent a precise match, but generally the number of teeth and relative intercanine distance can be determined. Ideally, a plaster cast of the biter's teeth could be fashioned and compared to the bite; but this is usually not possible or desirable. In a bite from another child which is not serious, there may not be child abuse per se but there can be child supervisory neglect. In this case, note the dentition of the biter (Image 51b) has diastemas present which were exhibited in the bite mark together with a small size of the incisal edges of the teeth. The biter was 6 years old.

1. Hammel PW. Recognition of child abuse by dentists, healthcare professionals and law enforcement. In: Palusci VJ, Fischer H, eds. *Child Abuse and Neglect: A Diagnostic Guide*. London, England: Manson; 2011:143–154.

CASE 52

Alan Sprigg

A 15-month-old girl was staying with her grandmother for the weekend. While bathing her on the first night, she noticed swelling over her forearm. She had fallen over earlier that evening but only cried for a short while and then continued playing normally. The next day she took her to her family physician who noted mild tenderness and some swelling. She was referred for a paediatric assessment. The paediatrician found a well-nourished, happy baby and wonders about a congenital anomaly of her forearm or a tumour. She requests a radiograph (Image 52).

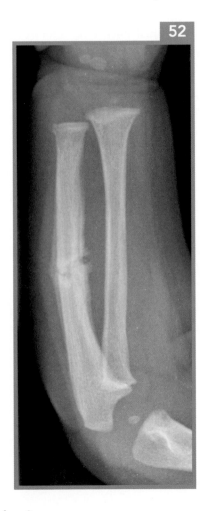

  i. What does this image show?
 ii. What would you do next?
iii. Could this be an accidental injury?

i. This single view shows a healing, undisplaced transverse fracture of the ulna, without a radial fracture. In a toddler this can be due to a fall onto the outstretched hand. More commonly both bones fracture together and may be angulated. When one bone fractures the intact bone may splint the fractured bone and may not be easy to identify clinically. The healing reaction on either side of the fracture site means this is an old injury. The tenderness suggests a recent fracture – in this case a re-fracture – at the site of old injury.

ii. Child protection investigations were started as there was no clear explanation for the original fracture at presentation. A full skeletal survey and biochemical assessment revealed no other injuries or underlying bone disorder.

iii. A few days later her parents recalled her falling off the sofa 3 weeks previously. They thought she had sprained her wrist and she was reluctant to use it. They gave her pain relief with paracetamol, for 2 days after which she used the arm normally. Not all carers bring their child to hospital rapidly. A casual observer may notice swelling or deformity when a regular carer did not. Once a bone is fractured (but not casted) it is relatively vulnerable to clinical re-fracture with minor trauma. It was appropriate to perform a full child protection assessment due to the initial absence of history to explain the fracture.[1] The final history offered was accepted as a reasonable explanation for the old injury at presentation.

1. Flaherty EG, Perez-Rossello JM, Levine MA, Hennrikus WL. Evaluating children with fractures for child physical abuse. *Pediatrics*. Feb 2014;133(2):e477–e489.

CASE 53

Patricia O. Brennan

This 6-month-old baby had been left with a babysitter for an evening. When the parents returned, the sitter reported the baby had been very unsettled for the first half of the evening. The baby was asleep when the parents went in to check her and so they left her asleep. The next morning, the mother changed the baby's nappy/diaper and discovered a rash over the baby's buttocks (Image 53). She was concerned about the nature of the rash, especially as there was no previous history of skin problems.

    i. What is the nature of the rash?

   ii. What is the most likely cause?

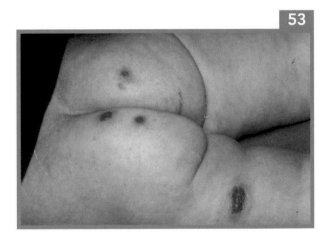

i. The infant has three circular red lesions on the buttocks and one oval blistered lesion on the posterior left thigh.

ii. The most likely cause of the lesions is burns from a cigarette. The lesions are circular and in an unusual position, have appeared suddenly for a nappy rash and are unlikely to be staphylococcal. The round blistered lesions are typical of stubbing burns as they are round. The oval blistered lesion is typical of a brushing burn from a cigarette. Accidental cigarette burns are usually on exposed surfaces and many are brushing flame-shaped burns. Intentional non-scald burns are relatively common and are often associated with other non-accidental injuries such as bruises. Contact burns are the most common non-scald intentional burns, especially from household items such as cigarettes, irons, cigarette lighters, hairdryers and curling tongs. They are usually clearly demarcated in shapes that mirror the causative object and usually occur in children older than 3 years of age. They are often on the backs of hands, limbs or trunk. However, accidental burns may be significant markers of child abuse as it has been reported that a child who suffers an accidental burn is seven times more likely to suffer future abuse or neglect.[1]

1. Kemp AM, Maquire S, Lumb RC, Harris SM, Mann MK. Contact, cigarette and flame burns in physical abuse: A systematic review. *Child Abuse Negl.* 2014;23(1):35–47.

CASE 54

Tor Shwayder

A 4-year-old girl presented with a slowly expanding rash on her right cheek (Image 54a). The rash has been in the same location for weeks. The central older part of the lesion was grey-brown in colour with a raised itchy rim. This was presumed to be tinea facei and was treated with topical anti-fungal creams with little effect. Several physicians considered this a thermal burn and possible child abuse.

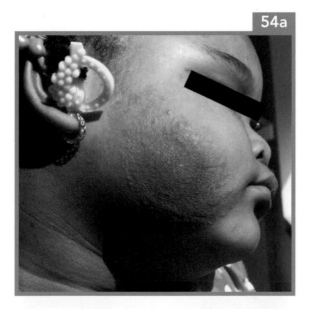

i. What is the diagnosis?
ii. Name two ways to make a definitive diagnosis.

i. Further history obtained from her mother notes the rash first appeared after the child was started on oral isoniazid for tuberculosis exposure. This is a fixed drug eruption as a result of treatment with isoniazid. Cutaneous drug eruptions are the most common adverse reactions attributed to drugs with the most common being fixed drug eruption.[1] Fixed drug eruption is a specific adverse reaction to medications that appears usually as a single or a few localized, sharply demarcated, round-to-oval, oedematous, dusky red macules or patches.[2] Lesions might appear locally as bullae or erosions. Rarely, some patients might have a severe clinical manifestation, such as extensive bullous eruptions.

ii. There are two ways to make the diagnosis: one would be a skin biopsy; another would be to stop the medication, isoniazid in this case and closely follow up the rash. These types of drug hypersensitivity reactions are unique. The offending agent can be ingested, inhaled or given via suppository. The lesions develop within 2 weeks after exposure. Subsequent exposure leads to a rash within a day. The unique feature of this rash is that it always appears in the same location, occasionally with new spots elsewhere. The eruption can be anywhere on the body, head to toe, but tends to favour the 'lips and tips' meaning face, lips, hands, feet and genitals. As the initial erythema resolves a 'gun metal gray' colour remains. The erythematous oedematous variant has very large plaques (over 10 cm) as seen in this photo. They do not leave scars. Offending agents are often NSAIDS, antihistamines, paracetamol, tetrahydrozoline eyedrops, sulphonamides, barbituates, tetracyclines, carbamazepine and various laxatives. Skin biopsy is the definitive diagnostic procedure. Another example of such a rash is shown (Image 54b). If one stops administering the causative drug the rash will slowly fade over several weeks as the antigen is cleared from the skin. The centre can become darker in colour and remains for many months. Treatment is to identify the offending agent – remembering the over-the-counter 'innocent' items like vitamins, antihistamines. Topical steroid creams help with the itch and inflammation.

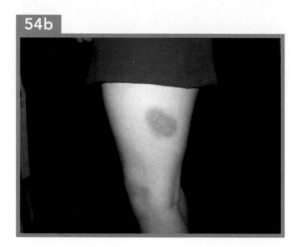

54b

1. Raksha MP, Marfatia YS. Clinical study of cutaneous drug eruptions in 200 patients. *Indian J Dermatol Venereol Leprol.* 2008;74(1):80.
2. Chen JF, Chiang CP. Dermacase. Can you identify this condition? Generalized fixed drug eruption. *Can Fam Physician.* 2012;58(6):659–661.

CASE 55

Vincent J. Palusci

A 10-year-old boy who had immigrated from the Middle East 5 years ago reported being burned by his sibling. He told his teacher that his older brother had taken a hot iron from the stove and burned his leg 'because I was bad'. He said this happened a week previously and he was worried about whether it would heal. He said it hurt 'a lot' and he told his mother, who reportedly told his brother to 'stop doing that'. The child reported this had happened before 'in my country' and that he had seen another child 'punished' with similar burning before he came to the United States. During examination, you noticed a healing lesion on his anterior thigh (Image 55a).

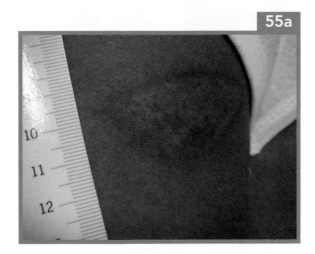

    i. What does Image 55a show?
   ii. Is this consistent with the child's disclosure?
  iii. Is this a commonly accepted cultural practice for discipline?

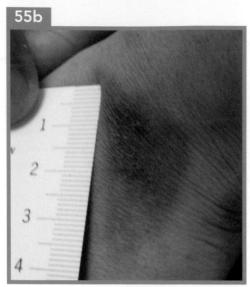

55b

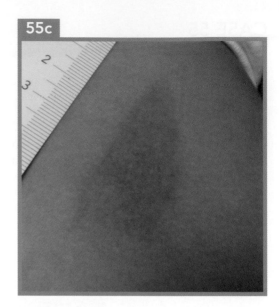

55c

i. The image shows a pattern skin lesion measuring 2 by 3 cm, with a hyperpigmented outline and pink, new skin with granulation. No eschar formation or superinfection is apparent. There is increased pigmentation at the base of the triangle shape. One possible interpretation is that the point or tip of the triangle-shaped object (consistent with an iron) was hotter or had longer contact with the skin, resulting in a deeper burn and pink skin formation.

ii. Given the healing nature and shape of the lesion, the disclosure seemed consistent with the injury. The cultural explanation for the injury and whether it was caused by another child were unclear. However, when you examined the 7-year-old sibling, she made similar disclosures and showed similar lesions (Images 55b and 55c). These appear smaller, healed and with uniform hyperpigmentation.

iii. There is consensus against using extremely harsh methods of physical punishment such as burning or smothering.[1] Many children have reported receiving violent punishment in countries ranging from Bosnia and Herzegovina (33%) to Yemen (94%); 1%–44% have experienced severe physical discipline. More violent discipline is used in countries where more domestic violence, polygamy and child labour are reported. More education and more books in the home were associated with a greater use of non-violent discipline strategies. In the United Kingdom, such violent discipline is not acceptable and is reported to Child Protective Services. However, it is usually managed by education for the parents rather than taking them to court for child abuse.

1. Palusci VJ, Nazer D. Maltreatment and advocacy. In: Kamat DM, Fischer PR, eds. *Textbook of Global Child Health*. Elk Grove Village, IL: American Academy of Pediatrics; 2011:127–152.

CASE 56

Pamela Wallace Hammel

An 18-month-old child was brought to the emergency department by his mother with extensive bruising of genitalia and inability to urinate. His mother stated that he fell from the jungle gym and had a straddling injury (Images 56a–e).

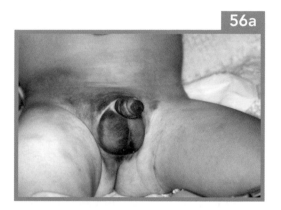

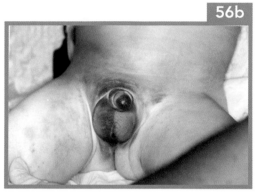

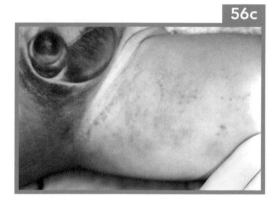

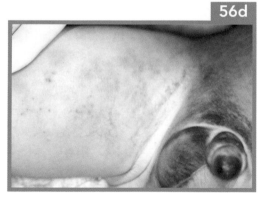

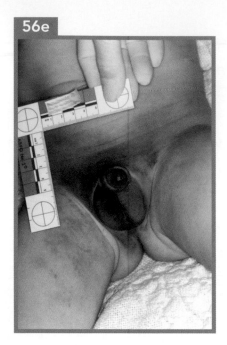

56e

   i. Is the explanation plausible?
  ii. What is the key element in the photos to prove or disprove the explanation?
 iii. What is the aetiology of this patient's presentation?

i. A straddling injury is not a consistent explanation for this injury, as it would not remove epithelium from the glans penis. These injuries are due to oral sexual assault.

ii. There are subtle injuries to the epithelium of both thighs, with slight bruising.

iii. While friction and abrasion injuries have been described in physical torture,[1] the aetiology of the thigh injuries in this case is rubbing from the whiskers of the assailant, also known as 'whisker burn'. A careful examination is essential in the presence of dramatic injuries to ensure important subtle injuries, i.e. the thighs, are not overlooked.

1. Ghaleb SS, Elshabrawy EM, Elkaradawy MH, Nemr Welson N. Retrospective study of positive physical torture cases in Cairo (2009 and 2010). *J Forensic Leg Med*. 2014;24:37–45.

CASE 57

Vincent J. Palusci

You were asked to consult on a 15-year-old obese Chinese male who was being treated for osteogenic sarcoma. During his back examination, you noticed several pattern marks which covered his back from his cervical to his lumbosacral paraspinal areas (Image 57a). Some were circular and others appeared to blend together and coalesce around the spine. They were red and purple in colour. The lesions are slightly tender to the touch, but there is no break in the skin.

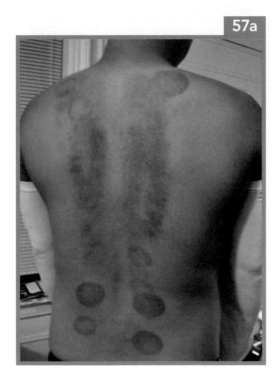

57a

   i. What are the possible causes for these findings?
  ii. Do you have any recommendations about further treatment?

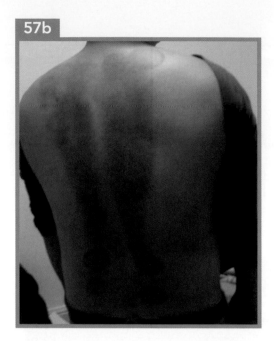

57b

i. The circular lesions suggest an object with a curved or curvilinear edge has been applied to the skin to cause bruises. Given that there is some bruising in the centre, additional pressure or force has been used within the outlined objects. The location of the lesion away from bony prominences suggest non-accidental trauma. This pattern is consistent with a complementary medical practice called cupping.[1] Cupping therapy is an ancient Chinese form of alternative medicine in which a local suction is created on the skin; practitioners believe this mobilizes blood flow in order to promote healing. Suction is created using heat or mechanical devices and is known in local languages as baguan, banki, bahnkes, bekam, buhang, bentusa, kyukaku and ciogio, among other names. The patient and his family confirmed that he had been treated with the practice 4 days before. The lesions appeared more extensive on day 1 (Image 57b).

ii. It is important to realize that families use a variety of traditional and non-traditional (complementary and alternative) treatments for cancer pain in their children. Depending on how it is applied, children often describe it as a soothing experience with little pain during the procedure and improvement in cancer pain for days or weeks afterward. In a review, psychoeducational interventions, music interventions, acupuncture plus drug therapy, Chinese herbal medicine plus cancer therapy, compound kushen injection, reflexology, lycopene, qigong, cupping, cannabis, Reiki, homeopathy and creative art therapies might have beneficial effects on cancer pain.[2] Results were inconsistent for massage therapy, transcutaneous electric nerve stimulation and music plus cancer treatment. Given that these lesions are not preventable and may actually reflect the appropriate application of cupping, parents and children should receive appropriate counselling regarding reducing the pain of the procedure as well as complications from heat or bleeding, particularly if the child has coagulation problems related to their underlying diagnosis.

1. Palusci VJ, Nazer D. Maltreatment and advocacy. In: Kamat DM, Fischer PR, eds. *Textbook of Global Child Health*. Elk Grove Village, IL: American Academy of Pediatrics; 2011:127–152.
2. Bao Y, Kong X, Yang L, Liu R, Shi Z, Li W, Hua B, Hou W. Complementary and alternative medicine for cancer pain: An overview of systematic reviews. *Evid Based Complement Alternat Med*.2014;2014:http://dx.doi.org/10.1155/2014/170396.

CASE 58

Dena Nazer

A 16-month-old Hispanic baby girl presented with a 2-day history of redness and swelling of the left side of her groin. Her mother thought she was bitten by an insect, however she did not witness the bite. The redness spread with areas of discolouration, and a blister developed the next morning. The creases were spared as shown in Image 58. The child protection team was consulted due to the suspicion of an abusive burn. The burn was thought to be inconsistent with the history provided of an insect bite.

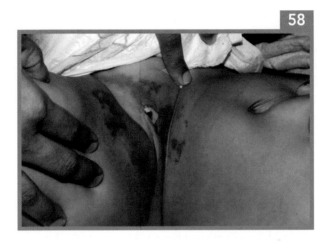

i. What further questions might you ask the mother?
ii. How would you further manage this case?

i. As the use of complementary and alternative medicine increases among children, it is important to ask parents about the use of herbs, folk remedies or other treatments as part of the routine paediatric history.[1] The mother of this child initially denied applying lotions or creams to the area, however she was not asked specifically about using complementary medicine. On further questioning the next day, the mother stated that she applied fresh crushed garlic directly to the child's skin overnight on the first day of symptoms to treat the suspected insect bite. She was advised to do so by her mother in Mexico. The crushed garlic was covered tightly by the child's diaper/nappy and caused second-degree burns to the groin. Chemical burns can result after the topical application of raw garlic, especially in young children whose skin is delicate and more susceptible than adults and particularly when applied for a long period of time such as in this child.[2] It is not unusual for parents not to volunteer the information regarding the use of complementary medicine or deny it initially. It is essential to address this respectfully with the families as well as to become familiar with different complementary and alternative medicine practices in order to be able to differentiate them from child abuse.[3]

ii. Folk remedies are well recognized as potential sources of confusion with child abuse.[2] While not intentionally abusive, they may lead to adverse effects and to delay in seeking definitive medical care.[4] The adverse effects of garlic were explained thoroughly to the child's mother and she was instructed not to apply any more garlic to her child's skin. The chemical burn was treated and she was seen by her paediatrician 5 days following discharge. The burn had healed well with no scarring. The Child Protective Services worker made a visit to the home and determined there were no concerning signs for child maltreatment.

1. Sawni-Sikand A, Schubiner H, Thomas RL. Use of complementary/alternative therapies among children in primary care pediatrics. *Ambul Pediatr.* 2002;2(2):99–103.
2. Nazer D, Saadeh S, Evans J, Sawni A, Palusci VJ. Child abuse or mimic: Child with bullous lesion on left side of groin. *Consultant for Pediatr.* 2007;6(4):240–246.
3. Palusci VJ, Nazer D. Maltreatment and advocacy. In: Kamat DM, Fischer PR, eds. *Textbook of Global Child Health*. Elk Grove Village, IL: American Academy of Pediatrics; 2011:127–152.
4. Nazer D, Smyth M. Cutaneous conditions mimicking child abuse. In: Palusci VJ, Fischer H, eds. *Child Abuse and Neglect: A Diagnostic Guide for Physicians, Surgeons, Pathologists, Dentists, Nurses and Social Workers*. London, England: Manson; 2011:69–90.

CASE 59

Mary E. Smyth

This 10-month-old male was left in the care of his 16-year-old uncle for several hours. When his mother returned home, she changed the baby's diaper/nappy and noted that he had profuse diarrhoea and bruises around his anus. Upon examination in the emergency centre, he was stable, consolable and had a normal physical examination except for the injuries shown (Image 59a).

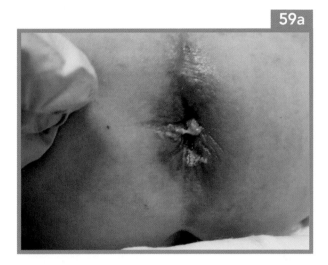

59a

i. What injuries are seen?
ii. What was the likely cause of these injuries?
iii. What is the appropriate management?

i. In addition to the bruises noted by his mother, the picture shows fissures and perianal tears distributed in a wheel-spoke appearance around the anus. Some appear to be actively bleeding.

    ii. These injuries are seen with penetrating and blunt force trauma to the anus, likely secondary to sexual assault.[1-3]

    iii. Child Protective Services and the police were notified and the uncle confessed to having penetrated the baby's anus with his penis. The uncle had a prior history of criminal sexual conduct. A sexual assault evidence kit ('rape kit') was used to methodically collect and store samples from the anus. The paediatric surgeons were consulted to evaluate the possibility of deep injuries to the rectum or pelvis.

1. Orr CJ, Clark MA, Hawley DA, Pless JE, Tate LR, Fardal PM. Fatal anorectal injuries: A series of four cases. *J Forensic Sci*. 1995;40(2):219–221.
2. Muram D. Anal and perianal abnormalities in prepubertal victims of sexual abuse. *Am J Obstetrics Gynecol*. 1989;161(2):278–281.
3. Kadish HA, Schunk JE, Britton H. Pediatric male rectal and genital trauma: Accidental and nonaccidental injuries. *Pediatr Emerg Care*. 1998;14(2):95–98.

CASE 60

Tor Shwayder

A 16-year-old African-American male is referred for evaluation. You notice these oddly similar scars on the dorsum of both of his forearms. They are of similar shape and size as shown in Image 60. He is reluctant to discuss the issue or the aetiology of these scars.

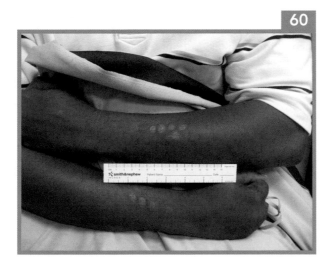

   i. What is the diagnosis?

  ii. What further actions should be taken, if any?

i. After some gentle probing, this young man admitted to burning his forearm with a lit cigarette. When asked for a reason, he stated, 'I was bored'. He declined to disclose if drugs or alcohol were involved in the incident. No other lesions compatible with abuse were noted on full skin exam. It appeared based on history to be a one-time incident. Definitive diagnosis in this case was by history and exam. A skin biopsy would show an 'old' scar which alone is not helpful. The exact 10 mm diameter of all the scars and the repetition of the marks suggest an external agent that could cause damage to the skin. Heat or cold would leave similar marks, however a hot object would cause damage to the skin more rapidly than would a cold object.

ii. Burns can be self-inflicted as found in deliberate self-harm syndromes, consisting of continual, sudden urges towards self-harm, and can be an attempt at suicide.[1] Self-mutilating behaviours are a known psychopathy and patients should be evaluated by a trained mental health professional in addition to the treatment of the burn injuries. These injuries are often seen in patients with a borderline personality disorder who may burn themselves repeatedly.[2] Patients with suicidal ideation should also be identified and followed up closely by mental health specialists. With regard to reducing the scar – great strides have been made with the newer lasers such as fractionated CO_2 lasers to 'break up' these scars and remodel the skin.

1. Toon MH, Maybauer DM, Arceneaux LL et al. Children with burn injuries—Assessment of trauma, neglect, violence and abuse. *J Inj Violence Res.* 2011;3(2):98–110.
2. Balakrishnan C, Greer KA, Tse KG, Hardaway MY. Specific pattern burn in a psychiatric patient. *Burns: J Int Soc Burn Injuries.* 1993;19(5):439–440.

CASE 61

Tor Shwayder

A 4-year-old girl presented with a 1-year history of genital and perianal pruritus. There was hypopigmentation of the labia majora, thickening to the clitoral hood, bruising to the labium minus on the right, and extension of the lesion to the perianal area (Image 61). Topical antifungal treatments had been tried without help. Sexual abuse was suspected based on the clinical findings. The child did not make any disclosure of abuse.

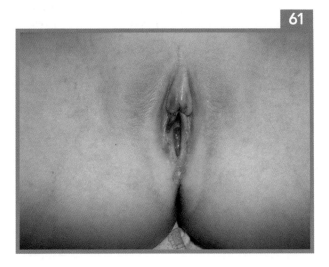

i. What is the diagnosis?
ii. What are the treatment options?
iii. Are there any cancer risks?

i. The diagnosis of this child's condition is lichen sclerosus (LS; previously known as lichen sclerosus et atrophicus). LS is an inflammatory affliction of the genitals. It occurs mainly in females, and 10%–15% of cases occur before puberty. The average age of presentation is 5 years but children may present as early as 6 months.[1] The main symptoms are irritation, itching, discharge, pain on urination, burning and bleeding (from the scratching). In boys, it can cause phimosis and difficulty voiding. The pruritus and itching cause most of the symptoms and signs such as lichenification, bruising and dyschromia. The bruising is often mistaken for child abuse. The involved skin is friable and may bleed which raises the concern of an acute trauma.[2] The classic findings are the whitened interior of the labia, perineum and perianal skin making a 'figure eight'. The classic distribution, symptoms and colour make the diagnosis. Biopsy is helpful in complex cases.

ii. Therapy for girls is high–potency topical steroid ointments or topical immune modulator ointments. The therapy of choice for phimosis in boys is circumcision.[3]

iii. Adult females with prolonged LS are at a low-level risk for squamous cell carcinoma of the perineal skin. This has not been seen in children.

1. Poindexter G, Morrell DS. Anogenital pruritus: Lichen sclerosus in children. *Pediatr Ann.* 2007;36(12):785–791.
2. Warrington SA, de San Lazaro C. Lichen sclerosus et atrophicus and sexual abuse. *Arch Dis Child.* 1996;75(6):512–516.
3. Powell JJ, Wojnarowska F. Lichen sclerosus. *Lancet.* 1999;353(9166):1777–1783.

CASE 62

Dena Nazer

A 6-year-old boy was brought to the emergency department for a medical evaluation. He was placed in foster care along with his 5-year-old sister that morning. He disclosed that his biological mother hurt him with a clothes hanger. He complained of pain and tenderness of his arms, back and buttocks. He did not complain of headaches, vomiting or abdominal pain. His sister made no disclosures and appeared shy. She elected to stay in the waiting room with her foster mother.

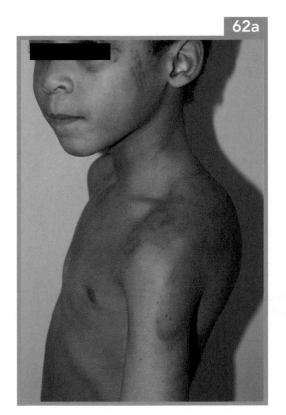

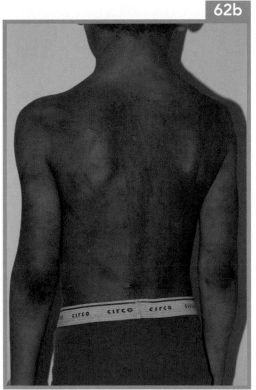

  i. What injuries are shown in Images 62a and 62b?
 ii. Would you have any further concerns regarding his sister?

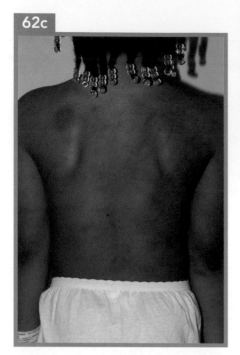

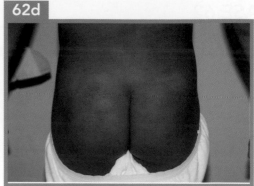

i. This child was noted to have a left black eye and linear bruises on his left cheek. He also had bruises and healed patterned marks over his back, buttocks and both arms. Most of the bruises were linear and semicircular which are consistent with the shape of the clothes hanger and consistent with his disclosure of physical abuse. His bruises were not on bony prominences or areas commonly injured accidentally. It is not possible to date bruises. Therefore children placed in foster care need to be evaluated at the time of placement to document the bruises present and any other medical concerns present prior to placement.[1]

ii. One would be concerned about his sister as she was living with him in the same household and was at risk of being abused. All siblings and children living in the same household would need to be evaluated. For those under 24 months of age, a skeletal survey is recommended when the index child is physically abused with serious injury, regardless of physical examination findings.[2] This child's sister was examined. She was noted to have similar marks on her back and buttocks, albeit less severe, as seen in Images 62c and 62d. Despite her not giving any disclosures, she needed to have a full medical evaluation. It would have been hard to notice these bruises without an evaluation due to the bruises involving areas of the body usually covered by clothing.

1. American Academy of Pediatrics Committee on Early Childhood Adoption and Dependent Care. Health care of young children in foster care. *Pediatrics.* 2002;109(3):536–541.
2. Lindberg DM, Shapiro RA, Laskey AL, Pallin DJ, Blood EA, Berger RP. Prevalence of injuries in the siblings and household contacts of abused children. *Pediatrics.* 2012;130(2):193–201.

CASE 63

Alan Sprigg

A 6-month-old baby presented to the emergency department as a 'collapse' at home. He was said to have stopped breathing and become blue. His father started mouth-to-mouth breathing and cardiac massage for under a minute. He responded rapidly. The parents called the ambulance and the baby was brought to the hospital. On assessment he was crying well and apyrexial and with normal oxygen saturations. He was assessed and investigations were performed to exclude sepsis including a chest radiograph which is shown below. This was an overexposed image which showed no evidence of pneumonia (Image 63). The baby was admitted and assessed and discharged home after 3 days. He was well and preliminary cultures were negative.

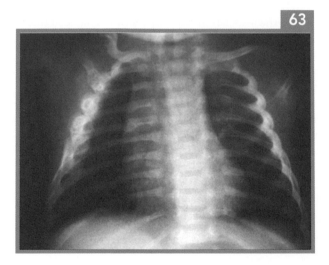

i. Five days after admission, the radiologist contacted you saying she was concerned. What do you see on the radiograph? What does this mean?
ii. Could these signs all be related to the inexpert cardiopulmonary resuscitation (CPR) that the father performed in his panic?
iii. What would you do?

i. The radiologist had identified a row of healing rib fractures laterally in the right third to fifth ribs and posteriorly in the right fifth rib. Do not be surprised if you did not see these on an x-ray taken for other purposes. Initial clinical and non-specialist radiology reviews often miss old rib fractures on an image performed for other reasons (e.g. to exclude pneumonia).

ii. Finding unexplained healing posterior or lateral rib fractures always raises the issue of non-accidental injury.[1] These all show healing reactions. In a 6-month-old these are over 10 days old and likely to be weeks old (e.g. 2–4 weeks). They do not relate to the acute event when the baby collapsed. Squeezing around the chest can cause lateral and posterior rib fractures. This may be associated with shaking injury. Baby ribs tend to bend with cardiac massage rather than fracture. The rib fracture rate even with prolonged cardiac massage is under 2% and these kinds of fractures are usually anterior.

iii. The baby should be recalled quickly, for clinical assessment and evaluation. Delay in reassessment may mean the baby is exposed to further trauma.

Underlying causes for rib fractures should be considered (e.g. metabolic bone disease if the baby was born prematurely). A full skeletal survey should be performed with a head CT scan as a minimum (or MRI) due to the association with rib fractures and head injury (squeeze and shake). Appropriate blood tests should be performed to exclude underlying bone disease. A follow-up chest x-ray should be performed at 2 weeks post-event as a routine. In this case it showed additional healing posterior rib fractures that would have been acute at presentation but undetectable. We recognize that initial chest x-rays are poor at identifying acute rib fractures unless they are displaced or angulated. The fractures may only become identifiable when they start to show healing reaction by about 2 weeks post-event. The extra radiation dose is small, but the information gained may make a significant difference to child protection. Some centres recommend a full repeat skeletal survey at follow-up.

1. *Child Protection Companion 2013*: Royal College of Paediatrics and Child Health, London; 2013.

CASE 64

Patricia O. Brennan

This 4-year-old African girl presented to the emergency department. Her parents said she had vaginal bleeding. She was otherwise healthy and there was no history of injury. On examination, she was apyrexial. General examination was normal. In the genital examination, the doctor saw a small amount of blood staining in her pants and thought the vulva looked 'odd' (Image 64). He could not identify exactly where the bleeding was coming from. A more senior doctor examined the girl and the genital findings are shown in the image.

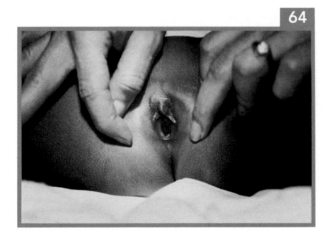

i. What are the clinical signs shown?
ii. What are the diagnosis and differential diagnosis?
iii. How should the condition be managed?

i. The illustration shows a red, doughnut-shaped swelling around the urethra covering the urethral meatus.

ii. The diagnosis, made clinically from the examination, is urethral prolapse. This benign condition is most common in prepubertal African-American girls and white post-menopausal women, although a series of urethral prolapse have been described in white girls.[1] The mucosa can become infected or ulcerated or necrotic. It usually presents with vulval bleeding (often minor) or blood on the undergarments, and sometimes with dysuria. It is thought to occur from weakening of the connections between the mucous and submucous membranes or from poor attachment between longitudinal and circular-oblique smooth muscle layers of the urethra. It is often associated with an acute episode of raised intra-abdominal pressure, such as coughing with asthma or vigorous physical activity and appears to be more common in overweight girls. It has also been associated with trauma and neurogenic abnormalities and constipation can exacerbate the condition through straining. Sexual abuse has also been reported before the urethral prolapse and must be considered in the differential diagnosis.[2] Differential diagnoses include bladder prolapse, ureterocoele prolapse, ectopic ureter, periurethral cyst, polyps and tumours such as rhabdomyosarcomas.

iii. Some centres initially try conservative management of urethral prolapse such as antibiotic and/or oestrogen cream, sitz baths and even bedrest. However, many of those which respond later relapse, some centres go straight to surgical management, particularly excision of the prolapsed mucosa round a Foley catheter and suturing the excised edges. Complications are rare, but urethral stenosis and recurrence can occur.

1. Rudin JE, Geldt VG, Alecseev EB. Prolapse of urethral mucosa in white female children: Experience with 58 cases. *J Pediatr Surg.* 1997;32(3):423–425.
2. Hillyer S, Mooppan U, Kim H, Gulmi F. Diagnosis and treatment of urethral prolapse in children: Experience with 34 cases. *Urology.* 2009;73(5):1008–1011.

CASE 65

Patricia O. Brennan

This 6-month-old boy presented to the emergency department as his mother noticed he had developed a squint. Image 65 shows his left eye and his right eye showed the same clinical sign.

    i. What does the illustration show?
    ii. What are the most common causes in this age group?
    iii. What other causes do you know?

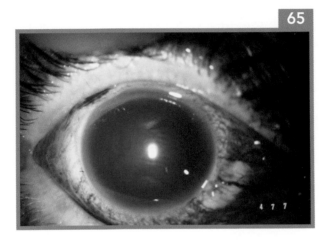

65

i. The image shows diffuse vitreous haemorrhage.

ii. There are many causes of this condition. The causes vary according to the age of presentation. Shaken baby syndrome is the most common cause in infants and toddlers and in one large series, this was the cause in 50% of cases of bilateral vitreous haemorrhage.

iii. In full-term infants, vitreous haemorrhage can be caused by birth trauma. Through childhood, other causes include accidental non-penetrating and penetrating trauma, regressed retinopathy of prematurity and tumours such as retinoblastoma. Idiopathic cases have also been described.[1]

The aetiology of vitreous haemorrhage varies in different parts of the world. In India, trauma and sequelae of retinopathy of prematurity and spontaneous haemorrhage are common causes, while child maltreatment has not been recorded there.[2]

1. Spirn MJ, Lynn MJ, Hubbard GB, 3rd. Vitreous hemorrhage in children. *Ophthalmology.* 2006;113(5):848–852.
2. Rishi P, Rishi E, Gupta A, Swaminathan M, Chhablani J. Vitreous hemorrhage in children and adolescents in India. *J AAPOS.* 2013;17(1):64–69.

CASE 66

Tor Shwayder

This 20-month-old baby girl presented with genital irritation and lesions of several months dura-tion (Image 66). Various topical creams have not been successful. Liquid nitrogen was tried but the child did not tolerate it. The child is otherwise healthy.

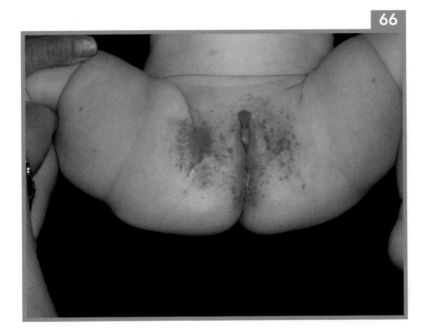

i. What are the diagnoses?
ii. How can you make these diagnoses?
iii. Is child abuse a serious issue to consider in this case?
iv. What are the treatment options?

i. This child has condyloma acuminatum (genital warts) on the clitoral hood, multiple mollusca in the area and an eczematous reaction to the mollusca.

ii. Diagnosis can be made clinically for all three. Molluscum lesions are dome-shaped pearl-coloured papules with a central umbilication. They maintain their single dome shape even when growing. Warts tend to grow in irregular masses. Biopsy of the papules will reveal warts or molluscum or eczematous skin or all three depending where you obtain the biopsy.

iii. One should always consider child abuse when sexually transmitted conditions are seen in the perineum. Molluscum in the genital region is seen frequently and is not a sign of sexual abuse when considered alone. Warts in the genital region can be a stand-alone infection. If the child or their caregiver has warts on their hands, these are readily transmitted to the genital region by activities of daily hygiene. Considering this child's age, a vertical transmission is still a possibility. A very careful examination of the child for other signs of abuse is warranted. If there are further concerns or any concerning history then a report to Child Protective Services is indicated.

iv. Treatment options include the following: For the eczema, a low-potency topical steroid such as 1% hydrocortisone ointment should be used. The mollusca and the warts will go away spontaneously – the mollusca in 2 months to 2 years, the warts in up to 5 years. Almost all the reports on topical creams for mollusca are anecdotal and not placebo controlled. The warts can be treated with topical acids, topical cantharidin, topical podophyllin extracts or topical imiquimod cream.[1] In extreme cases electrodessication and curettage under anesthesia are considered.

1. Moed L, Shwayder TA, Chang MW. Cantharidin revisited: A blistering defense of an ancient medicine. *Arch Dermatol.* 2001;137(10):1357–1360.

CASE 67

Vincent J. Palusci

You were asked to review pictures in the possession of the police. A 4-year-old boy was being cared for by his grandfather. When his mother returned home, the child told her that 'pop pop hurt me' and she saw a lesion on the boy's leg (Image 67a). She wrapped the leg in a cloth and immediately took him to an emergency room, where a more detailed examination revealed more characteristics of the lesion (Image 67b). Child Protective Services were notified.

   i. What do the images show?
  ii. Is this accidental or intentional?
 iii. What steps should be taken to protect the child during the investigation?

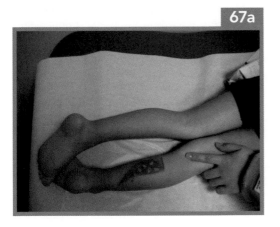
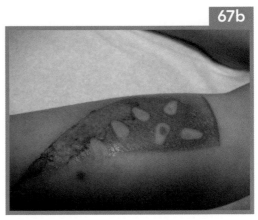

i. This image shows a recent pattern burn on the posterior calf, with evidence of at least partial thickness injury with sloughing and some sparing of the skin in the shape of holes in the heating plate of the iron. The entire shape is not depicted, but it appears that a good portion of the iron came in contact with the skin (Image 67b). No additional burns elsewhere on the legs are depicted. The second image highlights that one side of the burn appears deeper, suggesting the iron was applied with more force and/or at an angle to the leg, causing deep tissue injury on one side.

ii. Additional history was required to determine the mechanism of injury other than being caused by an iron since a plausible history of accident could be constructed based on the physical findings alone.[1] Additional information should be sought from witnesses (child, mother, grandfather) about the location of the iron, if it had been turned off, and the circumstances surrounding its contact with the child. If the iron had fallen off a table while hot onto the child's leg or whether the iron was on the floor and the child was playing/walking would help differentiate the mechanism of injury. Pictures of the iron and/or the iron itself should be obtained, and the temperature reached during use and the iron's settings should be noted by investigators.

iii. Regardless of whether the injury was intentional or accidental, there was an element of supervisory neglect present and steps should have been taken to supervise further contact with the grandfather pending investigation. Issues regarding discharge, home safety and appropriate supervision needed to be addressed before the child was discharged from medical care. Some legal authorities would prohibit any contact with the grandfather as to not taint any further interviews with the child. Education to be provided to the family to prevent burns must include the dangers of leaving hot irons and children unattended and encouraging parents to unplug irons when not in use, safely store the iron and the cord out of the child's reach, and not to leave irons on the floor or low tables.[2]

1. Berlin DA, Hughes WB. Iron burns in children under six. *Ann Burns Fire Disast.* 2001;14(4):171–172.
2. Batchelor JS, Vanjari S, Budny P, Roberts AH. Domestic iron burns in children: A cause for concern? *Burns.* 1994;20(1):74–75.

CASE 68

Carl J. Schmidt

This 4-month-old boy arrived unresponsive at the emergency room. The mother was at work when her partner called to tell her the child was unresponsive. The child was taken care of by a nanny occasionally, but she had not been in contact with the child for at least 3 or 4 days. A CT scan of the head showed intense cerebral oedema. Chest x-ray showed multiple rib fractures in various stages of healing. The child died from the head injury. External examination of the scrotum at autopsy showed the injury presented in Image 68a.

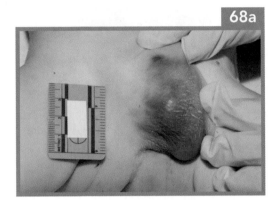

i. What is shown in Image 68a?
ii. What procedure is important for evaluation of the injury?

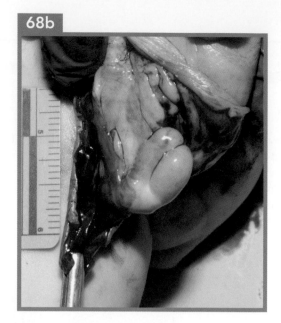
68b

i. This is a contusion of the scrotum. In a 4-month-old child, this is an inflicted injury. The bruise has multiple hues, from yellow to red-purple. One of the more common explanations for these bruises is that someone else other than the immediate caretaker caused it, and that was the case here – blame was placed on the nanny. Because of the multiple colours present on the skin, it was thought that the injury was inflicted multiple times. However it is not possible to date bruises accurately.[1,2]

ii. Extensive dissection of the skin by the forensic pathologist is essential for a complete evaluation of all cutaneous injuries. In these cases, multiple incisions on the back, groin and extremities are necessary with extensive separation of the skin to adequately evaluate subcutaneous haemorrhage, the main sign of an impact site. Even in light-skinned children, not all injuries may be apparent unless this is done. Image 68b shows that there is recent, red-purple haemorrhage of the subcutaneous tissue of the scrotum, which excludes the nanny as the perpetrator of this injury since haemorrhage with this appearance indicates the injury is not more than a day or so old. Also seen is the testicle with the epididymis.

1. Bariciak ED, Plint AC, Gaboury I, Bennett S. Dating of bruises in children: An assessment of physician accuracy. *Pediatrics*. 2003;112(4):804–807.
2. Byard RW, Wick R, Gilbert JD, Donald T. Histologic dating of bruises in moribund infants and young children. *Forensic Sci Med Pathol*. 2008;4(3):187–192.

CASE 69

Vincent J. Palusci

A 5-year-old African girl was brought to the emergency room by the police after she was noted to have several bruises and other marks. She spoke some words in English but had recently come from her home country in Africa at the beginning of the school year. The child reportedly told school officials that her mother had hit her with a belt. Her teacher reported that she had been given a 'red card' to take home to her mother the day before because of her bad behaviour. There were several red marks on her back as well as healed scars (Image 69a). A close-up image of a red lesion on her upper back showed a pattern (Image 69b). Another lesion on her right chest appeared fresh with signs of abrasion or superficial laceration (Image 69c).

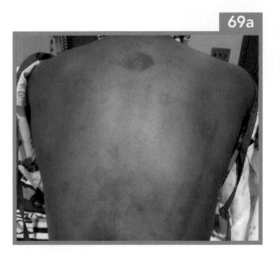

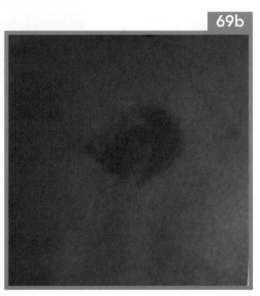

i. What are the possible causes for these findings?
ii. What additional steps could you take to help identify the sources?

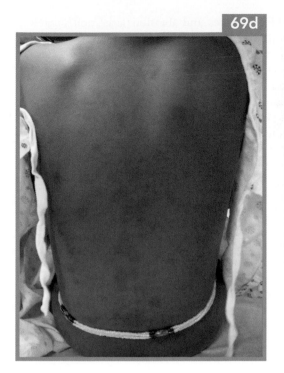
69d

69e

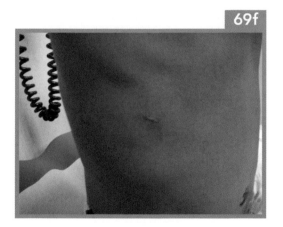
69f

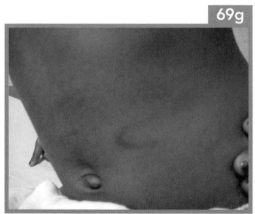
69g

157

i. The large red lesions appeared recent and the shapes and abrasion/laceration suggested impact by an object. While measurements were not provided, the lesions on the back and side seemed similar in size and shape. The disclosure by the child of a belt could be consistent with these shapes, depending on the belt and belt buckle configurations. The colour, size and shapes appeared to be consistent with recent physical abuse using a belt. The smaller circular brown marks over other areas of the back were nonspecific and may have been related to healed insect bites, eczema, impetigo or other conditions.[1]

ii. It is important to follow the course of these lesions to see how they heal. The rapidity of healing may help with assessing their depth and additional patterns may become apparent as tissue swelling resolves. One week later, the red marks had become brown on the back (Image 69d), including the large one over the upper thoracic vertebra, which had purple visible and suggested deeper injury as in a contusion (Image 69e). The lesion on the right chest was also healing (Image 69f). An additional brown cord pattern mark was seen on the left abdomen which was not noted during the emergency department visit (Image 69g). It is also important to seek out additional information about the child's medical history, immunizations and any other treatments. Another family member was contacted and reported that she had fevers and cough and was treated with a 'burning treatment'. This relative was not present when this occurred in Africa, but reports she was told by other family members that this is routinely done over the back for these types of illnesses in their village. The pattern depicted was consistent with a complementary medical practice called moxibustion.[2]

1. Hartwig E, Fischer H. Bruises. In: Palusci VJ, Fischer H, eds. *Child Abuse and Neglect: A Diagnostic Guide for Physicians, Surgeons, Pathologists, Dentists, Nurses and Social Workers*. London, England: Manson Publishing Ltd; 2011:13–41.
2. Palusci VJ, Nazer D. Maltreatment and advocacy. In: Kamat DM, Fischer PR, eds. *Textbook of Global Child Health*. Elk Grove Village, IL: American Academy of Pediatrics; 2011:127–152.

CASE 70

Nicholas Bishop

A 2-year-old boy presented with failure to thrive, developmental delay and refusal to walk. His parents said that he had become increasingly unsettled over the last 2 weeks. His left ankle appeared tender to the touch. An x-ray of his leg (Image 70) revealed fractures but the parents said they did not know how this had happened. On further clinical examination, the child had a slightly smaller than average head size, blue sclerae and no teeth. The child was fretful and there was increased work of breathing; the chest appeared to have a narrow inlet with a flared costal margin. The wrists appeared rather bulky. There was no obvious evidence of lax skin or joints. There were concerns about child maltreatment with neglect and possible non-accidental injury.

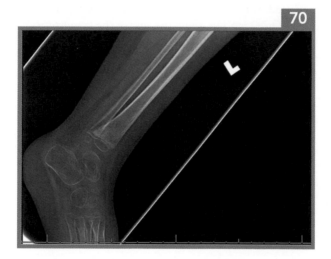

i. What changes do you note on the x-ray?
ii. What investigations would you do?
iii. What is your diagnosis and what would you do next?

i. The x-ray shows abnormal metaphyses of the distal tibia and fibula, sclerosis and periosteal reaction, compatible with healing. All the bones are demineralized.

   ii. This child needs to be evaluated for bone diseases and other metabolic conditions that may mimic child abuse due to the abnormal appearance of his bones as well as the symptoms associated with his presentation. Investigations should include routine (fasting/pre-feed) biochemistry in addition to a skeletal survey. This child had the following results:

      Ca 2.98 mmol/L (normal range: 2.1–2.7 mmol/L)

      PO_4 2.5 mmol/L (normal range: 1.2–2.0 mmol/L)

      Alkaline phosphatase 32 U/L (normal range: 76–310 U/L)

      His skeletal survey did not show any additional fractures but showed diffuse demineralization of all his bones as well as deformities of his rib cage.

  iii. Based on this child's clinical presentation and laboratory results, the diagnosis is hypophosphatasia. Hypophosphatasia is an inherited disorder of bone metabolism. Hypophosphatasia arises from loss-of-function mutations in the gene that encodes the tissue non-specific iso-enzyme of alkaline phosphatase.[1] This results in abnormal bone mineralization leading to rickets, fractures and other skeletal abnormalities as well as other systemic complications such as seizures, respiratory compromise, dental anomalies and nephrocalcinosis.[1] It may present in the perinatal, infantile, childhood or adulthood period with variable severity.[2] The earlier the age of presentation, the more severe the symptoms. It is most important to refer this child to a bone specialist as this condition can be associated with multiple fractures and developmental delays if not treated and is potentially lethal. He should also be referred to a geneticist for testing and counselling and a dentist for dental care.

1. Rockman-Greenberg C. Hypophosphatasia. *Pediatr Endocrinol Rev.* 2013;10 Suppl 2:380–388.
2. Bennett D, Pierce MC. Bone health and development. In: Jenny C, ed. *Child Abuse and Neglect: Diagnosis, Treatment, and Evidence.* St. Louis, MO: Saunders/Elsevier; 2011:261–274.

CASE 71

Dena Nazer

A 4-year-old girl was brought to the emergency department by her father. He states she fell off the sidewalk and bumped her head. The next morning she woke up with a swollen head and swollen eyes, as shown in Images 71a–71c. The father denied any further history of trauma. The child refused to answer questions in the emergency department. The following photos show her front face (Image 71a), right (Image 71b) and left sides (Image 71c) of her face, respectively.

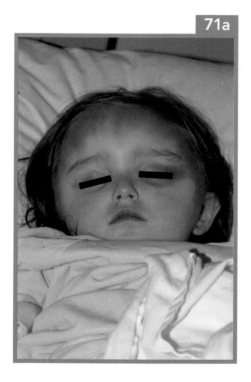

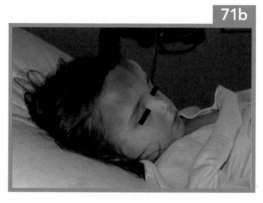

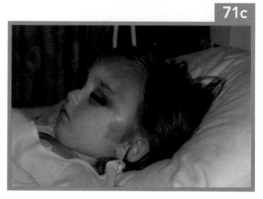

  i. What finding do you see?
 ii. What tests and imaging are important to determine the aetiology of this patient's presentation?
iii. Why did the child refuse to answer questions?

i. Examination of this child revealed a palpable, doughy swelling which was present both in the forehead as well as the hard skull areas. This is consistent with a subgaleal haematoma, which results from bleeding beneath the galea. It also resulted in tracking of the blood to the periorbital area, especially on the left side as noted in Image 71c. Mechanisms for subgaleal haematomas include falls, hair pulling, hair braiding and vacuum extraction with vaginal delivery.[1] The bleeding is located between the periosteum and the scalp's galea aponeurotica. Unlike cephalohaematomas, which are restricted by suture lines, subgaleal haematomas can cross suture lines and lead to significant blood loss and hypovolemia. The subgaleal space communicates anteriorly over the superior orbital ridge with the superior orbit, allowing blood to track into the periorbital space.[2] This can lead to swelling as in this child or proptosis and visual compromise.

ii. A full evaluation for child abuse is necessary. The history of falling off the sidewalk, which is less than a foot off the ground, would not cause the extensive subgaleal haematoma present in this child. Furthermore, her physical examination revealed multiple bruises on her body. Blood investigations including a complete blood count and liver and pancreatic enzymes were done. A skeletal survey was not needed due to her age greater than 2 years. A head MRI scan was done which was normal. In this child, the subgaleal haematoma resolved with conservative management and did not require surgical intervention.

iii. Children are often nervous when brought for medical care for a variety of reasons. In this case, the many new people and frightening nature of the emergency department environment could easily make the child mute. In addition, the presence of the potential offending parent, who may have threatened the child with physical violence if she spoke, could also frighten the child into not speaking. Steps can be taken to make the environment more child-friendly, and child life therapists can assist in making the medical evaluation less frightening for the child. Over time, the child may feel comfortable to disclose what occurred, which is more likely in the absence of an offending parent.

1. Seifert D, Puschel K. Subgaleal hematoma in child abuse. *Forensic Sci Int.* 2006;157(2–3):131–133.
2. Natarajan MS, Prabhu K, Braganza A, Chacko AG. Posttraumatic subgaleal and orbital hematoma due to factor XIII deficiency. *J Neurosurg Pediatr.* 2011;7(2):213–217.

CASE 72

Dena Nazer

A 4 year-old boy who was previously healthy was brought to the emergency department by the police. They were called by a neighbour who heard the boy screaming and crying. The boy disclosed that his mother's boyfriend held him against the wall and punched him with his fist twice on his abdomen. He complains of abdominal pain. When you examine him, you note abdominal tenderness and multiple healed patterned marks on his abdomen (Image 72) and on his arms and legs.

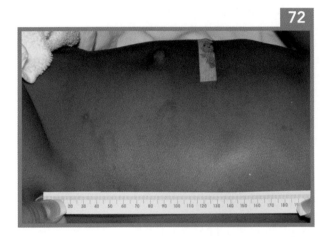

i. What does the image show?
ii. What tests and further imaging are important to evaluate this patient?

i. The image shows the left flank area and abdomen of the child. He has multiple patterned loop marks that have healed with hyperpigmentation. Loop marks result from being whipped with a cord or a belt and indicate this child has been physically abused. Although we cannot date when bruises originally occurred, these loop marks have healed so they must have occurred sometime before he was brought for medical care.[1] Children who disclose physical abuse need a detailed physical examination to further evaluate their presentation as well as document previous instances of abuse.

ii. Due to the child's disclosure of being punched in the abdomen, he needs to be further evaluated for internal injuries. Blood was drawn for a complete blood count as well as liver and pancreatic enzymes. His liver enzymes were elevated: alanine aminotransferase (ALT) 866 U/L, aspartate transaminase (AST) 478 U/L. The normal range for ALT is reported between 7 and 56 units per litre and for AST between 10 and 40 units per litre. It is recommended that children with transaminases levels >80 U/L should undergo definitive testing for abdominal injury in cases where physical abuse is suspected as in this child.[2] A CT scan of his abdomen showed a small liver laceration with mild periportal oedema as well as retroperitoneal fluid collection between the aorta and inferior vena cava. Due to the fluid collection an upper gastrointestinal series with barium as a contrast was done which showed thickened duodenal folds, which may be due to oedema secondary to the patient's history of trauma. An exploratory laparotomy was performed which confirmed the contusion of the liver. It also revealed contusions of the transverse colon and duodenum. This case highlights the importance of a full evaluation of children disclosing physical abuse. Children need to be screened for abdominal trauma initially with liver enzymes. Abdominal trauma is the second most common cause of death from abuse and needs to be recognized in a timely manner. However, children may have significant abdominal trauma with mild symptoms as in this case and with few or no physical findings on exam.

1. Bariciak ED, Plint AC, Gaboury I, Bennett S. Dating of bruises in children: An assessment of physician accuracy. *Pediatrics*. 2003;112(4):804–807.
2. Lindberg DM, Shapiro RA, Blood EA, Steiner RD, Berger RP. Utility of hepatic transaminases in children with concern for abuse. *Pediatrics*. 2013;131(2):268–275.

CASE 73

Margaret T. McHugh with Anastasia Feifer and Lori A. Legano

An 11-year-old boy is brought for physical examination prior to being placed in a foster home. His mother has a long history of drug abuse. While the boy lived with her and her boyfriend, Child Protective Services were called by the boy's teacher, who saw that he was coming to school hungry in unwashed clothes. She also told authorities that he had been found in the bathroom 'harassing' another boy by pulling his clothes off and locking him in a bathroom stall. Prior to his physical examination, he reveals to a skilled interviewer that his mother's boyfriend would often 'come in his bed' and 'hurt him' while his mother was asleep, but he has difficulty talking about the details as his attention and concentration are poor and he becomes angry and smashes toys when asked about the details of his abuse at home. His height and weight are below average for his age and he appears thin, with dry, scaling, eczematous patches on his skin. His anogenital examination is shown in Image 73.

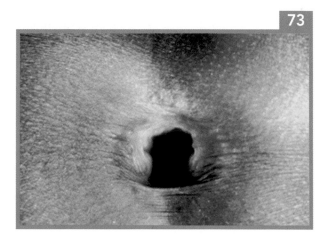

i. Are the physical findings consistent with sexual abuse?
ii. What laboratory testing was indicated for this patient?
iii. What medications were indicated for this patient?

i. The anogenital examination shows total anal dilation: specifically, dilation of the external and internal anal sphincter, so that the rectum is visible. Although the only finding diagnostic of penetration is semen (or other fluid or foreign body) in the anus (or vagina), total anal dilation has been shown to have a statistically significant correlation with penetration.[1] Findings with higher specificity for anal penetration include anal laceration, fissures and soiling. Yield of physical findings increases significantly when the patient is placed in the prone knee-chest position for examination. However, it is important to remember that a majority of cases, even in acute sexual assault, will have non-specific or absent physical findings.

ii. The boy should have been offered a complete evaluation for sexually transmitted infections, including anal, penile and pharyngeal culture for *Neisseria gonorrhoeae* and anal/penile culture for *Chlamydia trachomatis*. He can also be offered urine NAAT testing for *N. gonorrhoeae* and *C. trachomatis*. He should have also been offered baseline serologic testing for syphilis, hepatitis B and C (depending on the immunization status), and human immunodeficiency virus (HIV). Repeat serology testing should then have been performed at 3 and 6 months post-assault, although with newer more sensitive methods, fewer tests are needed.[2]

iii. Many experts do not indicate post-exposure chemoprophylaxis to prepubertal victims of sexual assault because the incidence of sexually transmitted infection (STI) in these patients is low. However, this patient underwent a high-risk exposure with an adult perpetrator and was offered post-exposure prophylaxis for *N. gonorrhoeae* and *C. trachomatis* as well as HIV (if an assault has occurred within the past 72 hours). Antibiotics can include a combination of a third-generation cephalosporin, such as a single intramuscular dose of ceftriaxone, as well as an oral macrolide (for prophylaxis of gonorrhea and chlamydia, respectively).[2] The patient should also be offered a course of antiretroviral medications for prophylaxis of HIV. As a full course of antiretroviral medication is indicated for 28 days, the patient should have frequent follow-up visits to monitor for tolerance of the medications as well as for emotional support.[2] A referral to a mental health specialist is indicated.

1. Myhre AK, Adams JA, Kaufhold M, Davis JL, Suresh P, Kuelbs CL. Anal findings in children with and without probable anal penetration: A retrospective study of 1115 children referred for suspected sexual abuse. *Child Abuse Negl.* 2013;37(7):465–474.
2. Pickering LK. *Red Book 2012:2012 Report of the Committee on Infectious Diseases.* Elk Grove Village, IL: American Academy of Pediatrics; 2012.

CASE 74

Dena Nazer

A 7-week-old baby boy presented to the emergency department with a 1-day history of swelling of his right thigh. His father stated that he was holding the baby and bent forward to pick up a dropped bottle and may have injured the baby at that time. He denied any other history of trauma and stated that there were no other complaints. On his physical examination, he had swelling and limited range of movement of his right thigh. He was noticed to be in pain. He had multiple bruises noticed on his right cheek, right palm, right wrist, right forearm, as well as on his scrotum. His bruises are shown in Images 74a–74c.

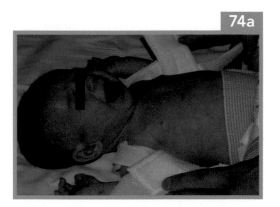

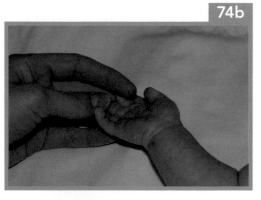

i. What is your major concern in regards to the bruises and thigh swelling?
ii. How would you further evaluate this patient?

i. Bruises are rare in infants and their presence in this baby should lead to the consideration of abuse or an illness as a cause.[1] The presence of the swelling and limited movement of his right thigh warranted an x-ray of his right leg, which showed a comminuted spiral fracture involving the mid-diaphysis of the right femur with 10 mm medial angulation of the dorsal fracture fragment. No callus formation was visualized, implying an acute fracture. In the presence of multiple bruises in an infant along with a fracture with no history to explain the injuries, our major concern was physical abuse. It is important when examining babies to perform a careful head-to-toe skin exam in order to be able to detect the presence of bruises and suspect physical abuse in order not to miss the opportunity of diagnosis and have the baby present later with more severe injuries.[2]

ii. This baby was evaluated with a skeletal survey that showed a nondisplaced fracture at the mid-portion of the left clavicle with exuberant callus formation. It also showed multiple non-displaced lateral rib fractures involving the right eighth and ninth ribs and left seventh through ninth ribs. No callus formation was seen. He had a complete blood count, prothrombin time (PT) and partial thromboplastin time (PTT) done as well as liver and pancreatic enzymes. His liver enzymes were elevated and an abdominal CT scan was done which was normal. His head MRI scan was also normal. A diagnosis of physical abuse was made and he was placed in a Pavlik harness and discharged home with his grandmother.

1. Sugar NF, Taylor JA, Feldman KW. Bruises in infants and toddlers: Those who don't cruise rarely bruise. Puget Sound Pediatric Research Network. *Arch Pediatr Adolesc Med*. 1999;153(4):399–403.
2. Thorpe EL, Zuckerbraun NS, Wolford JE, Berger RP. Missed opportunities to diagnose child physical abuse. *Pediatr Emerg Care*. 2014;30(11):771–776.

CASE 75

Tor Shwayder

A 6-year-old boy presented with these parallel brown hyperpigmented marks to the right side of his back (Image 75). He was previously healthy and asymptomatic. Physical abuse was suspected and he was referred for an evaluation. The remainder of his physical examination was normal. The child was in foster care and the foster parents denied any history of trauma or physically disciplining this child.

i. What is your diagnosis?

i. In this case as in all cases when child maltreatment is suspected, a thorough history needs to be obtained from the child as well as the caregivers.[1] The child needs to be asked separately about how he got the marks. When asked, this child states he was just playing in the wooded area by his house and scratched himself on a branch. He had bent down under a pine tree and when standing up scratched his back on two branches. This happened a while ago but he did not recall the exact time. The curvilinear lines fitted with his story of standing up (the straight parallel lines) and in that moment realizing he was catching his skin on a branch and twisting away (the curved lower segment). This child needed a thorough physical examination with particular attention to the skin examination for any other marks. The remainder of his physical examination was normal and he made no disclosures of physical abuse.

1. Kos L, Shwayder T. Cutaneous manifestations of child abuse. *Pediatr Dermatol.* 2006;23(4):311–320.

CASE 76

Patricia O. Brennan

A schoolteacher noticed these marks (Image 76) on this boy's chest when he said he was too ill to play at football practice. The boy's mother took him to the emergency department. The rash was non-blanching. The boy was afebrile and otherwise well.

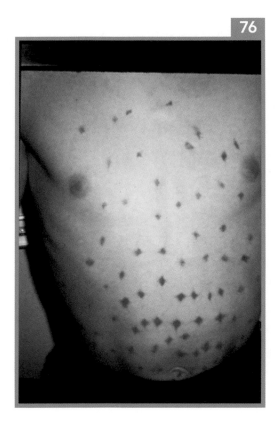

i. What is the diagnosis?
ii. What could be the underlying cause?

i. The purple lesions were diamond shaped and scattered randomly across the anterior chest and abdomen, within reach of the child himself. There were no other lesions anywhere on the child's body. This uniform rash, unlike any skin condition, was due to dermatitis artefacta and had been caused by the child himself.

ii. Dermatitis artefacta is skin damage caused by the child himself, but not acknowledged by the child. It is relatively rare and, although sometimes done for experimental reasons or under peer pressure, is usually a cry for help in a child who feels trapped in an intolerable situation. It may be a reaction to sexual abuse, social difficulty or bullying. Children who self-harm in other ways such as cutting or overdosing on medications usually acknowledge what they have done. This child will need careful and sensitive management, which may involve the input of a child psychiatrist or psychologist.[1,2]

1. Moss C. Dermatitis artefacta in children and adolescents. *J Paediatr Child Health*. 2015;25(2):84–89.
2. Finore ED, Andreoli E, Alfani S, Palermi G, Pedicelli C, Paradisi M. Dermatitis artefacta in a child. *Pediatr Dermatol*. 2007;24(5):E51–E56.

CASE 77

Dena Nazer

A 10-month-old baby boy presented with pain of his left leg and decreased movement. His mother gave the history of him falling off her bed. She was nursing him in bed and she fell asleep. When she woke up, she found him on the floor next to the bed. He was fine after the fall and continued to sleep and feed well. Later that day, when he was on his 'bouncy' seat, he started to bounce and attempted to push on both his legs. He cried when he did that and refused to bear weight on his left leg. On his physical examination, he had a slightly swollen left thigh that was tender. He did not have any other patterned marks or bruises or concerns of physical abuse on exam. X-rays are shown in Images 77a and 77b.

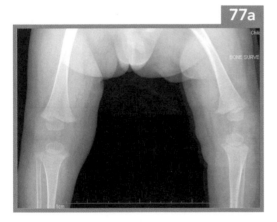

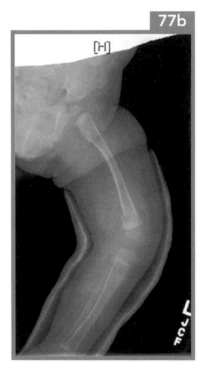

i. What do the x-rays show?
ii. Is the injury consistent with the provided history?

i. His left leg x-ray showed a cortical irregularity at the left femoral distal metaphysis consistent with non–displaced fracture (Images 77a and 77b). Child abuse was suspected due to the infant being immobile and due to the strong correlation of femur fractures with child abuse in this age. A skeletal survey was done that showed no additional fractures. He also had head imaging and a dilated retinal examination both of which were normal. Child Protective Services was notified for further investigation and to assess for any further safety concerns.

ii. The mother described her bed as a mattress on top of a box spring and frame. She stated that the frame sticks out several inches beyond the mattress. It is possible that the child impacted his knee when falling on the frame or the floor. Impacted transverse fracture of the distal femoral metadiaphysis may occur as a result of an accidental short fall of young children. An evaluation for child abuse should still be pursued in these cases, but with an absence of additional skeletal findings and a history of fall, it is likely that an accidental mechanism accounts for the injury.[1] It was felt that the bouncy seat elicited pain but was not the cause of the fracture. Fractures have been reported as caused by exersaucers, a stationary walker where the infant is seated with the ability to push up and bounce using his feet. However those have a different mechanism and are quite different from the bouncy chair in which the child was seated.[2] Upon obtaining history from the mother and reviewing of the chart and discussion with the radiologist, it was determined that it is possible for a fall from the bed with impact to the knee against the frame to result in this fracture. However, due to the fall not being witnessed, we discussed with Child Protective Services that an investigation was needed with home visits and evaluation of other children in the home.

1. Haney SB, Boos SC, Kutz TJ, Starling SP. Transverse fracture of the distal femoral metadiaphysis: A plausible accidental mechanism. *Pediatr Emerg Care*. 2009;25(12):841–844.
2. Grant P, Mata MB, Tidwell M. Femur fracture in infants: A possible accidental etiology. *Pediatrics*. 2001;108(4):1009–1011.

CASE 78

Vincent J. Palusci

Police brought a 16-year-old boy for evaluation of sexual abuse. He reported that his uncle had sexually assaulted him 1 week previously at his home, but he told no one at that time. He said that his uncle had forcefully pulled down his pants and forced him to bend over a chair as his uncle penetrated his anus with a finger and a penis. The police were skeptical about the teenager's report and were asking for a physical examination to determine whether this had occurred. You spoke with the boy in private and he confirmed the events. He stated he was not having pain, although it did hurt when this occurred, he noticed bleeding on toilet paper, and he had painful defecation for 1 or 2 days. He also reported he went to an emergency room the day after it occurred and they had done some tests, but he did not know the results. During your examination, you noticed some redness and normal anal rugae, no acute injuries or bruising and no evidence of sexually transmitted infections (STIs). There was, however, a thin, barely visible, white line extending outward from the anus from 1 to 2 o'clock, with him in the prone examination position (Image 78a).

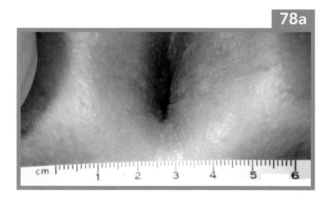

i. What is the significance of this finding?
ii. What are the important next steps in your evaluation?
iii. What source of information most accurately describes how this finding occurred?

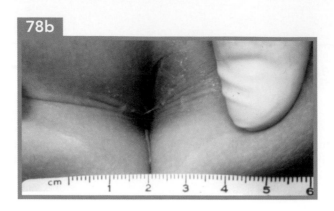

78b

i. Based on examination alone, the anal finding of a thin, white line represented a lesion of uncertain aetiology.[1] It is difficult to determine the cause of such a lesion without having seen it more acutely, since it may have occurred from abusive or non-abusive causes. By itself, a normal anal examination does not rule out or contradict the child's disclosure of abuse, although a paucity of physical findings may be detrimental to a criminal prosecution.[2]

ii. Given the disclosure that the child was seen previously in an emergency room, it was important to obtain the records from that evaluation to determine if images, tests or treatment were provided. Given the nature of the reported assault, there was increased risk for transmission of human immunodeficiency virus (HIV) and other STIs, although it was likely to be too late at this time to prevent their occurrence with prophylaxis. Thus, at that time, it was important to provide supportive counseling, work with his parents and the authorities to protect him from further abuse and arrange long-term mental health evaluation and treatment.

iii. When hospital records were obtained, it was found that the examining physician noted an acute, superficial perianal laceration at the location of the healing lesion (Image 78b).[3] Given the mucosal disruption, testing for gonorrhea, chlamydia and HIV had been done and preventative medications given. In addition, forensic specimens had been obtained, which were sent to the forensic laboratory. These revealed the presence of sperm and acid phosphatase, confirming the child's disclosures of sexual contact. The presence of recent injury and forensic evidence, while uncommon in child sexual abuse, is definitive evidence of sexual contact, and the disclosures by the child most accurately describe the context in which this occurred.

1. McCann J. The appearance of acute, healing, and healed anogenital trauma. *Child Abuse Negl.* 1998;22(6):605–615; discussion 617–622.
2. Palusci VJ, Cox EO, Cyrus TA, Heartwell SW, Vandervort FE, Pott ES. Medical assessment and legal outcome in child sexual abuse. *Arch Pediatr Adolesc Med.* 1999;153(4):388–392.
3. Palusci VJ. Anogenital findings and sexual abuse. In: Palusci VJ, Fischer H, eds. *Child Abuse and Neglect: A Diagnostic Guide for Physicians, Surgeons, Pathologists, Dentists, Nurses and Social Workers.* London, England: Manson Publishing Ltd; 2011:163–191.

CASE 79

Vincent J. Palusci

A 15-year-old girl had disclosed being sexually assaulted 2 weeks ago. She did not seek medical care at that time but was now concerned about possible pregnancy and sexually transmitted infections. During your evaluation, you noted that her external genitalia and anus appeared normal and there was no sign of discharge or infection. She revealed this lesion on her arm (Image 79a). She began her menses at age 13 years, her last period was 3 weeks previously, and her medical history was otherwise negative.

 i. What are the possible causes for this finding?
 ii. What is the best way to determine the aetiology of this finding?

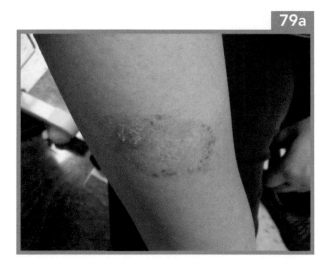

79a

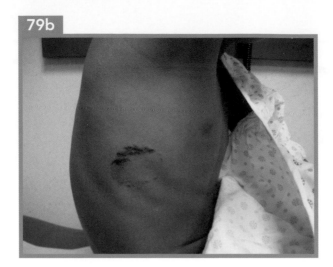

79b

i. This teen has an oval, patterned lesion on her anterolateral right arm with areas of central hypopigmentation, peripheral hyperpigmentation and scaling skin and some granulation tissue. No active cellulitis or vesicles are present. This could be caused by a healing burn, impetigo, atopic dermatitis, chemical contact reaction or trauma.[1]

ii. Given the healing nature of the lesion, determining the aetiology by observation or laboratory assessment is problematic. The shape is suggestive of a pattern and the best way to determine its aetiology, at this point, would be to ask the teenager or her parents if they know how it occurred. When asked directly, the teen responds: 'He bit me there when he was having sex with me'. While specific teeth marks are not visible, the shape and healing nature of the lesion are consistent with that disclosure. A similarly shaped, but more recent bite mark on a young child is also shown (Image 79b). Bite marks have been commonly noted in association with sexual assault and practices have been developed for evaluation and evidence collection.[2]

1. Hammel PW. Recognition of child abuse by dentists, healthcare professionals and law enforcement. In: Palusci VJ, Fischer H, eds. *Child Abuse and Neglect: A Diagnostic Guide*. London: Manson Publishing Ltd; 2011:143–154.
2. Verma K, Joshi B, Joshi CH, Paul R. Bite marks as physical evidence from the crime scene—An overview. Scientific Reports; 2013. Available at: http://dx.doi.org/10.4172/scientificreports.605 (accessed 12/30/2014).

CASE 80

Dena Nazer

A 6-month-old baby boy was brought to the emergency room with a swollen left leg for the past 3 days. His father stated he was changing his diaper on a changing table and the infant began moving and was about to fall off the table. To prevent the fall, his father held his leg. Afterwards, he noticed that the baby had decreased movement, pain and swelling of his left leg. His physical examination showed a tender and swollen left leg. He had radiologic evaluation of his left leg. X-rays of the femur are shown in the following images (Images 80a and 80b).

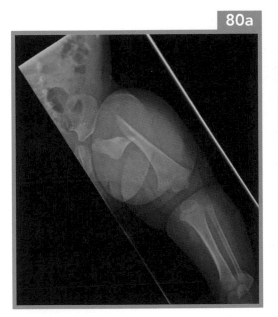
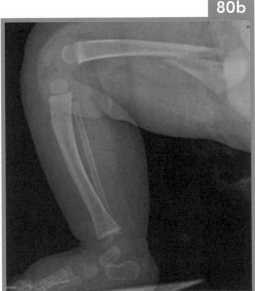

i. What injury do you see in the radiology images?
ii. Is the injury consistent with the history provided?
iii. Would you recommend any additional imaging or laboratory workup for this infant?

i. The images show plain x-rays of the left femur. They depict a complete oblique fracture of the proximal shaft of the femur with superimposition of the distal segment with lateral and anterior displacement. A large amount of soft tissue oedema is also seen overlying the fracture site.

ii. This infant is able developmentally to roll and fall off the changing table. However his father holding his leg to prevent his fall is not consistent with the resulting femoral fracture. The oblique nature of the fracture implies torsional loading (twisting or rotation). Femur fractures are the most common paediatric orthopaedic injury requiring hospitalization and the second most common diaphyseal fracture in children. As with all childhood fractures, it is essential to differentiate accidental from abusive fractures. Helpful details include the medical history, the child's age and developmental stage, an understanding of the mechanism that causes the particular type of fracture and the type, location and age of the fracture.[1-3]

iii. In non-ambulating children, 60%–70% of femoral fractures are caused by abuse. Child abuse was suspected as the likely aetiology of this infant's fracture based on his age, inconsistent history and delay in seeking medical care. The hospital child protection team was consulted and a thorough evaluation for other injuries was conducted. His skeletal survey revealed multiple healing posterior rib fractures which are highly specific for child abuse. Blood was drawn for a complete blood count and liver enzymes that were elevated. Due to the elevated liver enzymes, an abdominal CT scan was done which revealed a liver contusion. His head MRI scan was normal. The combination of fractures and abdominal injuries supported the diagnosis of child physical abuse that was made in this case.

1. Pierce MC, Bertocci GE, Vogeley E, Moreland MS. Evaluating long bone fractures in children: A biomechanical approach with illustrative cases. *Child Abuse Negl.* 2004;28(5):505–524.
2. Pierce MC, Bertocci GE, Janosky JE et al. Femur fractures resulting from stair falls among children: An injury plausibility model. *Pediatrics.* 2005;115(6):1712–1722.
3. Kemp AM, Dunstan F, Harrison S et al. Patterns of skeletal fractures in child abuse: Systematic review. *BMJ.* 2008;337:a1518.

CASE 81

Mary E. Smyth

A 3-year-old female was brought to the emergency centre by her father with fever and a 'rash' on her buttocks. The rash began a few days earlier as a bruise-like spot and was spreading. She had not had diarrhoea or any other symptoms. She had been in good health and was taking no medications. When asked 'what happened' the child replied 'a skeeter bit me'. Grandmother, who cared for the child, stated that there had been ongoing restoration work performed in the crawl space beneath the child's bedroom and they had seen many spiders in the house. On physical examination the child had a temperature of 39.8°C rectally. There was a 10 × 10 cm oval area on the left buttock which was warm to touch and erythematous with a darker centre. There was a 4 × 5 cm round, erythematous lesion on the right buttock. Both areas felt thickened and indurated with a rough surface (*peau d'orange*). There were no vesicles, blisters or bullae, as shown in Image 81.

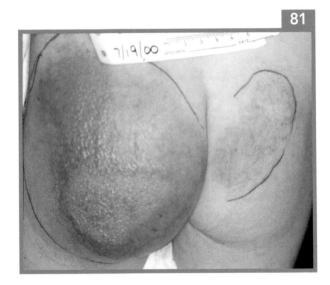

   i. What common form of inflicted injury was this mistaken for?
   ii. How can these conditions be differentiated?

i. The initial impression was that this child has been intentionally burned. Clinical laboratory testing for spider venom was not available but a presumptive diagnosis of spider bite was made. A complete blood count, blood and wound cultures and all other laboratory tests were normal.

ii. The lesion was undergoing the typical colour transition seen in venomous bites – 'red, white, blue' – as the cutaneous reaction to toxin progressed through vasodilatation, vasoconstriction and thrombosis. Fever, as noted in this child, results from systemic reaction to toxin. Other serious systemic reactions may occur such as haemolysis, rhabdomyolysis, methemoglobinemia, haemoglobinuria, platelet aggregation and renal failure. The child was monitored for several days.[1] Extensive skin necrosis resulted and the child underwent skin grafting of the affected sites.[2]

1. Quan D. North American poisonous bites and stings. *Crit Care Clin.* 2012;28(4):633–659.
2. Walker P, Morrison J, Stewart R, Gore D. Venomous bites and stings. *Curr Probl Surg.* 2013;50(1):9–44.

CASE 82

Vincent J. Palusci

A 16-year-old girl was brought to your office by her mother who had found pictures of her on her cell phone. The mother became concerned when she saw multiple red lines on her child's arm with the child holding a bottle of prescription pain pills. She asked her daughter about the pills and the child refused to disclose what they were or why she had taken pictures of them. The mother wanted you to speak with her daughter and find out 'what's going on'. You offered the child your female nurse as a chaperone and she agreed to your examining her. These findings were noted on her arm as shown (Image 82a).

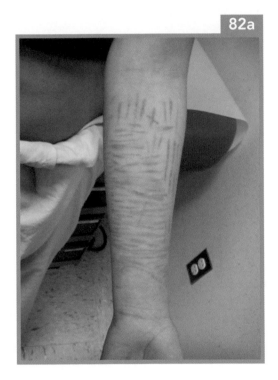

i. What does the image show?
ii. What are the possible causes for this finding?
iii. What are important next steps in the care for this patient?

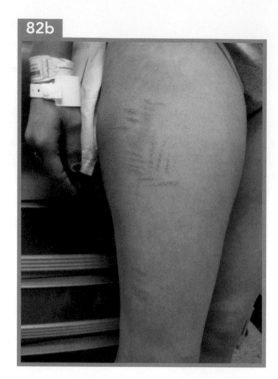
82b

i. The image shows multiple erythematous lines over the anterior forearm in varying transverse and vertical orientations. Some appear to have some eschar. Others appear more superficial. Note the sparing on the wrist and popliteal fossa. There is no apparent deep laceration with vascular or nerve involvement.

ii. This pattern of lesions does not follow dermatomal or vascular patterns. These are most likely inflicted by an object compressing against the skin or abrading/lacerating the skin. These lesions were also found on her thigh (Image 82b), and no natural process could cause these patterns in these isolated locations. In speaking with her, she told you she is having trouble in the tenth grade and was left behind a few years ago. She 'doesn't like' herself and her boyfriend said she was 'fat'. She started cutting her arm 'a couple of weeks ago' with a safety pin or a sewing needle. Since the weather had been cold, she had been wearing long sleeves to cover her arm but she did take a picture of herself in the bathroom with her mother's hydrocodone pills because she was thinking about how she would look with them 'if I were dead'. She had not been eating well and is trying to lose weight.

iii. 'Cutting' is a form of self-injury which begins as a defence against what is going on in the family and in the lives of children, usually teens. It is seen as a way to get control and for children with emotional problems, self-injury has an effect similar to cocaine and other drugs that release endorphins to create a feel-good feeling. Children who self-harm often have an eating disorder and may have a history of sexual, physical or verbal abuse and may be sensitive, perfectionist and overachieving. Self-injury by cutting can also be a symptom for psychiatric problems like borderline personality disorder, anxiety disorder, bipolar disorder or schizophrenia. Yet many children who self-injure are simply 'regular kids' going through the adolescent struggle for self-identity. However in this case, the teenager had also disclosed thinking about pill overdose and suicide. She needed urgent psychiatric evaluation to rule out suicidal ideation and long-term help and support of a trained therapist to overcome the self-harm habit, to develop new coping techniques and strategies to stop self-harming and to get to the root of the self-harm.[1]

1. National Collaborating Centre for Mental Health (UK). *Self-Harm: The Short-Term Physical and Psychological Management and Secondary Prevention of Self-Harm in Primary and Secondary Care.* Vol 16. Leicester, UK: British Psychological Society; 2004:19–21. Available from: http://www.ncbi.nlm.nih.gov/pubmedhealth/PMH0015739/pdf/PubMedHealth_PMH0015739.pdf

CASE 83

Alan Sprigg

An 8-month-old boy was brought to the emergency department (ED) as the parents noticed his wrist was swollen which they thought was causing him pain. He was the third child of unrelated African parents, his siblings being 18 months and 3 years old. They were all exclusively breastfed. He had not yet been weaned from breast milk. On examination both his wrists were swollen and uncomfortable, but there were no other significant findings. The ED doctor considered concealed trauma so he requested a wrist radiograph (Image 83).

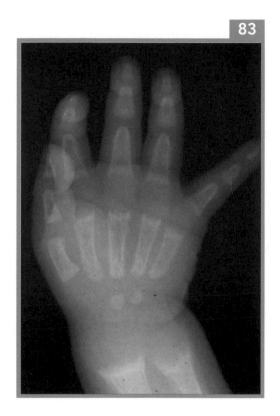

i. What do you see (or not see)?
ii. What is the most likely diagnosis?
iii. Are there concerns about non-accidental injury?

i. The image shows no fracture. However, the metaphyses are widened and splayed. They are irregular with loss of the normal dense end plate in the radius and ulna (the distal ulna is often slightly irregular on normal images). There is increased gap between the radius and the carpal bones due to unossified matrix. There is a trace of periosteal reaction along the metacarpals suggesting early healing reaction.

ii. This boy has rickets. Rickets does still exist and is usually seen with prolonged breastfeeding without formula or vitamin supplementation. There is an increased risk if the mother herself has dietary deficiency, has had multiple pregnancies close together and all the children were all breastfed or had poor exposure to sunlight, related to culture and country of origin. The boy's bone biochemistry was abnormal (calcium, phosphate, alkaline phosphatase [ALP], parathyroid hormone [PTH] and vitamin D). He responded to improved diet.

iii. The role of 'biochemical rickets' in non-accidental injury is an area of controversy. This issue arises when there are fractures in the presence of a radiographically normal skeleton, but the bone biochemistry results are mildly abnormal or the vitamin D levels are suboptimal. Fractures do not occur commonly in rickets and are usually 'insufficiency' fractures. Generalized radiographic changes are usually evident when rickets is sufficiently severe to predispose to fracturing.[1] Other disorders that may mimic non-accidental skeletal injury include

- Copper deficiency (rare) with metaphyseal spurs and reduced bone density
- Syphilis with metaphyseal 'lytic' areas
- Scurvy with osteoporosis and subperiosteal haematomas simulating fracture healing

1. Chapman T, Sugar N, Done S, Marasigan J, Wambold N, Feldman K. Fractures in infants and toddlers with rickets. *Pediatr Radiol.* 2010;40(7):1184–1189.

CASE 84

Mary Lu Angelilli with Sarah Hirschbeck

A 4-month-old baby girl presented with new-onset seizure-like movements. She began having rhythmic jerking of the right side of the body on the morning of presentation. She was previously healthy and has been afebrile. On physical examination, she was noted to have the lesion shown (Image 84) on her left leg. Her physical examination was otherwise normal.

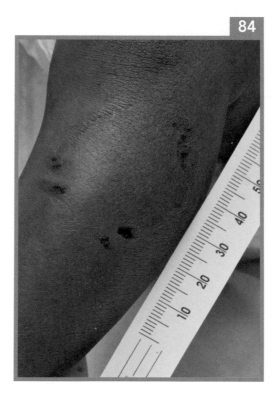

i. What is your diagnosis of the lesion on her leg?
ii. What is the management for the skin lesion?
iii. What further workup is needed?

i. The lesion pictured is a human bite mark. Human bite marks are typically located on the face, upper extremities and trunk. Human teeth may leave superficial abrasions or lacerations surrounded by soft tissue bruising. They generally appear as a straight line, are circular or oval shaped. Canine teeth leave the most prominent marks in the shape of a triangle or point. All human bite marks should raise suspicion for abuse.[1]

ii. Bite marks should be photographed individually. Serial photographs over several days may help a forensic odontologist evaluate the case. Photographs both with and without a ruler or scale in place should be taken. Intercanine distances measuring 3.5–4 cm are suspicious for bite marks left by an adult. Primary dentition (under 6 years old) typically has intercanine distances less than or equal to 3 cm. It has been shown that age, sex and race differences are insignificant in ages over 12 years. Each photograph should be taken with the camera lens positioned perpendicular to the skin to avoid distortion. Photographs should be taken by a person who is experienced with the camera and equipment being used. If available, pictures should be taken by a trained medical photographer. Location of bite marks should be documented on a body diagram and included in the medical record along with a detailed written description of the lesions.[2]

iii. The patient presented in the scenario needed to be evaluated for abuse because of the presence of the bite mark. It is important to take a detailed history and perform a full physical including a head-to-toe skin exam. A skeletal survey to evaluate for new and healing fractures, dilated retinal exam for retinal haemorrhages and head imaging are all warranted, especially considering this infant's age and her presentation with seizure-like movement.

1. Kos L, Shwayder T. Cutaneous manifestations of child abuse. *Pediatr Dermatol.* 2006;23(4):311–320.
2. American Academy of Pediatrics Committee on Child Abuse and Neglect and the American Academy of Pediatric Dentistry. Guideline on oral and dental aspects of child abuse and neglect. *Pediatr Dent.* 2008;30(7 Suppl):86–89.

CASE 85

Dena Nazer

A 19-month-old boy presented with bilateral burns in his hands. According to his father, the child was sitting at the dinner table. The father placed a cup of hot water on the table in front of the child to make some hot chocolate. The father stepped away for less than a minute and came back to the child screaming. The hot water was spilled on the table and he was shaking his hands in pain. The father washed the hands with cold water, noticed the burns and decided to seek medical care for his son. The photographs show the dorsum and palmer aspects of both hands (Images 85a through 85d).

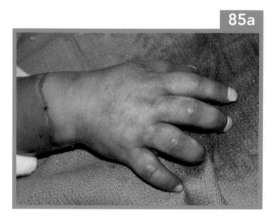
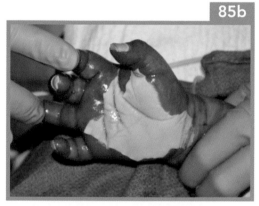
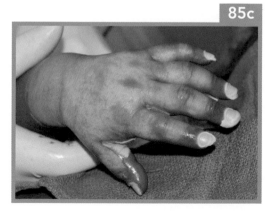
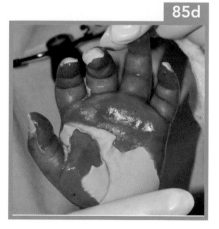

    i. Is the burn pattern consistent with the provided history?

    ii. What are some concerning features about this burn? What is your diagnosis?

i. There is a glove pattern and clear line of demarcation that is not consistent with the history provided by the father. When the Child Protective Services worker visited the home, the table was noticed to be small, the size of a corner coffee table. The cup was noted to be of a large size with a diameter of 20 cm. The child may have been able developmentally to reach the cup of hot water, however that would result in the water spilling and splashing the child and not in the burn pattern seen.

ii. When assessing a child who sustained a burn, we need to consider the location and configuration, as well as the compatibility with the mechanism or history provided.[1] This burn has many features concerning for abuse. It is bilateral, deep, symmetrical and with a clear line of demarcation separating the burned skin from the normal skin. There are also no splash marks.[2] As in this case, burns become more concerning for abuse when unwitnessed or with a poor history of events. The palms are partially spared due to the skin being thicker in that area and possibly being in contact with a cooler surface when the hands were immersed. The line of demarcation suggests the child was restrained when the hands were immersed in the hot water and thus no splash marks. This glove pattern results from the hands forcibly held in hot water and is consistent with an immersion burn. The diagnosis is physical abuse.

1. Thompson S. Accidental or inflicted? *Pediatr Ann.* 2005;34(5):372–381.
2. Maguire S, Moynihan S, Mann M, Potokar T, Kemp AM. A systematic review of the features that indicate intentional scalds in children. *Burns.* 2008;34(8):1072–1081.

CASE 86

Margaret T. McHugh with Anastasia Feifer and Lori A. Legano

A 4-year-old female had 1 day of bleeding noted in her underpants. Her mother said that when she checked her genitals, the area 'looked red'. The girl had been afebrile, active and playful, though was recovering from a mild upper respiratory tract infection. She denied any vaginal pain or dysuria. She was a healthy and developmentally normal child, attended school regularly and was toilet trained. She denied any sexual abuse when questioned in the office. Her physical examination is shown in Image 86.

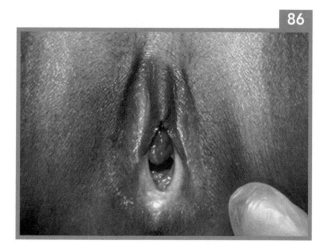

i. What was the diagnosis?
ii. What are the next steps in management of this condition?
iii. List other causes of bleeding in prepubertal girls.

i. This patient has a urethral prolapse, a relatively rare occurrence in prepubertal girls and mostly affecting patients of African descent.[1] The distal urethral mucosa protrudes beyond the urethral meatus, causing bleeding with or without urinary symptoms. Urethral prolapse may be caused by laxity of periurethral ligaments and low levels of oestrogen, and in some it has been shown to be associated with increased intra-abdominal pressure as with episodes of coughing or an asthma exacerbation.[2] The appearance of the prolapsed tissue is erythematous or even haemorrhagic and often obscures the anterior vagina (the 12 o'clock position) when the patient is examined supine. A 'donut-shaped' urethral opening can often be seen surrounded by prolapsed tissue. In this image, the extruded tissue is erythematous and highly vascular.

ii. The patient can be medically treated with topical oestrogen cream and sitz/salt baths to alleviate symptoms of bleeding and discomfort.[2] In some cases, this may resolve the prolapse; however, recurrence after a first episode is common and the patient may need surgical correction. Cases with persistence should be referred to a paediatric urologist.[1]

iii. Bleeding in a prepubertal girl can be distressing to patients and caregivers and should be evaluated thoroughly with a careful history. Child sexual abuse is part of the differential, and if there is concern, a verbal patient should be questioned carefully by a qualified interviewer. Physicians must always consider other non-abusive causes of bleeding, such as infections (Salmonella or group A strep), foreign body (especially toilet paper), accidental trauma such as a straddle injury, precocious puberty, including McCune-Albright syndrome or oestrogen secreting tumour, exogenous exposure to oestrogen and autoimmune conditions such as Behçet disease or lichen sclerosus et atrophicus.[1]

1. Vunda A, Vandertuin L, Gervaix A. Urethral prolapse: An overlooked diagnosis of urogenital bleeding in pre-menarcheal girls. *J Pediatr.* 2011;158(4):682–683.
2. Emans SJH, Laufer MR, Goldstein DP. *Pediatric and Adolescent Gynecology.* 5th ed. Philadelphia, PA: Lippincott Williams & Wilkins; 2005.

CASE 87

Tor Shwayder

A 9-year-old boy presented to the dermatology clinic with a brown streak on his right arm and forehead. The streak on his right arm is shown in Image 87 and was thought to be a 'whip mark' and child abuse was suspected. The family reported no history of trauma. The child was at a picnic recently and they did not recall him falling or injuring himself. The child made no disclosures of physical abuse.

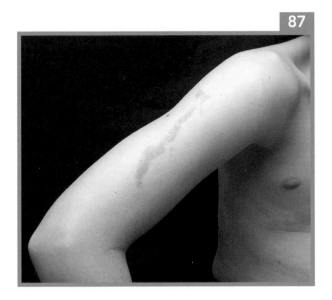

i. What is your diagnosis?
ii. How is the diagnosis made?
iii. What is the treatment?

i. The diagnosis of this child's lesion is lime-induced phytophotodermatitis. The child gave the history of lime juice spilling down his upper arm leaving a serpiginous trail while at the picnic. Plant-induced photosensitivity reactions are the most common phototoxic rashes seen in children.[1,2] Citrus fruit, especially lemon and limes, parsnips, carrots, dill, parsley, figs and celery (among others) contain furocoumarin, a phototoxic agent. This rash is activated by ultraviolet radiation (UVA), which has a reaction wavelength that can penetrate window glass. The reaction begins the day after the exposure and ranges from mild redness to severe blistering. Post-inflammatory hyperpigmentation is a common sequela as in this child.

ii. The diagnosis is made by recognizing the splash, spread or drip patterns made by external agents against the skin. When this is followed by sun exposure, the plant psoralens (furocoumarin) are activated. It is important to recognize this condition as it may be confused with child abuse.[3,4] A biopsy would show only inflamed or pigmented skin but will not give us clues to the cause. One can verify the diagnosis with photo patch testing but this is cumbersome and rarely needed in these cases of phytophotodermatitis.

iii. Treatment with topical steroids may be needed if the area is red and itchy. In cases where the patient is concerned about the hyperpigmented skin, bleaching creams may be used. Patients are advised to avoid contact with the triggering plant together with sunlight.

1. Chantorn R, Lim HW, Shwayder TA. Photosensitivity disorders in children: Part I. *J Am Acad Dermatol*. 2012;67(6):1093.e1-18; quiz 1111-1112.
2. Chantorn R, Lim HW, Shwayder TA. Photosensitivity disorders in children: Part II. *J Am Acad Dermatol*. 2012;67(6):1113 e1111–1115; quiz 1127, 1128.
3. Coffman K, Boyce WT, Hansen RC. Phytophotodermatitis simulating child abuse. *Am J Dis Child*. 1985;139(3):239–240.
4. Mehta AJ, Statham BN. Phytophotodermatitis mimicking non-accidental injury or self-harm. *Eur J Pediatr*. 2007;166(7):751–752.

CASE 88

Mary E. Smyth

This infant sustained burns when a cup of hot coffee was spilled on him. His father reportedly propped the cup on the baby inside his carrier while taking him to daycare. The coffee spilled, reportedly producing the burns seen (Images 88a and 88b). Treatment was sought immediately at the emergency centre.

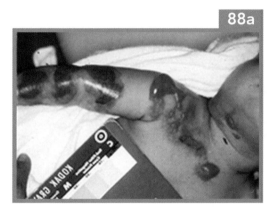

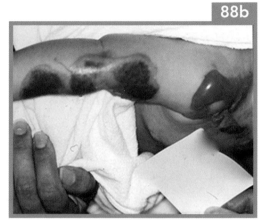

    i. What types of burns are seen?
   ii. Why is the burn not uniformly affecting the skin?
  iii. How is the diagnosis of accidental burn confirmed?

i. These pictures (Images 88a and 88b) show deep and superficial partial thickness burns with irregular margins on the neck, arm and chest of this infant. The burns continued onto the back of the neck and upper back (not pictured).

ii. This is a typical appearance of burns caused by hot liquids over clothing. The deeper, blistered areas are where the liquid made direct contact with the skin – note the triangular shape of a few areas, consistent with flowing liquid that cools as it flows in relation to gravity. The burns on the arms are not blistered because the clothing had a somewhat protective effect. Burns occurred, however, because the clothing held the hot liquid against the skin until it could be removed.

iii. The irregular margins of these burns are consistent with flowing liquid.[1] Inflicted, immersion burns have a sharp line of demarcation between the burn and the unaffected skin.[2,3] The father produced the infant carrier and the sleeper that the child was wearing which bore coffee stains that matched the injuries. In addition, Child Protective Services was able to interview witnesses to the accident at the daycare centre who confirmed the history. However, the practice of propping a cup of hot coffee on a child in a baby carrier is inappropriate and the father requires advice on safe parenting.

1. Daria S, Sugar NF, Feldman KW, Boos SC, Benton SA, Ornstein A. Into hot water head first: Distribution of intentional and unintentional immersion burns. *Pediatr Emerg Care.* 2004;20(5):302–310.
2. Greenbaum AR, Donne J, Wilson D, Dunn KW. Intentional burn injury: An evidence-based, clinical and forensic review. *Burns.* 2004;30(7):628–642.
3. Knox B, Starling S. Abusive burns. In: Jenny C, ed. *Child Abuse and Neglect: Diagnosis, Treatment and Evidence.* St Louis, MO: Elsevier Saunders 2011:232–233.

CASE 89

Pamela Wallace Hammel with Kenneth Cohrn

A teenager was attacked by a pack of seven dogs: pit bulls and mixed pit bulls. This injury was one of the superficial bites (Image 89a). A reverse image of the bite is shown in Images 89b through 89d. The total number of bites and severe injuries resulted in the teenager's death from multiple organ damage.

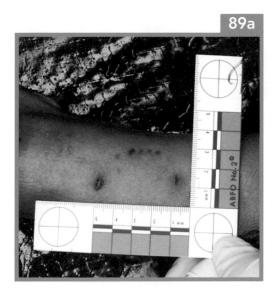

   i. What does Image 89a show?
  ii. When can such a death be the result of child abuse? How does one differentiate animal bites from human bites reliably? In cases of animal bites, how does one approach these fatal injuries as negligent homicide?
 iii. What is the role of the forensic odontologist in evaluating these cases?

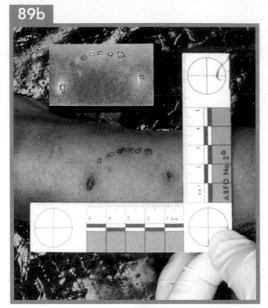

89b

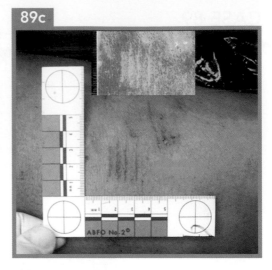

89c

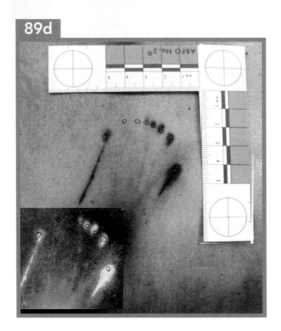

89d

i. Image 89a shows the typical pattern of a dog bite with short, straight, anterior segment and deep penetrations/punctures of the canines. The canines often produce tissue tearing. The child was attacked and killed by a pack of seven pit bull/pit bull mix dogs. She sustained mortal wounds over her entire body particularly the arms (defensive wounds) which were almost to the bone. She did not die during the attack but on the way to the hospital. The owner had been warned on several occasions to keep the dogs locked up and under control since they were terrorizing the neighbourhood. On this particular day, the pack of dogs got out and went down the road and killed the girl while she was getting groceries out of her car. The owner was arrested and was offered a plea but refused. He was convicted and sent to prison for 15 years.

ii. Animal bites are considered abuse/neglect when an infant or child is left unsupervised in the unrestricted presence of a dog or other animal.[1] Dogs are predators trained as pets, and children's play often mimics the dog's prey in the wild, with high-pitched screaming, random movements and no sense of space infringement. Distinguishing dog/cat bites from human bites involves comparing the morphology of the teeth as well as the shape of the jaw pattern.[2] The overall bite mark pattern is very different. Human bite marks are oval/ovoid; animal bites are longer, narrower, with a short straight anterior segment. The human dental formula is four incisors, two canines, four premolars and three molars. Canines and felines have six incisors, long curved canines, two premolars and three molars. Human bites usually leave contusions and superficial abrasions. Incisors leave a rectangular mark; canines leave a triangular mark. Image 89b shows the same image as 89a with the overlay of the teeth superimposed. The blue insert is simply an image adjustment to give a different colour perspective of the bite mark. Image 89c shows a scratch, which could be misinterpreted as a bite mark. Image 89d is a different bite mark. There were many additional bite marks which are not shown.

iii. The role of the forensic odontologist is to assess the overall bite pattern, its outline form and individual teeth markings, and come to a conclusion as to whether the bite is human or animal.[3] Also, if multiple dogs are involved the bite can be compared to the suspected animals, especially as to size of the arch. In this case, at least one bite mark could be matched to each of the dogs.

1. Naidoo S. A profile of the oro-facial injuries in child physical abuse at a children's hospital. *Child Abuse Negl.* 2000;24(4):521–534.
2. Senn D, Weems R. Animal bitemarks. In Senn D and Weems R (eds). *Manual of Forensic Odontology*, Fifth Edition. Albany, NY: Impress Printing and Graphics; 2013: Chapter 10, pp. 325–354.
3. Fischer H, Hammel P, Dragovic LG. Human bites versus dog bites. *New England J. Med.* 2003; 349(11):e11.

CASE 90

Alan Sprigg

A 5-month-old baby girl was brought to the emergency department by ambulance. The mother said she had been at home alone with the infant when she became pale, floppy and stopped breathing. Mother then noticed some twitching movements of her left arm and leg. She called the ambulance. The infant was mildly hypothermic, floppy and responding poorly to handling. She had a bulging fontanel. During assessment in the emergency department she had a generalized seizure needing intravenous medications to control it. She was then intubated due to apnoea. Once she was stabilized, a non-contrast CT head scan was requested (Image 90).

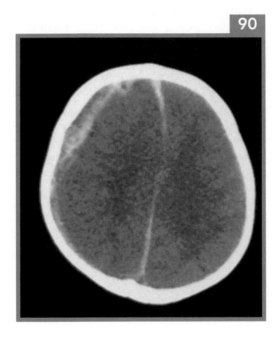

i. What diagnoses would you consider?
ii. What imaging would you request?
iii. What does the image show?

i. First consider meningitis and treat 'in case' then investigate, including blood count and blood cultures. Also, consider hypoglycaemia, head trauma, metabolic or biochemical disturbance.[1]

ii. Once the baby is stabilized then consider imaging tests:
   a. Chest x-ray to exclude pneumonia
   b. Computed tomography (CT) scan of the head to look for conditions such as haemorrhage and abscesses and exclude major haemorrhage that might need neurosurgical intervention
   c. Magnetic resonance imaging (MRI) to detect small areas of surface bleeding and focal brain change, as it is much more sensitive than CT (MRI is usually performed electively at about 3–7 days post-presentation.
   d. Skeletal survey
   e. Ophthalmoscopy

iii. The image shows acute blood (white) along the falx in the midline. This brightness is not due to the normal falx. Trauma scans are always performed without intravenous contrast being given. The dating of acute blood radiologically means bleeding at any time within 7 days or so. There is also midline shift from right to left due to a mixed density subdural collection over the right frontal lobe. Finding blood of two densities may mean bleeding of two different dates. It can also be explained by the mixing of clotted and unclotted (hyperacute) blood or mixing of acute blood with an acute traumatic effusion. There is subtle loss of grey white matter differentiation in the right frontal lobe which matches the clinical presentation with encephalopathy (better assessed with MRI). An MRI after a few days may assist in this differential diagnosis. Further investigations should exclude underlying coagulation disorder and metabolic disease. In addition, ophthalmoscopy revealed bilateral multilayer retinal haemorrhages. A full skeletal survey showed no bony injury. A follow-up chest x-ray at 2 weeks showed multiple unilateral healing posterior rib fractures even though no acute rib fractures were identifiable on the first chest x-ray of the skeletal survey even in retrospect. Later the mother admitted a squeeze and shake injury for a few seconds, when the baby would not stop crying in the early hours of the morning. The exact amount of force needed to cause subdural haemorrhage is unknown, as is the duration of the shaking. It is likely to involve a force well outside that of normal handling in a baby with immature neck control.

1. *Child Protection Companion 2013*. Royal College of Paediatrics and Child Health, London; 2013.

CASE 91

Patricia O. Brennan

A 12-year-old boy attended the paediatric department for an examination as an area of linear bruising across his left chest had been noted at school. He said he could not remember but thought he had knocked his chest on the floor when he fell the previous day. The paediatrician noted four bars of parallel bruising to the boy's left chest and a group of four small round bruises on his left upper arm. He also found a large area of depigmentation on the boy's face (Image 91) which was said to have happened when he pulled a hot cup of tea onto himself when he was 2 years old.

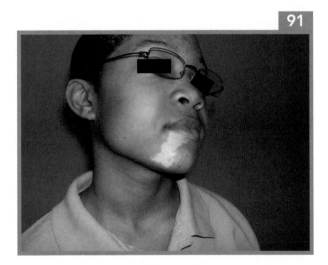

i. What is the diagnosis and differential diagnosis of the area of depigmentation?
ii. What is the aetiology of the condition?

i. This boy was the victim of non-accidental injury. He later said that the bruising to the chest had been caused when his mother hit him when she was angry after he had dropped a cup. The marks on his arm were where she gripped him. Vitiligo is the cause of the area of depigmentation. The differential diagnosis includes such conditions as tinea versicolor and post-inflammatory hypopigmentation or an area of scarring. The latter is unlikely as the surface of the depigmented skin is normal, the same as the adjacent area of pigmented skin.

ii. There is still a debate about the cause of vitiligo which is a polygenic disorder with complex pathogenesis, linked to genetic and non-genetic factors.[1] Suggested causes include destruction of the melanocytes because of an accumulation of a toxic melanin synthesis intermediate or that neurochemical factors damage melanocytes or even that immunological factors damage the melanocytes. The latter cause might explain why 80% of cases have an antimelanocyte antibody. There is also an incidence of autoimmune diseases such as Hashimoto thyroiditis and Addison disease in patients with vitiligo.

1. Laddha NC, Diwivedi M, Mansuri MS, Gani AR, Ansarullah M, Ramachandran AV, Dalai S, Begum R. Vitiligo: Interplay between oxidative stress and immune system. *Exp Dermatol*. 2013;22.4:245–250.

CASE 92

Carl J. Schmidt

This 6-month-old girl arrived at the medical examiner's office with extensive destruction of the parietal and occipital skull and partial evisceration of the brain. There are multiple linear abrasions in the forehead as seen (Image 92a). There were also some linear, parallel abrasions on the top of the right shoulder and the upper back. The scene report mentions the child being in a car seat during a motor vehicle accident, but further inquiry and a picture taken at the scene show the damage (Image 92b). The other occupants in the car survived and they were adamant that the child was in the car seat at the time the accident occurred.

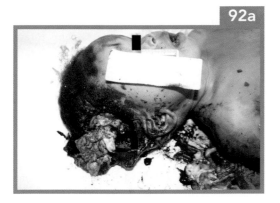

   i. Do you think the child was in the car seat when she was found?

  ii. From the scene picture of the car seat, where do you think the child was found? What can you say about how this child was restrained?

 iii. What do you think the manner of death should be (homicide or accident)?

i. It is apparent from the scene picture that the car seat was not adequately fastened to the car's bench seat by the adult seat belt. The child was not found in the car seat after the collision. Further inquiry revealed that the car seat was simply placed in the car without any actual restraint. Seat belt restraints are very good and are designed not to unlatch unless there is an extreme catastrophic event that essentially means the car is destroyed. The scene picture indicates the V-shaped straps are too close to the back rest for a child to actually have fit in there. When the car seat was inspected, the straps were found to be too short because they were adjusted that way. This child was simply placed on the car seat without being restrained in the seat, and the car seat was not restrained within the car.

ii. This girl was found approximately 30 feet from the car. The car was hit on the side and, as it rotated, the child was ejected through the left rear passenger window, which was open. Had she been properly restrained within the car seat and the latter ejected during the accident, death would still have been a possible outcome but the injuries would not have been as extensive as seen here because the frame of the car seat would have protected the head from injury.

iii. The certification of death in these cases always has controversy. However, infant and child car seats have been around for many years, so arguing ignorance is disingenuous. There are laws that cover the use of infant seats in all 50 states of the United States. This infant would likely have lived if the child seat had been properly latched to the car and the infant in turn properly placed in the seat.[1] A determination of homicide in this case is appropriate. Strictly speaking, homicide is the manner of death used when death is the consequence of the actions of another person. These can be from omission as well as commission.[2]

1. Decina LE, Lococo KH. Child restraint system use and misuse in six states. *Accid Anal Prev.* 2005;37(3):583–590.
2. Hanzlick R, Hunsaker JC, Davis GJ. *A Guide for Manner of Death Classification.* Marceline, MO: National Association of Medical Examiners, 2002. https://netforum.avectra.com/temp/ClientImages/NAME/38c0f1d2-11ec-45c7-80ca-ff872d0b22bc.pdf

CASE 93

Vincent J. Palusci

A 10-year-old white boy was brought to the emergency room after it was reported to Child Protective Services that he disclosed that his mother burned him with a hot fork. The child reportedly told school officials that her mother was very angry at him because of his poor behaviour and had taken a kitchen fork, heated it on the stove and had pressed it into his skin in several locations (Images 93a and 93b). He initially told no one, but one of his classmates noticed the marks and his teacher asked him how they occurred.

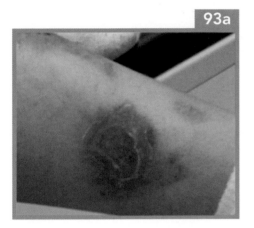

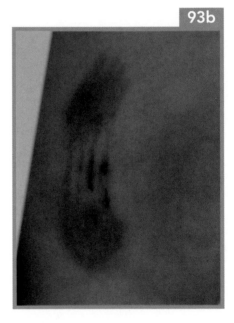

    i. Are these findings consistent with the child's disclosure?

   ii. What prognosis for healing and potential scarring should be considered?

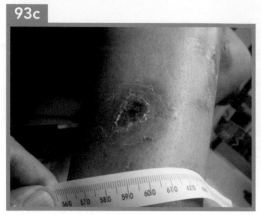

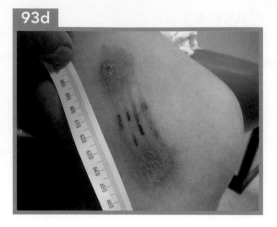

i. The images depict burns and other injury in non-specific and specific patterns. The linear patterns shown are very uncommon and are consistent with drawing the hot fork down the skin to cause linear burns. The pattern of burning suggested intentional injury with infliction of pain which should be considered by the investigators.[1,2] Given the prolonged painful contact with a hot implement, such practices have been considered 'torture' in certain circumstances.

ii. Two weeks later, the lesions were evident and showed evidence of early scar formation (Images 93c and 93d). The persistence of lesions and delayed healing suggested the increased risk of long-term scar formation.

1. Maguire S, Okolie C, Kemp AM. Burns as a consequence of child maltreatment. *Paediatr Child Health*. 2014;24(12):557–561.
2. Markman L. Abusive burns. In: Palusci VJ, Fischer H, eds. *Child Abuse and Neglect: A Diagnostic Guide*. London, England: Manson Publishing Ltd; 2011:43–68.

CASE 94

Vincent J. Palusci

A 6-month-old girl was brought to your office with a history of falling off the bed after her mother left the room. The child was able to roll and crawl and was found on the carpeted floor next to the bed after her mother heard her cry. There was no loss of consciousness. Her mother thought she was fine during the day since she acted normally, ate well and slept well overnight. The next morning, her mother noticed swelling over her forehead (Image 94a) which had become progressively worse over the day.

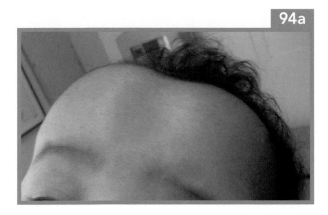

i. What does Image 94a show?
ii. What tests and imaging are important to determine the aetiology for this patient's presentation?

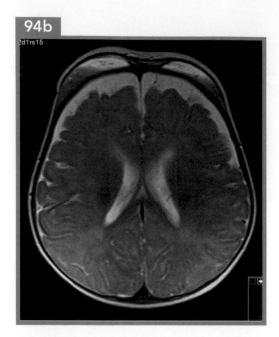

i. The child had bilateral swelling over the frontal bones without palpable fracture. No significant bruising was appreciated and the child appeared neurologically normal. A head magnetic resonance imaging scan was done (Image 94b) which showed the location of blood as being subperiosteal. These were thought to be traumatic cephalohaematomas consistent with a history of short fall. The imaging differentiated the location of bleeding from intracranial or subgaleal locations. While unusual, isolated and delayed extra-axial bleeding has been described from minor falls without overlying skin bruising or skull fracture.[1]

ii. Given the possibility of inflicted trauma in this presentation, full imaging of the axial skeleton using a skeletal survey was indicated. Coagulation tests such as a complete blood count, prothrombin time and partial thromboplastin times were also indicated to determine if the child had an underlying coagulation disorder contributing to the bleeding.

1. Agrawal A, Pratap A, Sundas A, Tiwari A. Delayed extensive subgaleal hematoma following minor head injury. *Pediatr Oncall [serial online].* 2006 (http://www.pediatriconcall.com/Journal/Article/FullText.aspx?artid=798&type=J&tid=&imgid=&reportid=158&tbltype=#).

CASE 95

Vincent J. Palusci

This 15-year-old girl had noticed a blister on her genitals. She scratched it and it broke but was not painful. No bleeding was noted. She had been having her menstrual periods for over a year and denied sexual contact. She has not noticed other blisters 'down there'. She had no other history of diseases, although sometimes she had ulcers in her mouth. She asked you to examine her private parts and you noted a non-tender, ulcerated lesion on her left labia majora shown (Image 95). There was no vaginal discharge or vesicles present. There was no palpable inguinal lymphadenopathy. No ulcerations were noted in her mouth or pharynx.

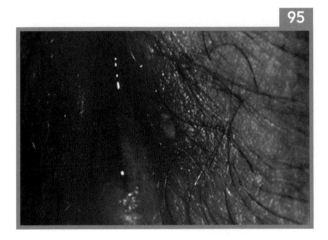

i. What does the image show?
ii. Is this caused by sexual contact?

i. The image shows an ulcer on the non-mucosal labial skin. There is no vesicle fluid present and there is no induration or signs of bacterial infection. This ulceration is not specific for sexually transmitted disease; while herpes viruses such as herpes simplex types 1 and 2 can cause painful vesicles, their presentation varies based on location.[1] Tests appropriate for this situation include viral culture as well as screening for additional sexually transmitted infections.

ii. Non-sexual causes for this type of lesion are common. In one series,[2] extensive workup failed to reveal a specific infectious or autoimmune aetiology in all but one patient, who was diagnosed with acute mycoplasma pneumonia. Acute genital ulcers in young girls who are not sexually active likely represent a form of idiopathic vulvar aphthosis. When present with other ulcerations this has been called Behçet's disease, which is characterized as a triad of symptoms that include recurring mouth ulcers (aphthous ulcers, canker sores), genital ulcers and inflammation of a specialized area around the pupil of the eye termed *uveitis*. The cause is not known. Both inherited and environmental factors are suspected to contribute to its development, but it is not contagious. The disease is relatively rare but is more frequent and severe in patients from Eastern Mediterranean countries and Asia than in those of European descent. Evaluation of a first episode of acute genital ulcers with mild prodromal symptoms should be limited. Treatment consists primarily of supportive care and symptom relief.

1. Palusci VJ. Anogenital findings and sexual abuse. In: Palusci VJ, Fischer H, eds. *Child Abuse and Neglect: A Diagnostic Guide for Physicians, Surgeons, Pathologists, Dentists, Nurses and Social Workers.* London, England: Manson Publishing Ltd; 2011:163–191.
2. Rosman IS, Berk DR, Bayliss SJ, White AJ, Merritt DF. Acute genital ulcers in nonsexually active young girls: Case series, review of the literature, and evaluation and management recommendations. *Pediatr Dermatol.* 2012;29(2):147–153.

CASE 96

Carl J. Schmidt

This 4-year-old boy arrived to the emergency room in an agonal state. He had multiple bruises on his head, bleeding in his mouth, a deformity of his left shoulder and scattered scars over his trunk and extremities. A CT scan of the head showed diffuse cerebral oedema and he died shortly after admission.

The autopsy showed at least 11 subcutaneous bruises in the scalp, all red-purple and recent. Extensive subcutaneous dissection showed similar multiple bruises in the back, forearms and lower extremities, each bruise representing an impact site. There was a laceration on the inner aspect of the upper lip with extensive separation of the soft tissue from the maxilla (Image 96a). The second image shows the deformity of the left shoulder (Image 96b). X-ray of the left shoulder revealed a fracture of the head of the humerus with extensive callus formation and dystrophic calcification (Image 96c). The child had no documented previous medical care.

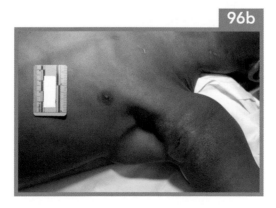

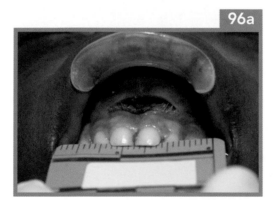

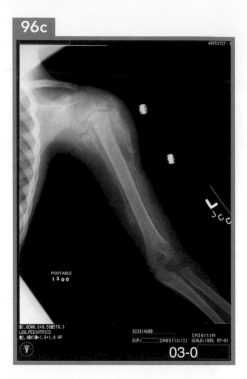

96c

i. What is the cause of death?
ii. Do you suspect an instrument was used to inflict the injuries?
iii. What is the significance of the shoulder injury?
iv. Can you affirm, if asked in court, that this child experienced pain?

i. This child has symmetric scald burns to both lower extremities that are consistent with immersion burns. Scald burns – both accidental and intentional – account for the majority of childhood burns seen by healthcare providers. This child had a burn with a stocking pattern, which was consistent with an abusive immersion burn. Forced immersion scald injuries are the most common mechanism of intentional scalding of children.[1] The patterns of these intentional scald injuries are mostly bilateral and symmetric, with clear upper margins and involving the lower extremities. This description clearly fitted this child's burn, and, coupled with the poor history of the event provided by the mother, our suspicion for an intentional scald injury was high. The genital burns were consistent with flexion of the hips and knees during the immersion and most likely occurred simultaneously.

ii. There are several features of scald burns that are suggestive of intentional burns, including (1) an absence of splash marks (indicating that the child was held tightly in position); (2) a uniform depth; (3) a well-demarcated burn area; (4) an involvement of dorsal hands or feet, face, buttocks or the backs of arms or legs; (5) a stocking or glove pattern; (6) a poor history of the event or an unwitnessed event; and (7) a delay in seeking treatment.[2] The presence of one or more of these features should raise a provider's index of suspicion for abusive scald burns.

1. Maguire S, Moynihan S, Mann M, Potokar T, Kemp AM. A systematic review of the features that indicate intentional scalds in children. *Burns*. 2008;34(8):1072–1081.
2. Markman L. Abusive burns. In: Palusci VJ, Fischer H, eds. *Child Abuse and Neglect: A Diagnostic Guide*. London, England: Manson Publishing Ltd; 2011: 43–68.

CASE 98

Pamela Wallace Hammel with Salwa Atwan

This 2-year-old child presented with almost total destruction of all primary maxillary teeth. Most were decayed to the gum line and only three teeth still have clinical crowns, but even these have caries present (Image 98). No previous dental care had been documented.

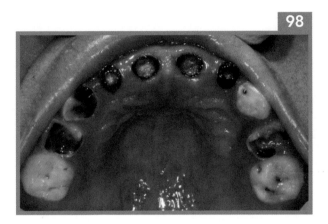

   i. What does the image show?
  ii. What are the potential consequences of these findings?

i. This is a classic case of dental neglect, with multiple caries likely reflecting 'nursing bottle caries' in response to the bottle being propped and extensive milk-tooth contact. Dental neglect has been defined as the willful failure of a parent to provide needed dental care.[1] In this case, the deliberate bottle propping in addition to the destruction of the teeth is consistent with a willful act.

ii. Untreated, this can lead to acute infection, pain and loss of function. This can harm life-time function, communication, nutrition and other activities necessary for normal growth and development. If infection progresses to sepsis or deeper infection, it may result in death. An assessment for other types of child neglect should be carried out in a child presenting with such dental caries. Any siblings of this child should also be assessed.

1. Kellogg N. Oral and dental aspects of child abuse and neglect. *Pediatrics*. 2005;116(6):1565–1568.

CASE 99

Alan Sprigg

A mother brought her 6-week-old baby to the emergency department. His arm was floppy and swollen and he was crying. The previous night, the mother had gone out with her friends for the first time since delivery, leaving the baby with her boyfriend. She arrived home at 3 a.m. The baby was asleep so she did not disturb him. The baby awoke at 6 a.m. crying in an unusual way. He was moving his hand and fingers but his arm was floppy and swollen. The boyfriend said he had not noticed any problems with the infant the previous evening before he put him in his Moses' basket/basinet. There was no history of trauma. An arm radiograph was requested (Image 99).

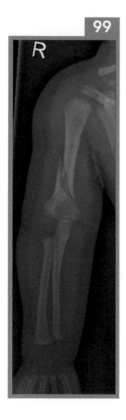

    i. What is your clinical differential diagnosis from the history alone?
   ii. What would you do first?
  iii. What do you do see on the radiograph?
  iv. What would you do next?

223

i. The most likely causes of the loss of use of the limb are sepsis or trauma (accidental or otherwise). If the diagnosis is a fracture, then non-accidental injury must be considered.[1]

   ii. A full history and body examination, including a temperature should be undertaken and inflammatory markers should be measured. A history of any incident which could result in injury and any family history of fragile bones should be particularly noted. A radiograph is then required.

  iii. The radiograph shows a minimally displaced spiral fracture through the shaft of the lower humerus. This implies a rapid forceful twist of the arm. The bone appears of normal structure. There is a little soft tissue swelling, but no healing reaction – hence a recent injury.

  iv. You should recheck the history and in the absence of any history of trauma consistent with the injury, explain the findings to the mother, together with your concerns about the possible origin of the fracture. You should then alert the paediatricians so that they can arrange treatment for the fracture and then make sure the child is in a safe place, often via admission to hospital. This is to ensure protection of the child while a safeguarding investigation is carried out. A full skeletal survey and magnetic resonance imaging (MRI) scan of the head, bone biochemistry and an examination of the eyes by a paediatric ophthalmologist should be carried out.[1] In this baby, there were no additional injuries. Bone biochemistry results were normal. There was no family history of fracturing with minimal trauma and no clinical features of bone diseases. With or without these underlying conditions the child would feel pain at the time the fracture was sustained and so the carer should be aware when the fracture was sustained although with bone fragility, the fracture could occur with lesser force. Although this boy had a difficult delivery (4 kg) with shoulder dystocia, the absence of healing callus and recent onset of symptoms excluded birth injury. The presentation with an unexplained spiral long bone fracture in a pre-mobile infant was highly suspicious for a non-accidental injury. It was a solitary injury with no features of underlying bone disease. There was no history of trauma so this injury was potentially non-accidental. Radiology cannot determine the exact time the fracture was sustained to aid agencies to determine whether the mother could have fractured the arm before she left or the boyfriend while she was out. Three months later, in a police interview, the boyfriend admitted to dropping the baby and grabbing him by his elbow to stop him hitting the floor. The baby's weight twisted rapidly, around the fixed arm. He said that he was too afraid to admit to this as an accidental event, as he was concerned the mother might leave him. Whether this was the true explanation is uncertain, but it is difficult to disprove.

1. *Child Protection Companion 2013*: Royal College of Paediatrics and Child Health, London; 2013.

CASE 100

Patricia O. Brennan

This 6-year-old girl was brought to the emergency department. She was said to have been play-ing at her grandmother's house and had caught her arm in the 'mangle'. She had a swollen arm, with some loss of skin and was complaining of great pain in the arm. The findings are shown (Image 100).

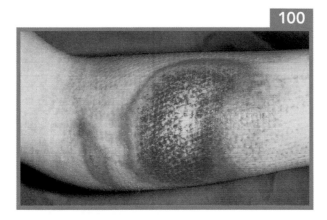

i. Does the injury shown fit the history or do you suspect non-accidental injury?
ii. What would your management of this injury be?

i. The injury shown is consistent with a severe crush injury, consistent with the arm being crushed between the rollers of the 'mangle' or wringer, a machine used to squeeze wet washing before tumbler driers were common. Production ceased in the early 1980s and the decline of wringer injuries occurred between 1993 and 2010. Wringer injuries can result in a burn-like condition with swelling and oedema to lacerations, torn ligaments and fractures. Non-accidental injury was not suspected, although there was an element of neglect as the child was not properly supervised during play.[1]

ii. Severe crush injuries cause severe injury to the deep tissues as well as to the skin. This occurs from direct trauma to tissues but also by changes indirectly related to the trauma, including oedema, increased intercellular fluid and fibrosis of the injured muscles and tendon sheaths. The skin requires repair and the fracture's stabilization, but the most important part of the initial treatment is prevention of the oedema by occlusive compression dressing and sometimes, splitting the muscle capsules to maintain blood flow within the muscles and preserve muscle function is required.[2]

1. Chesney RW. The disappearance of diseases, conditions, and disorders of childhood. *J Pediatr.* 2013;162(5):903–905.
2. Buck-Gramcko D. Severe crush injury of the hand. *Langenbecks Arch Chir.* 1972;332:465–468.

CASE 101

Patricia O. Brennan

This 9-month-old baby was failing to put on weight properly and had a small amount of blood in his nappy/diaper. On examination, a swelling was noticed protruding from the anus (Image 101).

  i. What conditions should you consider?
 ii. What aspects of management should be addressed?

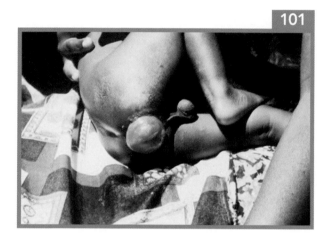

i. This infant has a rectal prolapse (protrusion of the rectal mucosa through the rectum), a common condition in children younger than 5 years. On examination, his weight was on second centile and had fallen from 50th centile since birth. A full medical history and examination were indicated. The conditions considered were chronic diarrhoea, constipation, frequent vigorous coughing, for example from whooping cough and failure to thrive. Neglect with an inadequate diet should be considered as a cause of poor weight gain in developed countries and malnutrition in underdeveloped countries. In view of the blood in the nappy, sexual abuse was also considered in this case.

ii. Most cases of rectal prolapse are mild and may spontaneously resolve. Medical management with stool softeners or laxatives is usually the first-line of management. Recurrences may occur but are rare after the age of 5 years. When conservative treatment fails, more complicated cases require further gastrointestinal investigation and referral to a surgeon for further investigation and possible surgical management is indicated.[1]

1. Laituri CA, Garey CL, Fraser JD et al. 15-Year experience in the treatment of rectal prolapse in children. *J Pediatr Surg.* 2010;45(8):1607–1609.

CASE 102

Dena Nazer

A 6-month-old baby girl was admitted to the hospital with failure to thrive. She was diagnosed with cystic fibrosis at birth and had a prolonged hospitalization. When discharged home, she continued follow-up with the pulmonary clinic. Her weight initially fluctuated. She then started losing weight and had not gained height for the past 2 months. Her mother was mentally ill and was overwhelmed with taking care of her. Her father was away in the military and was not involved in her care. Her paternal grandmother brought her in for medical care when she became concerned about her appearance. Images 102a through 102c show her right arm, thighs and buttocks, respectively.

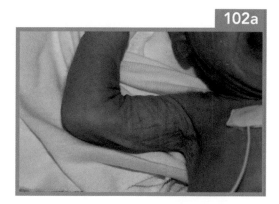

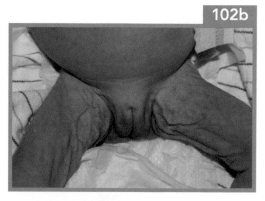

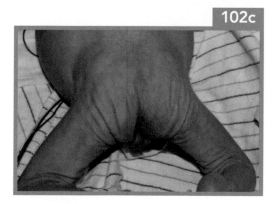

i. What do the images show?
ii. Do you have any further concerns regarding maltreatment in this child?

i. The images show the arm, thighs and buttocks of this baby that depict severe loss of subcutaneous tissue and malnutrition. She has no subcutaneous fat and her skin has a wrinkled appearance. There was also delay in her development. Failure to thrive to this degree without adequate medical cause is a concern for neglect. Her growth charts are shown in Images 102d and 102e, below. She was subsequently placed in foster care with her grandmother and gained weight and length over time with adequate feeding and care, as shown in her growth charts.

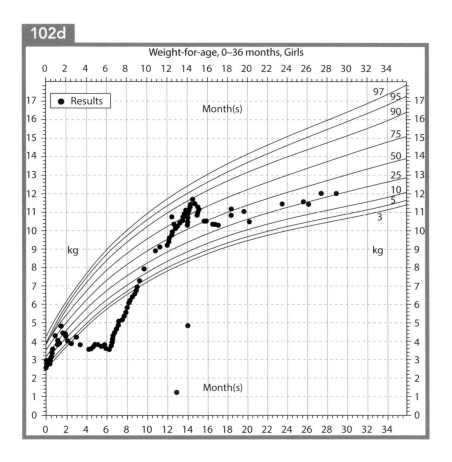

102e

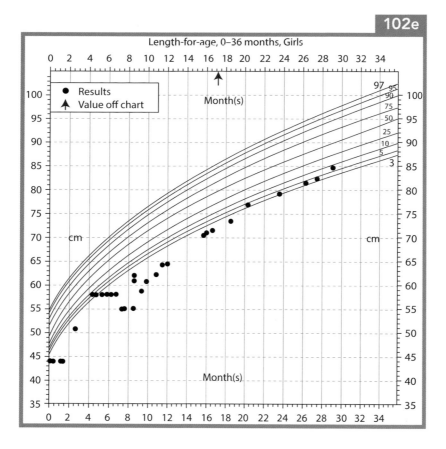

Length-for-age, 0–36 months, Girls

ii. Failure to thrive is not a diagnosis and its aetiology needs to be evaluated with a thorough history and physical examination.[1] Failure to thrive is multifactorial in most cases as in this child with organic (cystic fibrosis) and non-organic (neglect) causes. Recognition of neglect as a factor is important as it may lead to death in severe cases. The American Academy of Pediatrics has identified several risk factors that should alert the paediatrician to the possibility of neglect as the cause of failure to thrive.[2] These include mental health problems in a caregiver, lack of family support and resistance to recommended interventions despite multidisciplinary team approach as in this case. Additional evaluations should be carried out in this child to look for occult injury and to evaluate her emotional attachment to her mother. The contribution of the cystic fibrosis to her malnutrition should be assessed in the hospital with direct observation of her ability to eat and digest food and her weight over time. Formal evaluations for other medical conditions can be made depending on the results of her examination, basic screening tests and progress.

1. Yetman RJ, Coody DK. Failure to thrive: A clinical guideline. University of Texas. Houston Health Science Center. *J Pediatr Health Care.* 1997;11(3):134–137.
2. Block RW, Krebs NF. Failure to thrive as a manifestation of child neglect. *Pediatrics.* 2005;116(5):1234–1237.

CASE 103

Vincent J. Palusci

A 4-year-old girl was brought to the emergency room 2 days after sustaining a burn. Her mother reported she was making hot tea and placed it on the table in the dining room and the child walked up to the table and pulled the cup, spilling its contents onto herself. The mother removed her clothes, applied aloe and bandaged the skin and did not seek medical care because she thought Child Protective Services would be notified. The child sustained the injury over her abdomen as depicted in Image 103.

    i. What does the image show?
   ii. What are the possible causes for this finding?
  iii. What are important next steps to determine the aetiology for this patient's presentation?

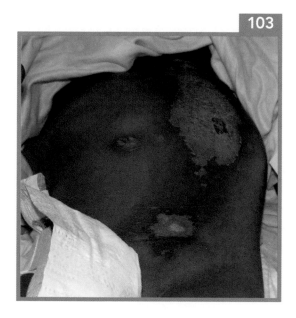

i. The child had an asymmetric skin lesion with hyperpigmentation surrounding new tissue/granulation tissue, with increasing width caudally. There was a 'sweep' from the left to the right, moving from left mid-quadrant to suprapubic location. There was also eschar formation present centrally, with diffuse crusting but no evidence of cellulitis. There were separate areas of granulation tissue, suggesting separate areas of superficial and deep partial thickness burns. There was sparing of the umbilicus, inguinal creases and genitals.

ii. The pattern was consistent with an accidental drip or splash burn, modified by the position of the child, clothes and temperature of the liquid involved.[1] Clothing can modify burn patterns either by increasing contact time (and therefore increasing burn depth) or by absorbing heat and liquid to decrease thermal energy transmission. A thermal liquid burn as reported was likely, but chemical burns are possible.

iii. In addition to routine care of the burn, the child should be interviewed. A normally developing child at this age should be able to disclose important details concerning how the burn occurred. Consideration should also be given to evaluation for other trauma and some have noted the value of skeletal surveys in detecting occult trauma in younger children.[2]

1. Maguire S, Moynihan S, Mann M, Potokar T, Kemp AM. A systematic review of the features that indicate intentional scalds in children. *Burns*. 2008;34(8):1072–1081.
2. Degraw M, Hicks RA, Lindberg D. Incidence of fractures among children with burns with concern regarding abuse. *Pediatrics*. 2010;125(2):e295–e299.

CASE 104

Carl J. Schmidt

A 6-month-old infant boy was brought unresponsive to the emergency room of a community hospital. He was asystolic and declared dead shortly thereafter. There were obvious deformities of all four extremities (Image 104a). X-rays showed deformed, shortened extremities, some with healing fractures (Images 104b and 104c). The sclera were grey. The caretakers were equivocal as to the time when last seen alive. They stated that care was provided in a specialized paediatric clinic at another hospital system. Child Protective Services were called to interview the caretakers. An autopsy was performed.

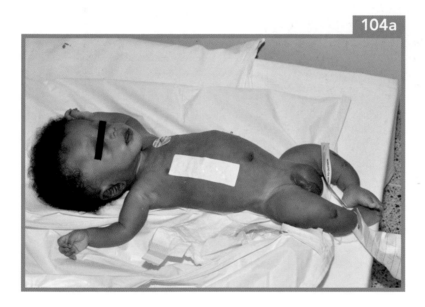

104a

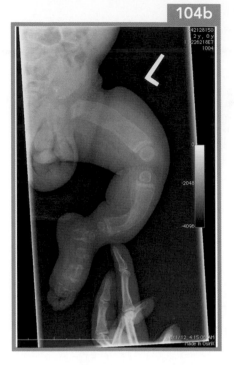

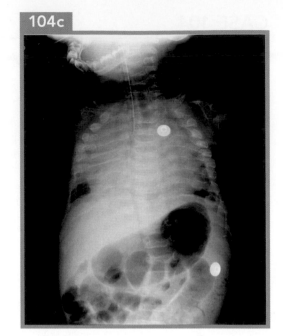

i. What is the diagnosis?
ii. What is the cause of death?
iii. Would you report this case to Child Protective Services?

i. This infant suffered from osteogenesis imperfecta, a rare disorder characterized by a mutation in the gene encoding type 1 collagen. The main clinical manifestations are osteoporosis, brittle and easily fractured bones, blue sclerae, dentinogenesis imperfecta and hearing impairment. There are several subtypes characterized by different degrees of clinical severity, from fatal in the perinatal period due to extreme bone fragility, to a variant that allows for a normal life except for somewhat increased susceptibility to fractures.[1]

ii. There are a number of reasons why children with osteogenesis imperfecta die.[2] The more severe variants cause death due to respiratory infections and heart failure secondary to scoliosis. Pneumonia is frequent due to decreased respiratory effort that accompanies the multiple rib fractures. There are complications inherent to osteogenesis imperfecta, such as basilar invagination of the skull (projection of the tip of the odontoid process into the foramen magnum) that can also cause death. In this particular case, the variant was of the severe, progressive deforming type, with multiple fractures in the trunk and extremities. Pneumonia was present on autopsy.

iii. In this case, it was apparent from the appearance of the child that, in spite of the parent's educational limitations, the child was as well cared for as one could expect. He was clean, reasonably well nourished and there was no diaper/nappy rash. It was easy to discern that progressive, fatal congenital disease was present. Discrepancies in the parent's stories were resolved and the medical records obtained from the medical centre where this child was routinely seen clarified the story. This is not always the case, especially with the more common variants that survive into adulthood but are more prone to fractures in childhood.[3] To a great extent, the decision to involve other authorities depends on the knowledge and experience of the nurses and physicians who see children like this, because child abuse can also happen to severely incapacitated children.

1. Rauch F, Glorieux FH. Osteogenesis imperfecta. *Lancet.* 2004;363(9418):1377–1385.
2. McAllion SJ, Paterson CR. Causes of death in osteogenesis imperfecta. *J Clin Pathol.* 1996;49(8): 627–630.
3. Singh Kocher M, Dichtel L. Osteogenesis imperfecta misdiagnosed as child abuse. *J Pediatr Orthop B.* 2011;20(6):440–443.

CASE 105

Dena Nazer

A 3-month-old baby girl was brought to the emergency department by her parents with a history of spitting up blood. Medical staff noticed some marks on her face and left eyelid. Her parents reported no history of trauma. Images 105a through 105d depict her face and the inside of her mouth.

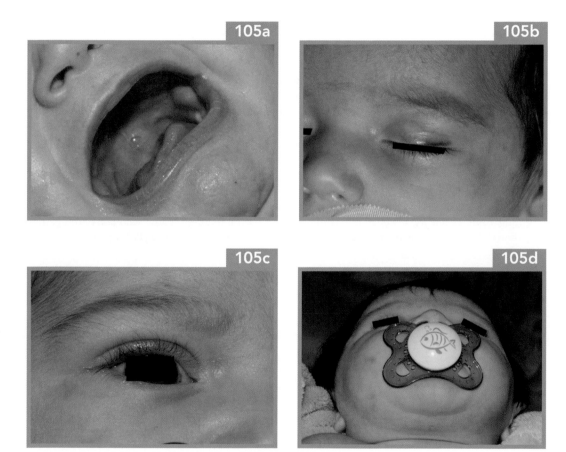

i. What do the images show?
ii. What tests and imaging studies are important to further assess this infant?

239

i. Image 105a shows an abrasion of her left hard palate at the junction with the soft palate. Image 105b shows bruises on the infant's left side of her face and left upper eyelid. Image 105c shows a subconjunctival haemorrhage of her right eye and Image 105d shows further bruises on the right side of her face. On further questioning, her father stated he is not able to handle the baby's crying. He added that when she cries, he wraps his finger with a towel and inserts it into her mouth to make her stop crying, which could explain the palatal abrasion. There was no explanation given by either parent for the facial bruises. However, based on their shape and location along with the history, they could be sustained when holding the baby's jaw forcefully by the father to insert his finger in her mouth. It is important to determine whether the bruises in children resulted from abuse or an accident. Medical assessment starts with a thorough history and a complete physical examination with documentation of findings.[1] When child abuse is suspected, a report needs to be made to Child Protective Services to prevent further abuse and possibly death.

ii. 'Those who don't cruise rarely bruise'.[2] Bruises on the face and inside the mouth are particularly concerning for child abuse. Although the bruises were partially explained by the father's actions, those actions are abusive in nature. To evaluate for associated injuries, she had blood drawn for a complete blood count, liver enzymes, prothrombin time (PT), partial thromboplastin time (PTT), all of which came back normal. She had skeletal survey x-rays, which showed multiple posterior rib fractures and metaphyseal corner lesions, both of which are highly specific for child abuse. Her head magnetic resonance imaging (MRI) scan was normal. A report to Child Protective Services was made based on the diagnosis of physical abuse and the infant was placed with her grandparents.

1. Kellogg ND. Evaluation of suspected child physical abuse. *Pediatrics*. 2007;119(6):1232–1241.
2. Sugar NF, Taylor JA, Feldman KW. Bruises in infants and toddlers: Those who don't cruise rarely bruise. Puget Sound Pediatric Research Network. *Arch Pediatr Adolesc Med*. 1999;153(4):399–403.

CASE 106

Vincent J. Palusci

A 6-year-old boy was brought to your office after he was removed from his parents' care. He and other children were found unattended in a filthy apartment and police noticed he appeared dirty, with poor hygiene and rashes on his arms. During physical examination in the emergency room, a physician became concerned about additional lesions noted over his back and buttocks as shown in Image 106. You were asked to determine whether these were bruises and what additional evaluation is needed.

    i. What does the image show?
   ii. Are these lesions bruises?
  iii. What additional evaluation is needed?

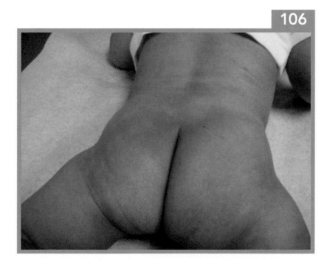

i. This child demonstrated several irregularly shaped blue/purple lesions which were homogeneous and extended over the lower back onto the buttocks and sacrum. There were no ecchymotic areas or pattern marks which would suggest bruises.

ii. These lesions were not bruises. They are commonly called 'Mongolian spots' or 'Mongolian blue spots' and they are more properly called congenital dermal melanocytosis.[1] They are present from birth, generally fade during the early years, are more prominent among dark-skinned individuals and may persist into adulthood. They are superficial and, while often seen in this area, may also be seen on the abdomen, extremities and other areas.

iii. Nutritional and developmental assessments would be helpful given the reported chronic neglect to determine if special education services or therapy (physical, occupational, speech) are needed. The statewide registry for immunizations should be checked as well as any available medical records to determine if he had any underlying chronic diseases needing treatment. Children with neglect may also have exposure to environmental lead and anaemia, and screening tests for red blood count and serum lead level are indicated.

1. Rapini RP, Bolognia JL, Jorizzo JL. *Dermatology: 2-Volume Set.* St. Louis, MO: Mosby; 2007.

CASE 107

Dena Nazer

A 6-month-old baby boy presented with a mark on his cheek as shown in Image 107a. His father gave a history of the baby sleeping with his cheek on top of his pacifier/dummy (shown) all night, which resulted in this mark.

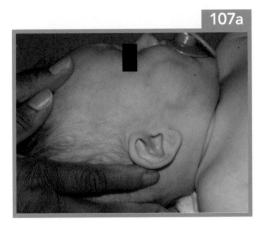

i. What is your diagnosis?
ii. Is the injury consistent with the provided history?

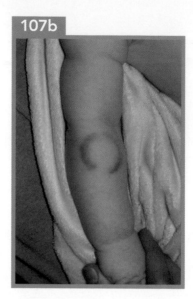

107b

i. Image 107a shows a patterned bruise on the child's right cheek. It shows a circular mark made by two opposing concave arcs, consistent with a bite mark. The intercanine distance was more than 3.5 cm in this infant, suggesting a human adult-sized bite. The diagnosis is a bite mark.

ii. The injury is not consistent with the provided history. Sleeping with his cheek on his pacifier will not result in bruising of the skin. Furthermore, the diameter of the patterned bruise is not consistent with the measurement of the pacifier. Children with bite marks need to be fully evaluated for associated injuries. A complete skin exam in this infant showed a similar mark on his left forearm (Image 107b). After the mark was noted, his father stated that a few days prior he was playing with the baby and the baby grabbed the father's hair. The father stated he 'had to bite' the baby's arm to release his hair. Unlike the injury to the cheek, the injury to the forearm is consistent with the history provided and is consistent with an adult-sized bite mark. However, it is still considered an abusive injury. Bite marks should be carefully documented with photos and measurements.[1] An intercanine distance of 3.5 cm in this child suggests a human adult-sized bite. In children where the bite marks appear fresh, it should be swabbed with a pre-moistened sterile cotton-tipped applicator for forensic analysis of potential genetic markers found in saliva.[2] If available it is also recommended to consult a forensic odontologist for further analysis of the bite mark. The perpetrator may be identified from the dental characteristics of the bite. It is also important to recognize that bites, especially those with a thrust mark or a suction mark may be a sign of sexual abuse. A suck mark appears as a bruise or area of haemorrhage in the centre of the bite mark and occurs when the skin is drawn into the mouth in a forceful manner and held. A thrust mark occurs when the tongue is pushed against the lingual aspect of the teeth with the skin located between the two.[2]

1. Kellogg ND. Evaluation of suspected child physical abuse. *Pediatrics*. 2007;119(6):1232–1241.
2. Kellogg N. Oral and dental aspects of child abuse and neglect. *Pediatrics*. 2005;116(6):1565–1568.

CASE 108

Vincent J. Palusci

A severely developmentally-delayed toddler with chronic seizures was admitted for intractable seizures and a cast was noted over her right leg. She has received anticonvulsant medications since infancy. When asked what had happened, the mother replied that the child was found to have a fracture after a 'crack' was heard during transfer from her bed to her wheelchair. Her leg was caught under her as she was placed into the chair and she did not have sufficient muscle tone or strength to protect her extremities. Initially she cried, but then was consoled in the chair. Later that evening, her mother noted swelling of her right leg and knee and she took her to her paediatrician. There, x-rays were ordered which demonstrated a right distal femur fracture (Image 108a) and a cast was placed. The next day she began having an increase in her seizures and she was brought to your hospital for management. X-rays were again obtained, this time with the cast (Images 108b through 108d).

   i. What do the images show?
  ii. Should this be reported as suspected physical abuse?
 iii. What further evaluation should be done?

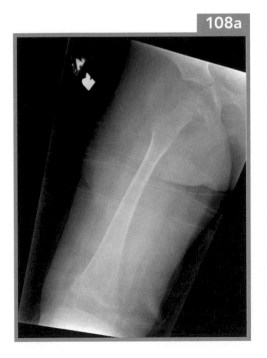

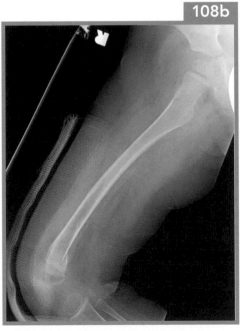

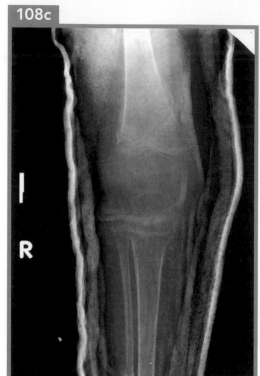

108c

I

R

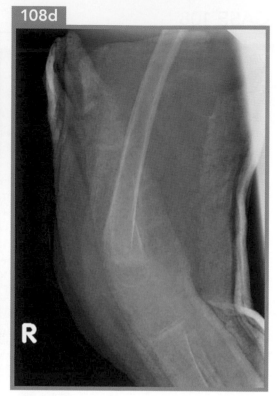

108d

R

i. There is a fracture extending through the metaphysis to the distal diaphysis with angulation in a Salter-Harris type 2 distribution. Irregular bone edges are visible bilaterally, but there is no periosteal new bone formation. The bones appear hypodense, although no ricketic changes are seen.

ii. The presence of an unexplained fracture in a developmentally delayed child is concerning for abuse. Children with associated intellectual or developmental disability who cannot disclose what has happened to them are at a significantly higher risk for maltreatment. The assessment for physical abuse involves considering any history of accidental injury, the child's developmental capabilities and the contribution of any underlying medical conditions which may have made an injury possible with less force.[1] Given that the child received anticonvulsants and was hypotonic and immobile, there are several medical risk factors pointing to decreased bone strength. The appearance of the bones on x-ray supported a diagnosis of metabolic bone disease which may have contributed to easy fracturability as described during transfer from the bed to the wheelchair. While a report to Child Protective Services could have been made for abuse, further evaluation may have obviated the need for such a report. Follow-up imaging 2 weeks later shows healing at the edges, early callus formation and growth arrest lines in multiple metaphyses, further supporting metabolic bone disease or deficiency as a cause.

iii. A well-defined protocol for skeletal survey with 20 or more dedicated images would help identify additional fractures and further clarify the metabolic bone disease. Serum blood tests for basic metabolic components, including calcium, phosphate, alkaline phosphatase, vitamin D and parathyroid hormone would also assist in identifying potential underlying causes.[2] Tests for osteogenesis imperfecta and other collagen or metabolic deficits can also be considered. While standard reference values are not readily available, a bone density test could also be considered. If there has been continued concern for abuse, brain imaging should have been considered given the child's multiple delays.

1. Kellogg ND. Evaluation of suspected child physical abuse. *Pediatrics*. 2007;119(6):1232–1241.
2. Flaherty EG, Perez-Rossello JM, Levine MA, Hennrikus WL. Evaluating children with fractures for child physical abuse. *Pediatrics*. 2014;133(2):e477–e489.

CASE 109

Dena Nazer

This 2-year-old patient was found to have multiple bruises. Her mother stated that when she came home from work she went straight to the room to check on her and noticed the bruises. The babysitter reported that she fell down the stairs. The child was noted to have extensive bruising to the buttocks and posterior thighs, linear streaks on the back and also on the face, left shoulder, left wrist area and bilateral knees (Images 109a through 109d).

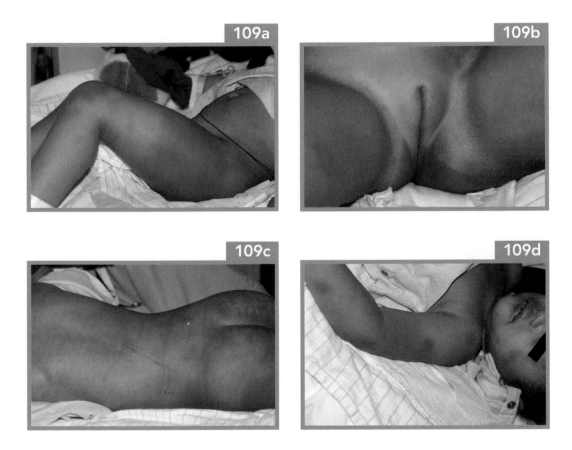

i. Is the injury consistent with the history provided?
ii. How would you further evaluate this child?

i. This child had multiple bruises in areas not commonly injured by accidents. The location and the extent of bruising were not consistent with falling down the stairs. Bruises in toddlers that are located in atypical areas, such as the trunk, hands or buttocks, should prompt concern for physical abuse which was our major concern in this child.[1]

ii. In this child an evaluation for physical abuse was initiated. A complete blood count, liver enzymes and pancreatic enzymes were done. A skeletal survey was done which was normal. A head CT was done due to the bruising of the head and neck and its results were also normal. Due to the liver enzymes being elevated, an abdominal CT was done which was normal. The diagnosis was physical abuse.

1. Sugar NF, Taylor JA, Feldman KW. Bruises in infants and toddlers: Those who don't cruise rarely bruise. Puget Sound Pediatric Research Network. *Arch Pediatr Adolesc Med.* 1999;153(4):399–403.

CASE 110

Dena Nazer

A 1-year-old girl presented for medical care with rectal bleeding. Her mother stated she was walking in the home and tripped. When she fell, her mother describes the child's bottom hitting a metal rod that was sticking out of the child's crib. Her mother stated she was setting up the crib and the rod was perpendicular to the floor, so when the child fell on top of it, it pierced her diaper/nappy. The child cried immediately and the mother noticed the blood in the diaper/nappy and brought her to the emergency department where an examination was done (Images 110a and 110b).

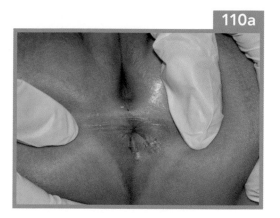
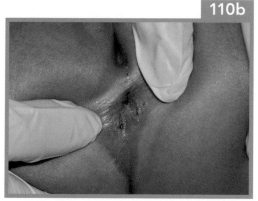

i. What injury do the images show?
ii. Is the injury consistent with the history provided?

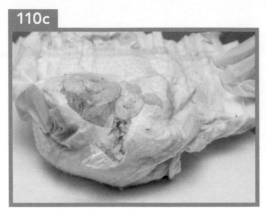

110c

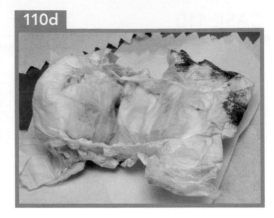

110d

i. Images 110a and 110b show two anal lacerations at the areas of 4 and 6 o'clock, which were 1 cm in length. The bleeding stopped when the wound was cleaned. Her genital examination was normal with no acute or chronic signs of trauma as was the remainder of her physical exam.

ii. The injury is thought to be consistent with the history provided. The mother had saved the diapers as seen in Images 110c and 110d. The diaper/nappy was full when the child tripped and a full diaper can be pierced much easier than a dry one. It was felt that the fall on top of the metal rod would puncture the diaper and cause the injury to the anus. The mother stated that when she saw the blood, she used the diaper to wipe the child's bottom, thus the blood on the diaper/nappy in different places. There was no delay in medical care and the remainder of the physical examination was otherwise normal. Child Protective Services were notified and they visited the home to make sure there were no other safety concerns. The child was followed up at the children's advocacy centre and the wounds had healed well with conservative management. It is important in these cases to obtain a full medical history and examination as well as a social work assessment of the family to identify any additional concerns. Anal injuries heal externally very quickly and it is important to ascertain whether there is potentially deeper, more life-threatening injury and to document these injuries.[1,2] Forensic trace evidence can also be collected before any cleansing or operative repair.

1. Berkowitz CD. Healing of genital injuries. *J Child Sex Abus*. 2011;20(5):537–547.
2. Finkel MA. Anogenital trauma in sexually abused children. *Pediatrics*. 1989;84(2):317–322.

CASE 111

Pamela Wallace Hammel

This 8-year-old boy was undergoing orthodontia with a palatal expander. He came in with the expander broken and the ecchymosis shown. There was no history of thumb sucking, falling with something in his mouth or other accidental trauma. There was no disclosure of abuse, but the examining dentist was concerned about possible sexual assault and collected specimens for pharyngeal gonorrhea.

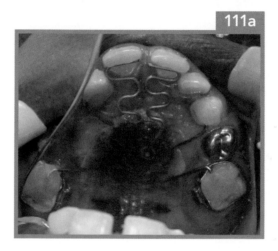

   i. What does Image 111a show?

   ii. What is the possible aetiology of these injuries?

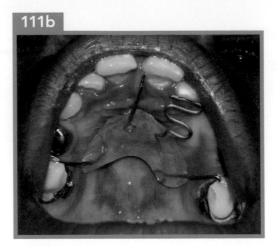

111b

i. A large bruise is noted over the hard palate in a pattern similar to the plastic frame of the expander. No active bleeding is noted. The shape of a similar expander is shown in a child without a bruise (Image 111b).

ii. Any palatal bruising should be viewed with suspicion. Palatal expansion is used to correct cross bites and to relieve crowding in the maxillary arch. While petechial hemorrhages of the soft palate have been noted in fellatio,[1] the palatal inflammation is located under the palatal acrylic strap that fractured, most likely during the assault. The child firmly denied being assaulted, and it was only because of his being positive for oral gonorrhea that sexual assault was confirmed.

1. Schlesinger SL, Borbotsina J, O'Neill L. Petechial hemorrhages of the soft palate secondary to fellatio. *Oral Surg Oral Med Oral Pathol.* 1975;40(3):376–378.

CASE 112

Nicholas Bishop

An infant was born at 28-weeks' gestation weighing 800 grams and had multiple problems during his stay in the neonatal intensive care unit (NICU), including necrotizing enterocolitis which did not require resection, delayed enteral feeding (fully fed enterally only by day 45), prolonged intravenous feeding to day 38 and conjugated hyperbilirubinaemia. He initially received ventilatory support for 4 weeks and remained on oxygen for 8 weeks. His chest x-ray at 7 weeks age showed patchy lung disease, but no fractures. He had biochemical profiles undertaken weekly during his stay in the NICU; his serum phosphate was recorded on two occasions as being <1.0 mmol/L (normal range >1.5 mmol/L); calcium, parathyroid hormone (PTH) and vitamin D were all within the normal range. He was discharged home at 38 weeks' equivalent gestation, but was readmitted 4 weeks later with increased work of breathing and an episode of possible apnoea. His oblique chest x-ray (Image 112) revealed healing fractures of the fifth and sixth left posterior ribs as shown.

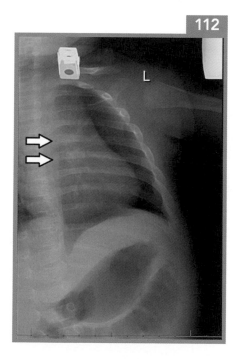

i. What are the factors in this infant that contribute to increased fracture risk?

i. Prematurity and diseases during the neonatal period can adversely affect bone health.[1,2] Factors in prematurely born infants that contribute to an increased risk of fractures include
   a. Gestational age ≤32 weeks
   b. Metabolic bone disease of prematurity, suggested by low PO_4 estimates
   c. Cholestatic jaundice
   d. Prolonged total parenteral nutrition
   e. Prolonged oxygen requirement to 36 weeks' gestation equivalent age
   f. Physiotherapy and procedures

It is critical that one obtains a careful history that investigates the neonatal course in the evaluation of preterm infants with a coincidental finding of rib fractures due to their increased risk of fractures.[3] However, due to the increased risk of abuse in premature infants, child abuse also needs to be considered and evaluated further on a case-by-case basis.

1. Bennett D, Pierce MC. Bone health and development. In: Jenny C, ed. *Child Abuse and Neglect: Diagnosis, Treatment, and Evidence.* St. Louis, MO: Saunders/Elsevier; 2011:261–274.
2. Dahlenburg SL, Bishop NJ, Lucas A. Are preterm infants at risk for subsequent fractures? *Arch Dis Child.* 1989;64(10 Spec No):1384–1385.
3. Lucas-Herald A, Butler S, Mactier H, McDevitt H, Young D, Ahmed SF. Prevalence and characteristics of rib fractures in ex-preterm infants. *Pediatrics.* 2012;130(6):1116–1119.

CASE 113

Patricia O. Brennan

This 4-year-old boy had chronic severe asthma necessitating frequent admissions to hospital. During an outpatient clinic at the tertiary care hospital, his parents said he had a bad nappy/ diaper rash, despite being dry during the day. This healing rash was noted on examination (Image 113). On further examination, he was also noted to have a large healing ulcerated lesion, diameter 3 cm on his left forearm, which the parents had failed to mention and for which they had no explanation. The general examination was otherwise unremarkable although the boy appeared anxious and withdrawn.

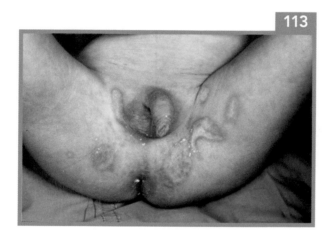

  i. What are your concerns?
 ii. What other information would you seek?
iii. How would you manage the case initially?

i. The boy has healing ulcers in the nappy area. These are unusual in shape and site, especially in a boy who is not in nappies/diapers continuously. They are not characteristic of napkin/diaper dermatitis or of a rash from a systemic disease. This together with the unexplained ulcerated lesion of his left forearm lead to concerns about inflicted injury with a caustic substance or factitious illness.

ii. The doctor asked the parents about the boy's past medical history and they said he had fractured his left femur 5 months previously when he was playing on a sofa. They had taken him to their local hospital for treatment and the parents appeared to be very caring. The doctor also reviewed the boy's attendances at all the tertiary care hospital departments and found an attendance with an injury to the upper right humerus resulting in subperiosteal new bone but with no fracture recognizable on x-ray. There was no history of any injury. The doctor also consulted the childcare agencies, but the child and family were unknown to the police or social care. However, despite this, the doctor had increasing concerns about child maltreatment. He considered the skin marks on the nappy area and the left forearm could be due to the application of a caustic substance.

iii. In view of the doctor's concerns, he did not allow the child home with the parents, but admitted him to the hospital. He also referred the case to social care services and the police and a full child protection investigation followed. The child was subsequently taken into the care of the local authority and placed with foster carers. After family law proceedings, he was eventually adopted. Neither parent was charged with any criminal maltreatment.[1]

1. Maguire S, Okolie C, Kemp AM. Burns as a consequence of child maltreatment. *Paediatr Child Health*. 2014;24(12):557–561.

CASE 114

Nicholas Bishop

A 4-year-old girl of African origin presented to an emergency department with a convulsion and was found to be hypocalcaemic (Ca 1.2 mmol/L; normal range: 2.1–2.65 mmol/L) with a serum 25-hydroxyvitamin D of 6 nmol/L (normal range: 50–125 nmol/L). She was admitted, received intravenous calcium and was discharged home after 3 days when the blood calcium had risen to 2.1 mmol/L, on oral calcium supplements and vitamin D 3000 units (75 mcg) daily. The parents were asked to return for further blood tests to assess the adequacy of supplementation, but failed to attend and could not be contacted at the given address or by telephone. Six weeks later the girl was seen again in the same emergency department. She was not moving her leg and an x-ray showed several findings (Images 114a and 114b).

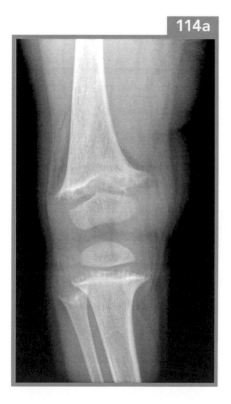
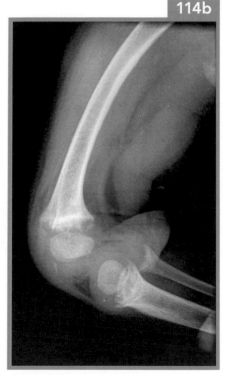

i. Is this a non-accidental injury?

259

i. The x-ray shows abnormal bones with frayed metaphyses and osteopenia. These are signs of rickets. These findings are not from abuse, however, they may result from medical neglect if the parents have not been providing recommended vitamin D and mineral supplementation. Rickets result in weakening of bone tissue; bone demineralization results in a loss of bone stiffness, which in turn means that the bone cannot resist deformation due to mechanical loading. It is difficult to know how much bone demineralization needs to occur to make a functional difference in the growing skeleton; however, when there are radiologically clear signs of rickets, it is likely that bone strength has been lost.[1,2] The bone changes on x-ray would therefore suggest that the child is at risk of easy fractures. However, bone disease and non-accidental trauma can co-exist and this child may be found to be abused in the future. Preliminary checks should therefore be undertaken to make sure there are no concerns about the parenting before the child is discharged from hospital. Failure to attend health appointments or to give medications can be a sign of poor parenting.

1. Chapman T, Sugar N, Done S, Marasigan J, Wambold N, Feldman K. Fractures in infants and toddlers with rickets. *Pediatr Radiol.* 2010;40(7):1184–1189.
2. Perez-Rossello JM, Feldman HA, Kleinman PK et al. Rachitic changes, demineralization, and fracture risk in healthy infants and toddlers with vitamin D deficiency. *Radiology.* 2012;262(1):234–241.

CASE 115

Mary E. Smyth

This 4-month-old baby was admitted to the intensive care unit after an apparent life-threatening event (ALTE). He was reported to be previously healthy except for one visit to the emergency centre at 2 months of age for vomiting when he was diagnosed with formula intolerance. Chest x-rays performed during the evaluation of his ALTE are shown (Images 115a and 115b). One week previously, he was admitted with burns to the burn unit at a different hospital. The burns that necessitated hospitalization in the burns unit are also shown (Images 115c and 115d). The explanation given for the burns was that the water accidently got too hot as the baby was being rinsed in the bath.

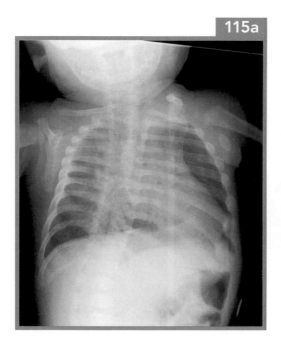

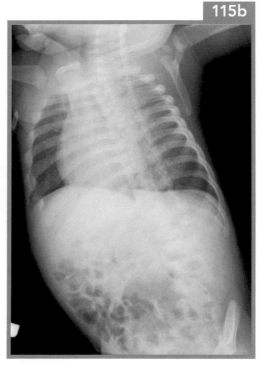

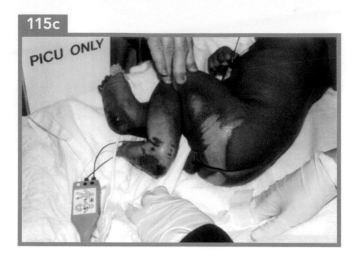

115c

PICU ONLY

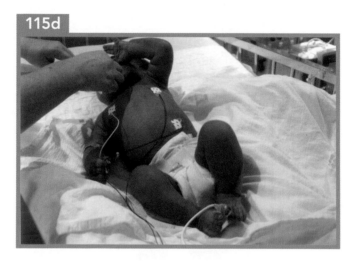

115d

i. What are the findings shown on x-ray and what is the significance?
ii. Is the appearance of the burn consistent with a burn from hot running water?
iii. What other tests could have been done when the child was hospitalized for the burn?

i. The chest x-rays show healing rib fractures, right fourth to eighth and possibly left fourth to sixth ribs. A review of x-rays obtained in the emergency centre at age 2 months showed these fractures in the acute stage. The fractures had not been identified at that time.

ii. These burns are consistent with the baby being placed in hot water, an immersion burn. Note the sparing of the posterior legs. The sheet beneath the baby mirrors where the water was at the time of the burn. Running water would not spare the posterior legs, yet burn the buttocks and feet.[1,2]

iii. This case is an example of previously missed abusive injury, which was diagnosed upon subsequent injury. It is estimated that up to one-third of children with abusive burns will have evidence of unsuspected fractures revealed by a skeletal survey.[3] Skeletal survey is recommended for all children with suspicious burns under 2 years of age, and specially trained radiologists should review the images.

1. Daria S, Sugar NF, Feldman KW, Boos SC, Benton SA, Ornstein A. Into hot water head first: Distribution of intentional and unintentional immersion burns. *Pediatr Emerg Care.* 2004;20(5): 302–310.
2. Greenbaum AR, Donne J, Wilson D, Dunn KW. Intentional burn injury: An evidence-based, clinical and forensic review. *Burns.* 2004;30(7):628–642.
3. Fagen KE, Shalaby-Rana E, Jackson AM. Frequency of skeletal injuries in children with inflicted burns. *Pediatr Radiol.* 2015;45:396–401.

CASE 116

Mary Lu Angelilli with Priyanka Nanjireddy and Autumn Atkinson

Case A: A 6-month-old infant presented to the emergency department with swelling and blistering of the left hand. His parents stated he woke up in this state and they deny any history of trauma, injury or burn. Image 116a depicts his hand.

Case B: An 8-month-old infant presented to the emergency department with blisters and swelling of his hand. His family stated he sustained the burn when the hot water knob was hit accidently while the patient was in the sink for a bath (Image 116b).

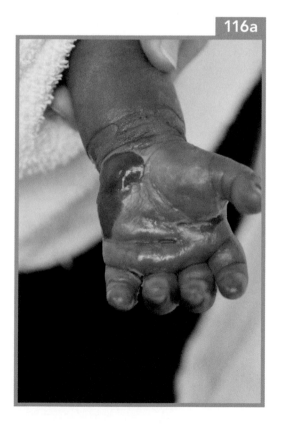

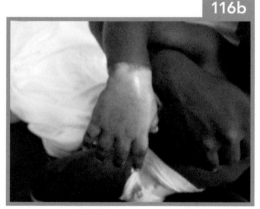

    i. What is your diagnosis in the two children? Accident or abuse?
   ii. How would you further evaluate these two children?

i. Case A is consistent with tourniquet syndrome, which in this case was believed to be accidental. The family reports that the child was put to sleep with mittens on each hand to prevent him from scratching his face. Each mitten had a string that was tied around the wrist. The mitten on the right hand had fallen off by morning. When the mitten on the left hand was removed in the morning, the mother noticed the swelling. Tourniquet syndrome, also known as hair-thread tourniquet syndrome, is an entity characterized by strangulation of appendages (toes, fingers, genitals) by hair or synthetic fibers.[1-3] This occurs when there is wrapping of material around tissue causing occlusion of venous return, oedema, inflammation and in prolonged cases, necrosis. The tourniquet may not be easily evident, especially when involving the penis. This condition is in the differential diagnosis of irritability in an infant. While tourniquet syndrome is usually accidental, intentional placement of the tourniquet is possible.

   Case B is consistent with a non-accidental abusive immersion burn. Similar to case A, there is a clear line of demarcation without signs of splash marks.[4] The burn in case B is of uniform depth. These findings are not consistent with the history that water was running down the child's hand after accidentally placing the hand under the running water.

ii. In both cases, a thorough history and physical examination are necessary. In simple hair-thread tourniquet syndrome where an accidental cause is more likely, further workup is at the discretion of the physician. If the extremity were still occluded, removal of the tourniquet is of utmost importance. If abuse is of concern, as in presentation B, a skeletal survey to evaluate for new or healing fractures, fundus exam to rule out retinal haemorrhages and head imaging to evaluate for head trauma should be completed.

1. Klusmann A, Lenard HG. Tourniquet syndrome – Accident or abuse? *Eur J Pediatr*. 2004;163(8):495–498; discussion 499.
2. Narkewicz RM. Distal digital occlusion. *Pediatrics*. 1978;61(6):922–923.
3. Conners G. Index of suspicion. Case 2. Hair tourniquet syndrome. *Pediatr Rev*. 1997;18(8):283, 285.
4. Peck MD, Priolo-Kapel D. Child abuse by burning: A review of the literature and an algorithm for medical investigations. *J Trauma*. 2002;53(5):1013–1022.

CASE 117

Margaret T. McHugh

This is a 9-year-old girl who was brought from school after school staff made a Child Protective Services report about possible burns on the child's buttocks. The lesions as shown in the image were noted when the child was changing for gym class (Image 117).

i. Are the school staff's concerns reasonable given the image provided?
ii. What additional information would be helpful to determine the aetiology?

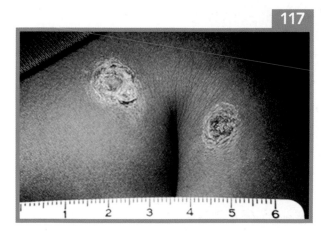

i. The lesions are consistent with healing staph impetigo. While this could be confused with cigarette burns based on their size, the location and appearance suggest an infection or other cause.[1]

ii. The child denied that these are cigarette burns. Her mother gave a history that the child had been wearing a pair of jeans with large metal studs above the back pockets. The child had a history of a metal allergy in the past. The areas under the studs became very irritated and the child scratched them. She developed impetiginous lesions with large bullous lesions that healed in this circular fashion.

1. Bays J. Conditions mistaken for child physical abuse. In Reece RM, Ludwig S, eds. *Child Abuse Medical Diagnosis and Management*. 2nd ed. Philadelphia: Lippincott Williams & Wilkins; 2001:177–206.

CASE 118

Dena Nazer

A 10-year-old girl presented with severe dysuria and mild diabetic ketoacidosis. She was a known diabetic. She also noticed bumps on her privates. She denied sexual abuse and was not sexually active. Her 16-year-old sister had similar symptoms. The child's sister denied sexual abuse but was sexually active. The physical examinations of the child and her sister are shown in Images 118a and 118b, respectively.

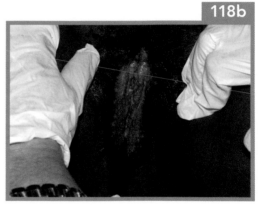

i. What do the images show?
ii. How would you further evaluate these sisters?

i. Both children had vulvar erythema with multiple vesicles. The 10-year-old child had severe pain and discharge and subsequently her infection was complicated by diabetic ketoacidosis. Her 16-year-old sister had more visible vesicles. Both sisters tested positive for herpes simplex type 2 (HSV-2). Children infected with HSV usually present with ulcers and/or vesicles.[1]

ii. Due to both children testing positive for HSV-2, which is a sexually transmitted disease, both were tested for other sexually transmitted infections. They both tested negative for *Chlamydia trachomatis, Neisseria gonorrhoeae, Trichomonas vaginalis*, human immunodeficiency virus (HIV), hepatitis B and syphilis. The type of virus (HSV-1 or HSV-2) does not rule out sexual abuse since 10%–20% of genital herpes in adults can be due to type 1.[1] Herpes simplex in the genital area is suspicious for sexual abuse, and it is recommended that cases of genital herpes be reported to Child Protective Services unless there is a clear history of auto-inoculation.[2] This case was reported despite the absence of any disclosure by the girls when they were seen. The 10-year-old child subsequently disclosed sexual abuse by her uncle.

1. Hammerschlag MR. Sexually transmitted diseases in sexually abused children: Medical and legal implications. *Sex Transm Infect*. 1998;74(3):167–174.
2. Kellogg N. The evaluation of sexual abuse in children. *Pediatrics*. 2005;116(2):506–512.

CASE 119

Vincent J. Palusci

A 6-year-old male was brought for medical attention after sustaining a leg injury while playing soccer. The soccer ball struck him below his knee and he fell, complained of sharp pain and was carried off the field. The leg became swollen and he was unable to bear weight. He was brought to a local emergency room where an x-ray was obtained (Image 119a) followed by a computed tomography (CT) scan (Image 119b).

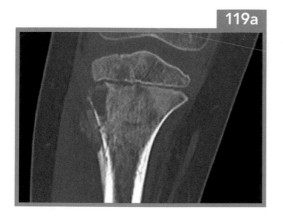

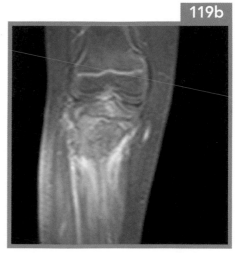

  i. Are these findings consistent with the reported accidental injury?
  ii. What are the possible causes and treatments for these findings?

i. The CT scan shows marked demineralization of the proximal tibia, with fracture and disruption of the cortex which was not consistent with the history of single blunt trauma during the soccer game. There was additional periosteal reaction and disruption of the fat pads indicative of swelling. However, these findings suggested chronic changes and bone destruction in a pathologic manner. While a report for suspected physical abuse could have been made because of these inconsistencies, there needed to be further evaluation for these findings before abusive trauma could be determined to be the cause.[1]

ii. Referrals were made to a paediatric orthopaedist who immobilized the leg but was concerned about underlying cancer or neoplasm. A biopsy was performed which indicated osteogenic sarcoma. A referral to a paediatric oncologist was made and chemotherapy was begun with methotrexate. After 8 weeks, a limb-sparing tumour removal was made and additional chemotherapeutic agents were added based on the current children's cancer study group protocol. Referrals were made for paediatric rehabilitation, orthotics and home schooling.

1. Brill PW, Winchester P, Kleinman PK. Differential diagnosis I: Diseases simulating abuse. In: Kleinman PK, ed. *Diagnostic Imaging of Child Abuse.* 2nd ed. St. Louis, MO: Mosby; 1998:178–196.

CASE 120

Dena Nazer

A 3-month-old baby girl was brought to the emergency department by her mother who was concerned about bruises. The baby was left in the care of her father overnight while her mother went to work. The next morning, her mother noticed bruises on her left side, shoulders and buttocks. The baby had otherwise been acting normally. Her mother commented that the baby had several bruises in the past on different areas of her body including forehead. There was no history of trauma given except for the bruise she once had on her face as a result of hitting herself with her toy. Her mother mentioned that some of these bruises have been present since birth. Images 120a through 120c show her buttocks, left flank and left shoulder.

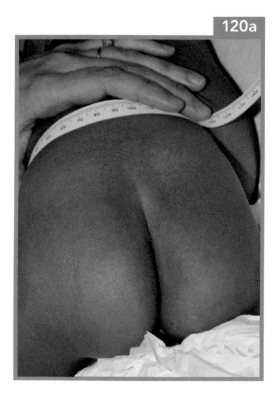

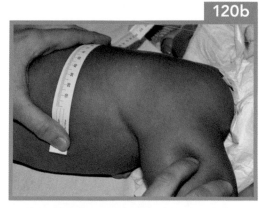

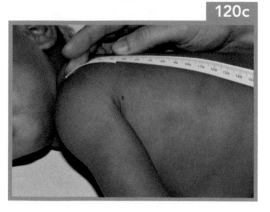

i. What is your diagnosis?
ii. Would you recommend any additional testing?
iii. How do you confirm your diagnosis?

i. The child has a combination of dermal melanosis (commonly called Mongolian spots) and bruises. Mongolian spots are ill-defined grey to greenish-blue patches that are usually present at birth or develop within the first few weeks of life. Mongolian spots are commonly located on the buttocks or the lumbosacral area. They can be mistaken for bruises due to their colour, especially when they are located on atypical sites.[1] When asked specifically about each of the marks, the mother mentioned the ones on the buttocks were present since birth, consistent with Mongolian spots. The one on her left lateral thigh was also from birth. However the ones on her side as well as her left shoulder were new. The mother stated that she noticed they were tender as well.

ii. An evaluation by a child abuse paediatrician may be valuable in identifying cutaneous mimics of physical abuse, relieving abuse concerns and recognizing children who have mimics but also have been abused as in this child.[2] A thorough history was obtained as well as a physical examination with photography. Marks were noted as either present since birth or of recent onset. Due to the presence of bruises, this child had a skeletal survey that showed multiple acute posterior rib fractures, which are highly specific for abuse. She also had a complete blood count, prothrombin time (PT), partial thromboplastin time (PTT) and liver enzymes, all of which were normal. Head imaging was also normal. There was no history to explain the bruises, and a 3-month-old is not mobile and not able to harm herself with a toy and cause bruises. The diagnosis was therefore physical abuse.

iii. The diagnosis was confirmed when the infant presented for her 2-week follow-up for a repeat skeletal survey. Unlike bruises, Mongolian spots are not tender and do not evolve over time. They usually fade in early childhood but can persist indefinitely. She was examined again and the Mongolian spots that the mother thought were bruises since birth on her buttocks and lateral left thigh remained unchanged. The remaining bruises on her left side and shoulder had resolved. Her repeat skeletal survey showed healing of the posterior rib fractures with no additional fractures.

1. AlJasser M, Al-Khenaizan S. Cutaneous mimickers of child abuse: A primer for pediatricians. *Eur J Pediatr.* 2008;167(11):1221–1230.
2. Schwartz KA, Metz J, Feldman K, Sidbury R, Lindberg DM. Cutaneous findings mistaken for physical abuse: Present but not pervasive. *Pediatr Dermatol.* 2014;31(2):146–155.

CASE 121

Tor Shwayder

An 11-year-old boy presented with a history of a red swollen scaly penis, scrotum and anus for more than 1 year's duration. His genitals are shown in Image 121. He denied any further symptoms and kept this 'hidden' from his parents. His family history was positive for psoriasis. Topical steroids and topical immune modulators were tried and had little to no effect. Due to the persistence of symptoms and the further development of oedema, a skin biopsy was performed which showed many granulomas. He was referred to a colleague for confirmation of the suspected diagnosis.

   i. What is the diagnosis?
  ii. How was the referral and second biopsy helpful in making the diagnosis?

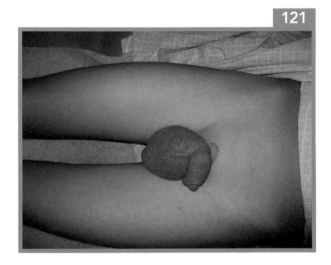

i. This child has granulomatous lymphangitis (a variant of cutaneous Crohn's Disease).

ii. The child was referred to a gastroenterologist. An oesophagogastroduodenoscopy and a colonoscopy with biopsies were performed which revealed no evidence of active ileitis or colitis. However rectal biopsies revealed isolated microgranulomas. Laboratory studies showed high anti-*Saccharomyces cerevisiae* antibodies (ASCA). Tuberculin test and chest x-ray were normal. The gastroenterologist's conclusion was metastatic (cutaneous) Crohn's Disease (CD). The penile and scrotal swelling improved dramatically within a 9-month period of treatment. The child continued to feel well without any gastrointestinal symptoms related to CD.[1] In some cases, a rare condition such as CD may lead to concerns of child abuse. It is essential to recognize these diseases and refer to the appropriate specialist in order not to misdiagnose or delay required treatment.

1. Zabetian S, Lowe L, Shwayder, T. An adolescent boy with persistent penile and scrotal erythema and swelling. *Pediatr Dermatol*. 2012;29(6):765–766.

CASE 122

Vincent J. Palusci

A 9-year-old prepubertal girl was referred for evaluation for genital pain, itching and discharge 2 days before. She was seen in a local emergency department, where sitz baths were prescribed. The mother reported the child had something similar 3 years ago and hydrocortisone cream was prescribed. There were no concerns of sexual abuse reported by the mother or the child and no laboratory tests were done. Today, the physical examination shows pigmentary changes and erythema, as shown in Image 122.

   i. What is the cause for this finding?
  ii. Is this finding indicative of sexual abuse? What are the complications?
 iii. What treatments have been shown to improve a child's symptoms?

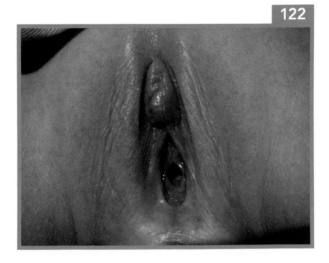

i. The genital examination in the supine, frog-leg position revealed hypopigmented labia majora and minora, extending to the clitoral hood. There was friable tissue with minimal bleeding. The posterior commissure and fossa navicularis were friable with visible excoriations. The annular hymen was unaffected and the urethra also appeared normal. There were no hymenal bumps, clefts, bruises, abrasions, laceration, warts or other signs of acute or chronic hymenal trauma. No intravaginal foreign body was seen. Sexual maturity rating was Tanner stage 1. There was mild clitoral enlargement. There was no perianal involvement.

ii. Childhood lichen sclerosus is an uncommon and often misdiagnosed inflammatory dermatitis with an unpredictable course. It is not associated with child sexual abuse but may cause pain and bleeding which are mistaken for trauma. No laboratory tests are indicated, although a bacterial culture may identify the cause of bacterial superinfection, which was not present in this case. Chronic complications include architectural changes of the vulva and extremely rare malignant transformation. The clinical depiction varies and is thought to be dependent on low oestrogen levels such as in autoimmune disorders, Turner's syndrome and chronic kidney disease. Treatment is symptomatic, with soaking, moisturizers and topical corticosteroids.[1]

iii. With long-term corticosteroid treatment, some patients develop architectural changes of the vulva. Some patients who are 'cured' experience a recurrence of symptoms. Many have no recurrence once puberty ensues. The prognosis cannot be predicted, so long-term follow-up is recommended.

1. Poindexter G, Morrell DS. Anogenital pruritus: Lichen sclerosus in children. *Pediatr Ann.* 2007;36(12):785–791.

CASE 123

Dena Nazer

A 2-month-old baby boy was brought for evaluation because of bleeding that was noticed in his diaper. His mother noticed bleeding from his penis and a few red drops of blood on his diaper/nappy. There was no history of trauma. His mother stated he was in an infant carrier and maybe the straps were too tight around him. He had been active and eating well with no other complaints. His exam is shown in Image 123.

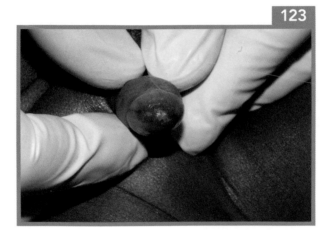

   i. What injury does the image show?
  ii. Would you have any further concerns?

i. The image shows this child's penis. There was an abrasion noted to the tip of his penis measuring 1 cm and involving the urethral meatus. The abrasion was surrounded by ecchymosis. The remainder of his physical examination did not show any further bruises or signs of trauma.

ii. In a 2-month-old child, a genital injury raised the possibility of sexual as well as physical abuse.[1] Anogenital injuries may result from accidents or from abuse. Straddle injury is the most common mechanism of accidental anogenital injury which is a blow to the perineum as a result of falling or striking a surface or an object with the force of one's own body weight. Male straddle injuries most commonly involve the scrotum, followed by penile trauma.[2] An investigation was initiated for this child due to his young age and the absence of history to explain the clinical finding. A complete blood count, liver enzymes and skeletal survey were done and were normal. An investigation by Child Protective Services was also conducted in this case.

1. Hobbs CJ, Osman J. Genital injuries in boys and abuse. *Arch Dis Child.* 2007;92(4):328–331.
2. Dowd MD, Fitzmaurice L, Knapp JF, Mooney D. The interpretation of urogenital findings in children with straddle injuries. *J Pediatr Surg.* 1994;29(1):7–10.

CASE 124

Vincent J. Palusci

A 10-year-old African-American boy had been removed from his home by the police when a neighbour noted that the boy was home alone over the weekend without parental supervision. The mother reportedly left this child with developmental disability and mental retardation at home with food and water and thought he could take care of himself. The police were concerned that he had skin lesions from abuse (Image 124a).

    i. What are these lesions?
   ii. Are these lesions from abuse?
  iii. What treatment does the boy need for these lesions?
  iv. How would neglect contribute to these lesions?

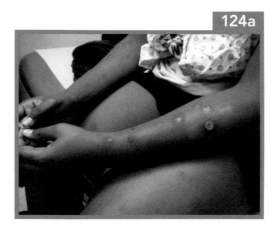

124a

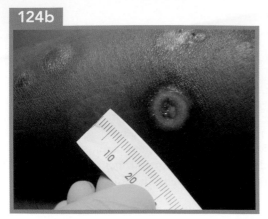

124b

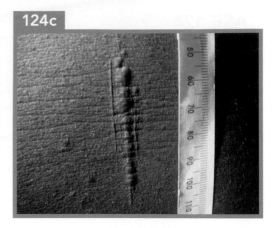

124c

i. The round lesions over the arms and legs with surrounding hyperpigmentation, eschar or central granulation tissue appear to be untreated furuncles or boils (closed), some of which have progressed to carbuncles (open). Boils are localized suppurative staphylococcal skin infections originating in a gland or hair follicle and characterized by pain, redness and swelling. Necrosis deep in the centre of the inflamed area forms a core of dead tissue that is spontaneously extruded, eventually resorbed or surgically removed. These may progress to carbuncles, which are deep-seated pyogenic infections, often preceded or accompanied by fever, malaise and prostration. In milder form, these can appear to be large, deep skin abscesses formed by a group or cluster of boils. There can be a large site of staphylococcal infection containing purulent matter in deep, interconnecting subcutaneous pockets. Pus eventually discharges to the skin surface through openings. Common sites for carbuncles are the back of the neck and the buttocks.[1]

ii. While these infections are not caused by abuse, it is easy to confuse them with a cigarette burn. A closer view of a lesion (Image 124b) reveals it is 9–10 mm diameter across, close to the size of a cigarette. The 'punched out' middle may suggest a deep burn caused by pressing the cigarette directly into the skin near a 90° angle. However, the number and distribution of the lesions and how they are healing suggests these are not thermal burns. Unfortunately, the child's delayed development precluded obtaining meaningful information by interview.

iii. Treatment may include antibiotics, local moist heat and when there is definite fluctuation and the hard white core is evident, incision and drainage. It is important to avoid irritating or squeezing the lesion to prevent spread of the infection. Many of the lesions would have to be covered. Given the number, oral as well as topical antibiotics will be needed and consideration should be given to the incidence of methicillin resistance in the community.

iv. There are additional hypertrophic linear scars (Image 124c) which could suggest inflicted lesions. However, the total pattern of festering carbuncles with hypertrophic scarring is most likely due to poor nutrition and inadequate medical care, both caused by neglect. In addition, the act of leaving this child alone in a house over the weekend constitutes neglect.

1. Pubmed Health. Carbuncle. 2013-05-15. http://www.ncbi.nlm.nih.gov/pubmedhealth/PMH 0001828/.

CASE 125

Margaret T. McHugh

A 12-year-old girl presented to the emergency department with her aunt, who was her guardian, for evaluation of vomiting. On routine lab work, she was found to have a positive pregnancy test. The young person was reported to be 'reluctant' to talk with staff. Examination revealed a finding seen in Image 125a. Image 125b is another example of this clinical finding in a pregnant adolescent.

    i. What is the finding demonstrated?
   ii. What procedures can be done to better delineate the genital findings?

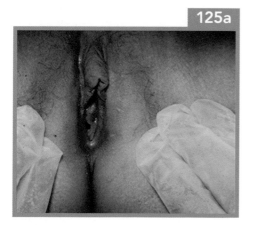
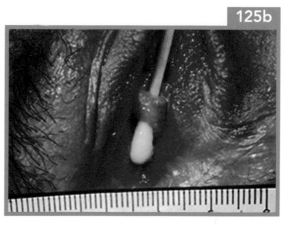

i. The picture demonstrates a persistent, septate hymenal remnant. During the forensic interview, it was learned that the 12-year-old attended special education classes. She reported that her uncle would come into her bedroom at night, lie down on top of her, 'jump up and down' on her and 'white stuff' would come out of her. A Child Protective Services investigation and a full evaluation for sexually transmitted diseases and collection of forensic specimens were indicated.[1] Hymenal septa generally do not require surgical intervention but may be associated with difficulties during intercourse.

ii. In menstrual females with effects of oestrogen, the hymenal tissues are less sensitive and a Q-tip or other small swab can be used to demonstrate the septum. It is important to differentiate this finding from a vaginal duplication, which will require additional intervention.

1. Kellogg ND, Menard SW, Santos A. Genital anatomy in pregnant adolescents: 'Normal' does not mean 'nothing happened'. *Pediatrics.* 2004;113(1 Pt 1):e67–e69.

CASE 126

Mary E. Smyth

These pictures show burns on both feet of two different children. They have a similar appearance. The first two images (Images 126a and 126b) show burns on the feet of a 4-year-old boy who was left in the care of his mother's boyfriend overnight while his mother was at work. The child had language and developmental delays and did not speak. Upon returning home in the morning, his mother found his feet wrapped in bandages. The boyfriend stated that the child had stepped into a pan of hot grease the night before. The second two images (Images 126c and 126d) show burns on the feet of a 9-month-old girl. Her mother stated that she was rinsing the baby in the utility tub in the laundry room after the baby had a dirty diaper. The baby screamed and mother noted burns immediately as she placed the baby feet-first in the tub.

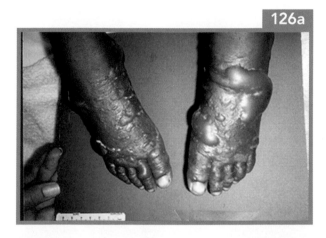

126a

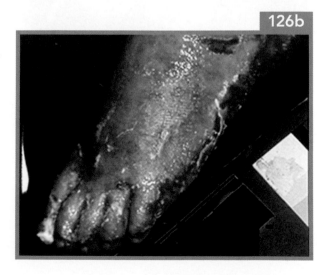

126b

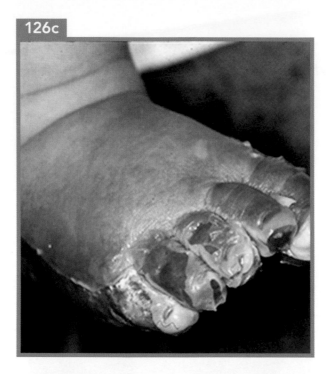

126c

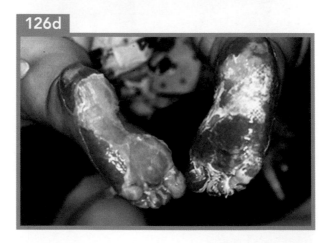

126d

i. Which of these cases should be reported to Child Protective Services (CPS)?
ii. What features help to make the diagnosis of non–accidental immersion burns?

i. Both cases should be reported to Child Protective Services (CPS). CPS can make a referral to local law enforcement who can investigate the scene of the injury and in the case of burns, measure the water temperature at the scene.

ii. The first case was felt to be clearly non-accidental. The history of the child stepping into hot grease seemed highly implausible.[1,2] Humans step one foot at a time. If the child were stepping into something hot he would withdraw his foot and not step in with the other foot. In addition, it is unclear where the pan of hot grease that the child could step into was located.[3,4] The second case was also reported to CPS. After thorough questioning and scene investigation, the mother's account of the incident was corroborated. In the emergency room she stated that she was rinsing the baby in the laundry tub because there were multiple workers in her home doing reclamation work and she did not want to leave them to go upstairs. She was distracted and did not realize how hot the water was. Investigators confirmed the presence of the workers, reviewed the recording of the call for emergency medical services and measured the water temperature to be 160°F (71°C).

1. Daria S, Sugar NF, Feldman KW, Boos SC, Benton SA, Ornstein A. Into hot water head first: Distribution of intentional and unintentional immersion burns. *Pediatr Emerg Care.* 2004;20(5): 302–310.
2. Feldman KW, Schaller RT, Feldman JA, McMillon M. Tap water scald burns in children. *Pediatrics.* 1978;62(1):1–7.
3. Greenbaum AR, Donne J, Wilson D, Dunn KW. Intentional burn injury: An evidence-based, clinical and forensic review. *Burns.* 2004;30(7):628–642.
4. Murphy JT, Purdue GF, Hunt JL. Pediatric grease burn injury. *Arch Surg.* 1995;130(5):478–482.

CASE 127

Carl J. Schmidt

A 26-month-old girl and a 15-month-old boy were found submerged, one on top of the other, in a bathtub. Their father said he fell asleep for about 4 hours and later found the children in the bathtub. The tub had water and also contained a large amount of toilet paper and assorted debris. The children wore diapers/nappies and light clothing. The water temperature was 130°F (54.4°C) as measured at the tap. The children are shown in Images 127a and 127b.

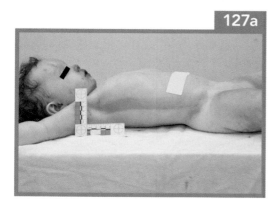
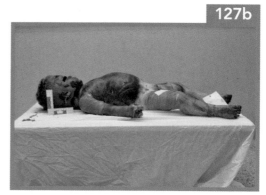

i. Which child was completely submerged? Why?
ii. Is the history consistent with the burn patterns seen in the photos?
iii. Would it be possible to determine if they drowned and were scalded while still alive or did the skin changes occur after death?

i. The boy (Image 127b) was completely submerged. Erythema and skin slippage shown is diffuse except for an area on the back where he was in contact with the bathtub. Skin slippage indicates more advanced decomposition. The reddened skin felt stiffer and blood was clotted within superficial skin vessels due to the increased water temperature. The girl (Image 127a) has a distinct immersion line on the right chest and abdomen indicating she was face down in the water. There is clear groin sparing because she wore a diaper/nappy while immersed in the water.

ii. The burn pattern is not consistent with the history given by the father. These children's motor and cognitive development was not yet at the point where they could turn on the hot tap water, fill the bathtub and then immerse themselves in the water. Based on the temperature measured at the tap, the water was hot enough to elicit pain in a conscious child. The boy is in a more advanced state of decomposition than was the girl. He therefore died first and was submerged for a longer time.

iii. While we cannot be absolutely certain about what happened, we can infer several facts as seen in the previous questions.[1] Microscopically, cellulose material identical to the toilet paper fibers was found in the deep alveoli of the lungs of both children. This happened due to active inhaling of water, which already contained the toilet paper. The perpetrator spread large amounts of toilet paper in the bathroom after they died in an attempt to simulate that the toddlers were playing while he was asleep. The cause of death in these cases was drowning and certified as homicide. The scalding was determined to be post-mortem.

1. Spitz WU, Spitz DJ, Fisher RS. *Spitz and Fisher's Medicolegal Investigation of Death: Guidelines for the Application of Pathology to Crime Investigation.* 4th ed. Springfield, IL: Charles C. Thomas; 2006.

CASE 128

Patricia O. Brennan

An 8-year-old girl presented to the emergency department with abdominal pain and dyschezia. She would not allow examination of the anogenital region and child abuse was suspected and a referral was made to the child care agencies. Examination under anaesthetics revealed severely inflamed tissues as illustrated (Image 128).

    i. What is the diagnosis?
   ii. What features of this condition can mimic child sexual abuse?

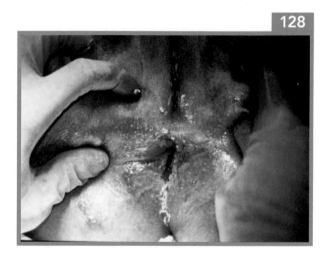

i. This child has Crohn's Disease with perianal complications of perianal abscess and these occur in 25%–50% cases.

ii. Sexual abuse can be suspected in Crohn's Disease, particularly if perianal involvement occurs with recurrent bleeding from multiple perianal fissures at various sites of the anal margin and oedema and soreness of the perianal tissues, extending to the vulva. These signs can be the presenting features when the gastrointestinal symptoms can be very mild or even absent. Other dermatological conditions such as lichen sclerosus atrophicus, Behçet syndrome, bullous diseases, contact dermatitis and neoplastic lesions can also be mis-diagnosed as child sexual abuse.[1,2]

1. Palder SB, Shandling B, Bilik R, Griffiths AM, Sherman P. Perianal complications of pediatric Crohn's disease. *J Pediatr Surg.* 1991;26(5):513–515.
2. Porzionato A, Alaggio R, Aprile A. Perianal and vulvar Crohn's disease presenting as suspected abuse. *Forensic Sci Int.* 2005;155(1):24–27.

CASE 129

Mary E. Smyth

This toddler presented to the emergency room after sustaining a burn to his mouth and face (Image 129). He was drooling profusely but was otherwise stable. His mother and grandmother had been stripping wax off a floor and while they were not watching, he took the rag out of the bucket and began to suck on it.

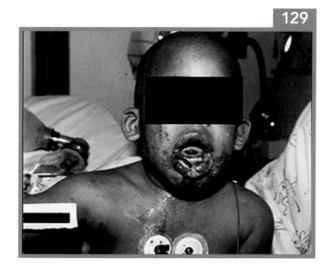

i. What features of this child's injury confirm the aetiology as a caustic burn?
ii. Is there a role for Child Protective Services in this type of case?

i. The child's injury is clearly confined to the areas where the caustic floor cleaner came into contact with his mouth and face causing swelling and tissue damage. He was drooling because the caustic that was swallowed had produced injury to his oral cavity, throat and oesophagus.[1]

ii. When a child sustains a significant injury such as this and there may be an element of 'supervisional neglect', a report to Child Protective Services (CPS) is warranted. The CPS worker visited the home and was able to see where the injury occurred. His mother produced the bottle of wax stripper, clearly labelled for industrial use, which had been improperly diluted. The caseworker identified several other unsafe conditions in the home, which led to a finding of neglect. Reporting these types of cases is important to address any concerns of neglect and ensure future safety of this child and his siblings.

1. Hettiaratchy S, Dziewulski P. ABC of burns: Pathophysiology and types of burns. *BMJ*. 2004;328(7453):1427–1429.

CASE 130

Margaret T. McHugh, with Anastasia Feifer and Lori A. Legano

A 6-year-old female presented with vaginal pain and itching that she had for several weeks. Her mother noted a few spots of dried blood in her underwear 1 day prior, prompting her visit to the paediatrician. She had also had constipation intermittently for the past several weeks and one episode of encopresis at daycare. Her development had been normal for her age, and she was toilet trained at age 3 and a half years. She lived with both of her parents and her 10-year-old brother. She had not missed any school, but appeared clearly uncomfortable, and teachers reported that she often asked to go to the toilet. When her mother asked if anyone 'touched' her, she shook her head 'no'. The results of her urinalysis were normal. Her physical examination is shown in Images 130a and 130b.

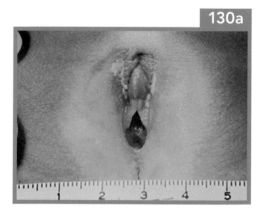
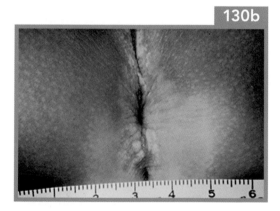

   i. What does the image show?
   ii. What is the treatment for this condition?
   iii. Is a report to the authorities for suspected child abuse appropriate?

i. The patient had lichen sclerosus, an inflammatory dermatitis most commonly affecting pre-menarchal girls and post-menarchal women. Lichen sclerosus affects the vulva and can extend perianally as seen in this patient, resulting in the classic 'figure eight' pattern of hypopigmentation and inflammation. The involved skin becomes atrophic and parchment like. The skin changes can lead to pruritus, fissures and bleeding. Patients can present with intense vaginal soreness and irritation, dysuria and bowel symptoms such as painful defecation, constipation or encopresis.[1] Some patients can also be asymptomatic in spite of skin changes. Physical findings of bleeding, fissures and irritation can often be mistaken for child sexual abuse.[2]

ii. Lichen sclerosus is treated with topical corticosteroids.[1]

iii. Lichen sclerosus can be prone to the Koebner phenomenon (skin lesions following lines of trauma or external irritation) and can be exacerbated by abuse such as fondling or penetration, but the cause of this skin condition is low oestrogen in conjunction with an inflammatory response that is possibly autoimmune in nature.[2] The classic skin changes in a figure-eight pattern in this child should prompt the diagnosis, and the mother can be reassured and no report needs to be made.

1. Emans SJH, Laufer MR, Goldstein DP. *Pediatric and Adolescent Gynecology.* 5th ed. Philadelphia, PA: Lippincott Williams & Wilkins; 2005.
2. Lagerstedt M, Karvinen K, Joki-Erkkila M, Huotari-Orava R, Snellman E, Laasanen SL. Childhood lichen sclerosus—A challenge for clinicians. *Pediatr Dermatol.* 2013;30(4):444–450.

CASE 131

Margaret T. McHugh

A 3-year-old boy was brought to the emergency department (ED) with a scrotal laceration. The mother stated that she was changing the boy in the kitchen after he had soiled his clothes while playing. She left the room to get a new outfit. She heard a thud and the child screaming. She found him on the floor with a bloody wound to 'his privates'. She described the child as very active and believed that he fell from the kitchen counter while climbing up to retrieve a toy. She stated that he hit a cabinet drawer handle. The ED staff were concerned that the laceration was not consistent with the history. The laceration was length-wise on the scrotum and handles on drawers are usually horizontal and concave. A report was made to Child Protective Services to investigate further (Images 131a and 131b).

  i. Were the ED staff's concerns reasonable given the images provided?
 ii. How can a scene evaluation provide the needed information? What would be helpful?

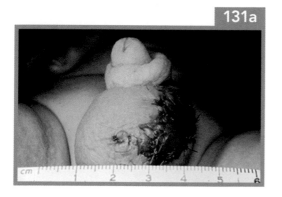
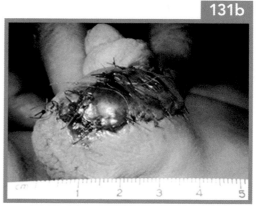

i. Scrotal injuries in young children are unusual and warrant further investigation.
ii. On inspection of the kitchen, it was found that the drawer handles were designed as an H configuration with a horizontal element to pull the drawer open with a decorative, spiral-shaped metal ornament on either side of the bar in a vertical direction. Such a decorative pull could account for the scrotal laceration since the child was totally undressed at the time of the injury.[1,2]

1. Adams JA. Medical evaluation of suspected child sexual abuse: 2011 update. *J Child Sex Abuse.* 2011;20(5):588–605.
2. Widni EE, Hollwarth ME, Saxena AK. Analysis of nonsexual injuries of the male genitals in children and adolescents. *Acta Paediatrica.* 2011;100(4):590–593.

CASE 132

Vincent J. Palusci

A 5-day-old girl was brought to the emergency department after she was noted to have seizures. Her mother noticed that her breastfeeding had decreased and first brought her to the primary care physician where the infant was noted to have repetitive movements of her left arm. There was no history of trauma. She was born at 4 kg after a term pregnancy with uneventful prenatal care. Ultrasound at 30 weeks' gestation was normal. Delivery was complicated by a prolonged second stage of labour and her Apgar scores were 5, 7 and 9 at 10 min. She required several minutes of positive pressure ventilation after birth but was later transferred to the well-baby nursery in good condition. She was discharged on day three of life. In the emergency department, she began to have bilateral tonic–clonic seizures and she was sent for CT scan of her head. Her breathing became depressed. A lumbar puncture was performed, antibiotics and anticonvulsants were given, and she was intubated and transferred to the paediatric intensive care unit for further management. No bruises, bleeding or oral injuries were noted. Fontanelles were normal and there was no swelling palpable on her scalp. Head imaging noted intracranial blood (Image 132a) and posterior skull fracture (Images 132b and 132c).

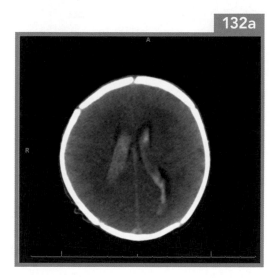

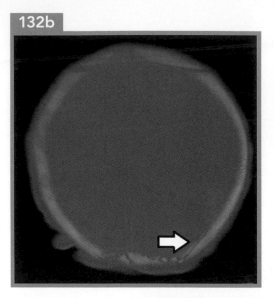

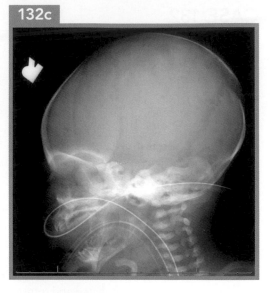

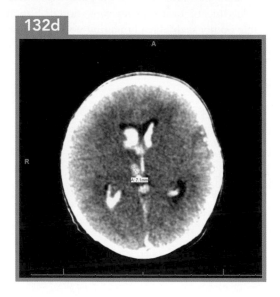

i. What does Image 132a show?
ii. What does Image 132b show?
iii. What additional testing and evaluations are helpful to evaluate potential abusive head trauma?
iv. What further imaging is needed to determine the aetiology for this patient's presentation?

i. A large amount of intracranial blood is visualized on this head CT. The blood is located primarily in both lateral ventricles and on additional images was also seen in the third and fourth ventricles and on the left in the subdural space on the left.

ii. A small, non-displaced lucency is noted (arrow) in the left posterior skull on this CT bone window. There is a small degree of overlying soft tissue swelling of the scalp.

iii. Given the possibility of inflicted trauma in this presentation, full imaging of the axial skeleton using a skeletal survey was indicated.[1] The retinae should be examined for haemorrhage. Coagulation tests such as a complete blood count, prothrombin time and partial thromboplastin times were also indicated to determine if the child had an underlying coagulation disorder contributing to the bleeding. The American Academy of Pediatrics has recommended additional testing of factor VIII and factor IX levels in addition to D-dimer and fibrinogen levels to exclude additional medical causes for bleeding.[2] A clinical decision rule has concluded that a thorough evaluation should be performed when children with potential head trauma present with (1) unexplained respiratory depression, (2) bruising to the head or neck or torso, (3) subdural and/or interhemispheric intracranial bleeding, or (4) any skull fractures other than a unilateral, single, non-diastatic, linear parietal fracture.[3]

iv. Magnetic resonance imaging (MRI) of the head offers several sequences to further evaluate the blood as well as the brain and other intracranial structures with greater precision and without radiation. On the second day in the hospital, the head MRI (Image 132d) showed blood throughout the ventricular system with fluid levels layering in the bilateral occipital horns, compatible with acute intraventricular haemorrhage. Skeletal survey confirmed a small, nondisplaced parietal fracture. Susceptibility artefact in the region of the right thalamus is also compatible with haemorrhage. There are several punctate and linear areas of susceptibility artefact with associated T2 hyperintense signal in the right frontal and parietal corona radiata/centrum semiovale which may represent additional small foci of haemorrhage. In addition, there is a suggestion of diffusion restriction seen in the region of the right thalamus, right centrum semiovale and corona radiata suggestive of ischaemia. There is moderate dilatation of the ventricular system compatible with hydrocephalus. There is no abnormal parenchymal or leptomeningeal enhancement and no midline shift. The basal cisterns are patent. Additional MRI vascular sequences were obtained and showed normal internal carotid artery and branches at the level of the circle of Willis bilaterally with no evidence of vascular stenosis, occlusion, aneurysm or malformation. Evaluation of the posterior circulation demonstrated normal vertebrobasilar system with no evidence of filling defect within the dominant venous sinuses including the superior sagittal sinus, the transverse and sigmoid sinuses.

1. Christian CW, Block R. Abusive head trauma in infants and children. *Pediatrics*. 2009;123(5):1409–1411.
2. Anderst JD, Carpenter SL, Abshire TC. Evaluation for bleeding disorders in suspected child abuse. *Pediatrics*. 2013;131(4):e1314–e1322.
3. Hymel KP, Armijo-Garcia V, Foster R et al. Validation of a clinical prediction rule for pediatric abusive head trauma. *Pediatrics*. 2014;134(6):e1537–e1544.

CASE 133

Vincent J. Palusci

A developmentally delayed 2-year-old girl had a second surgical repair for congenital heart disease with pulmonary hypertension and was requiring multiple medications. In the postoperative care suite, you were asked to examine her anus because there were 'concerns of sexual abuse'. The nurse caring for her had noticed perianal bruising (Image 133). She also had some genital redness which was noticed when her urinary catheter was placed for the operation.

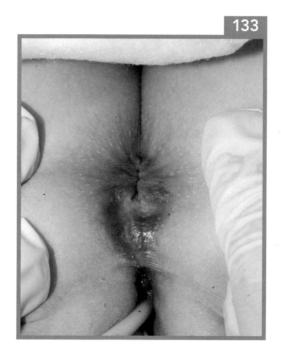

i. What does the image show?
ii. What are the possible causes for this finding?

i. This child had significant perianal venous distention which extends anteriorly to the perineum. The incompletely seen posterior commissure of the labia appears slightly erythematous, but no lacerations or other signs of trauma are depicted. Some swelling of the anal folds or rugae is suggested. The child is in the prone position and it is unclear whether her knees are drawn up beneath her.

ii. Given that this finding was not noted during prior procedures and there was no history of sexual abuse provided, these findings were most likely related to the child's underlying congenital heart disease and effects from anaesthesia. Positive perianal findings are uncommon after child sexual abuse,[1] and chronic pulmonary hypertension with associated increases in pressures in the inferior vena cava may have, over time, chronically enlarged the perianal venous vascular bed. In addition, anaesthetic agents may result in decreased peripheral venous tone. If used, a prone, knee–chest position with resulting increased abdominal pressure (Valsalva) can also increase venous prominence and distention. The genital findings are nonspecific for sexual abuse and may be related to poor hygiene or, in this case, medical procedures.

1. Myhre AK, Adams JA, Kaufhold M, Davis JL, Suresh P, Kuelbs CL. Anal findings in children with and without probable anal penetration: A retrospective study of 1115 children referred for suspected sexual abuse. *Child Abuse Negl.* 2013;37(7):465–474.

CASE 134

Vincent J. Palusci

A 14-year-old pubertal girl complained of burning with urination. In her medical chart, you noticed that she had her first menstrual period last year and that your examination was 'normal genitalia' at that time. You inquired as to how her periods were and she tells you that she did get 'belly aches' every month but that she leaked blood for a week. She had also noticed it took her longer to urinate and she had begun having 'accidents' with leaking urine during the day. You considered urinary tract infection, but then spoke with her mother privately about the need for an examination. Her mother told you she thought the girl was having sex with her boyfriend and was worried about her having a sexually transmitted infection. During genital inspection, you noted she has some genital redness (Image 134a).

i. What other exam manoeuvres are needed?
ii. What are the possible causes for this finding?

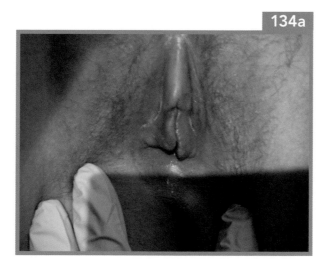

134a

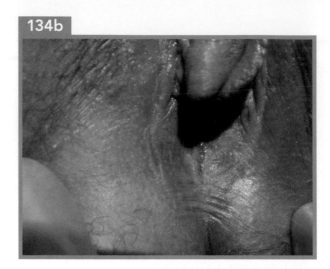

134b

i. The girl demonstrated pubic hair and oestrogenization of her labia and clitoral hood (Image 134a). No discharge was appreciated. A visible urethra or hymenal opening was not seen with simple labial separation and there was increased erythema extending to the perineum. Closer visual inspection with positioning using stirrups could have better depicted her external genital findings. When this was done with continued labial separation, a fine, superficial labial fusion line was noted centrally, extending posteriorly to the labial insertions (Image 134b).

ii. Labial adhesions, also known as labial agglutination or labial fusion, constitute an acquired condition in which the labia are adherent in the midline. The estimated incidence of labial adhesions in prepubertal girls was typically 0.6%–3%, but more recent studies have revealed that it may be present in as many as 38.9% of healthy girls.[1] It has been suggested by some authors that labial adhesions should arouse suspicion of sexual abuse, but given how frequently labial adhesions occur, this is an unlikely major cause. They are less common after puberty, suggesting the possibility of congenital absence of the vagina, ambiguous genitalia or imperforate hymen unless prior exams have demonstrated normal genitalia.

1. Van Eyk N, Allen L, Giesbrecht E et al. Pediatric vulvovaginal disorders: A diagnostic approach and review of the literature. *J Obstet Gynaecol Can.* 2009;31(9):850–862.

CASE 135

Carl J. Schmidt

This 2-month-old female infant was found unresponsive, face down, with her face embedded in soft bedding. The infant's mother attempted resuscitation briefly before calling for help. Emergency medical personnel responded but left the infant at the scene as she was obviously not able to be resuscitated. The mother was single and lived with her parents. This infant was the mother's first child and was the product of a normal pregnancy with adequate prenatal care. The mother's sister also had children but lived in another state. She had an infant that died suddenly and was diagnosed as having sudden infant death syndrome (SIDS). The mother wondered if her infant suffered the same fate. A picture was taken at the scene (Image 135a). Image 135b was taken the next morning just before the autopsy.

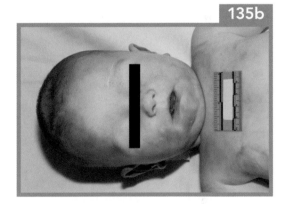

   i. What else would you ask the caretaker?
  ii. Is there a significant difference between the scene and autopsy pictures? If so, why is this important?
 iii. How can physicians prevent these deaths?

i. The history in cases of unexpected infant death is the most informative part of the assessment and therein often lies the clue to the cause of death. All pertinent facts regarding the prenatal and obstetrical history need to be gathered. A history of sudden infant death in the family is important because it means either that there is a genetic trait that causes sudden death in the family (rare) or there are cultural practices that predispose to sudden infant death (much more common). As much detail as possible should be sought regarding sleep practices for the infant because this is a major source of risk for sudden infant death.[1] In this case, the mother mentioned that she often placed her child next to her at night with the soft bedding seen in Image 135a. The mother also often had one or two glasses of beer before going to sleep, although she denied using other drugs. The infant was a 'good baby' who slept at least 6 h every night. She had been given safe sleep instructions before discharge from the hospital, which consisted of a nurse who provided her with some brochures and she signed a form that she had received them. Her own mother told her she had slept with all her newborn children and they were all 'fine' so it would be 'ok' if she did, too. The American Academy of Pediatrics has developed a series of recommendations regarding a safe sleep environment which include using firm sleep surfaces and room sharing without bed sharing.[2] If these had been followed and more than a cursory explanation had been given to the mother of what they mean, it is likely that this infant would have survived infancy. The dead infant that fits the criteria for the literal definition of SIDS is now extremely rare, given that this determination should only be made after a full autopsy, scene investigation and review of medical history are completed.

ii. The most significant difference between the pictures of the death scene and those taken the next day is in the prominence of the lividity pattern. The scene picture clearly shows blanching of the face with a lividity outline that shows that the infant's head was turned so that the left cheek was pressed against the mattress cover and the right cheek had nothing pressing against it. This proves the infant was supine when found dead. The picture taken the next day does not show a pattern that is as prominent because the lividity has shifted; the infant was placed prone in the body bag for overnight storage, which allowed the blood to shift again by gravity. Hence, it is very important that a picture be taken as soon as possible after the infant is found because it is definitive documentation of the position the infant was found which can help corroborate (or not) the narrative describing how the infant was found.

iii. In addition to providing anticipatory guidance for parents during the prenatal, perinatal and postnatal periods on the dangers of unsafe sleep environments, physicians can assist their communities in the investigation and prevention of sudden infant death by participating in child death review. The American Academy of Pediatrics had identified potential roles for paediatricians and other physicians which include advocating for proper death certification for children, recognizing that such certification is only possible for sudden, unexpected deaths after comprehensive death investigation that involves an immediate evaluation at the scene of the death and includes an autopsy, supporting state legislation that requires autopsies in deaths of children younger than 6 years, advocating for state legislation to establish comprehensive and fully funded child death investigation and review systems at the local and state levels, serving as expert members in reviewing case files of the agency investigating the deaths of children, and serving as consultants to the child fatality teams.[3] Primary care physicians, emergency medicine physicians and child abuse specialists are ideally suited for participation on such review teams and other physicians, such as obstetricians, would be valuable partners in reviewing deaths from specific causes, such as prematurity.

1. Pasquale-Styles M, Tackitt PL, Schmidt CJ. Infant death scene investigation and the assessment of potential risk factors for asphyxia: A review of 209 sudden unexpected infant deaths. *J Forensic Sci.* 2007;52(4):924–929.
2. American Academy of Pediatrics. SIDS and other sleep-related infant deaths: Expansion of recommendations for a safe infant sleeping environment. *Pediatrics.* 2011;128:1030–1039.
3. Christian CW, Sege RD, and the American Academy of Pediatrics Committees on Child Abuse and Neglect, Injury, Violence, and Poison Prevention, and the Council on Community Pediatrics. Child death review. *Pediatrics.* 2010;126:592–596.

INDEX

AAP, *see* American Academy of Pediatrics
Abdomen, 49–50; *see also* Blunt trauma;
      Dermatologic injury
    trauma in, 163–164
Abusive burns, 261–264; *see also* Burns
Accident, automobile, 207–208
Activated partial thromboplastin time
      (aPTT), 70; *see also* Partial
      thromboplastin time
Alanine aminotransferase (ALT), 164
Alkaline phosphatase (ALP), 188
ALP, *see* Alkaline phosphatase
ALT, *see* Alanine aminotransferase
ALTE, *see* Apparent life-threatening event
American Academy of Pediatrics
      (AAP), 2
Anal injury
    anogenital injuries, 280
    Crohn's disease, 291–292
    dilation, 165–166
    fissure, 47–48
    granulomatous lymphangitis, 275–276
    laceration, 175–176, 251–252
    rectal prolapse, 227–228
    trauma, 135–136
    venous distension, 303–304
Animal bites, 201; *see also* Bites
Anogenital injuries, 280
Anti-*Saccharomyces cerevisiae* antibodies
      (ASCA), 276
Apparent life-threatening event
      (ALTE), 261
aPTT, *see* Activated partial thromboplastin
      time, Partial thromboplastin time
ASCA, *see* Anti-*Saccharomyces cerevisiae*
      antibodies
Aspartate transaminase (AST), 164
AST, *see* Aspartate transaminase
Asymmetric skin lesion, 233–234; *see also*
      Burns
Automobile accidents, 207–208; *see also* Blunt
      trauma

Battered child syndrome, 215–218; *see also*
      Craniofacial injury
Behçet's disease, 214
Bilateral burns, 191–192; *see also* Burns
Bites
    adult, 189–190, 243–244
    dog, 199–201

    foot, 61–62, 177–178
    paediatric, 117–118
    sexual assault, 177–178
    spider, 181–182
Black eyes, 79–80; *see also* Ocular injury
Blunt trauma; *see also* Craniofacial injury;
      Trauma
    abdomen, 163–164
    automobile accidents, 207–208
    back, 73–74, 169–170
    head, 215–218
Bones, *see* Fractures, Osteopenia
Bruises, *see* Dermatologic injury
Buried penis, 103–104; *see also* Genitourinary
      injury
Burns; *see also* Dermatologic injury
    abusive burns, 261–264
    bilateral, 191–192
    caustic, 257–258, 293–294
    chemical, 133–134
    cigarette, 121–122, 137–138
    contact burns, 122
    drip, 233–234
    fork, 209–210
    with fractures, 261–264
    garlic, 133–134
    genitals, 7–8
    hand, 81–82
    hyperpigmented marks due to, 7–8
    immersion, 191–192, 265–266,
      285–288
    infants and children, 82
    iron, 125–126, 151–152
    linear, 209–210
    non-accidental, 82
    scald, 219–220
    scalp, 9–10
    splash, 197–198
    stocking, 219–220
    types of, 82
    whisker, 127–130

Carbuncles, 281–282; *see also* Infections
Caries, 221–222; *see also* Oral injury
Caustic burns, 257–258, 293–294; *see also*
      Burns
CBC, *see* Complete blood count
CD, *see* Crohn's disease
Cephalohaematoma, 211–212; *see also*
      Craniofacial injury

Chemical abuse, *see* Ingestions
Chemical burn, 133–134; *see also* Burns
Childhood anaemia, 28
Child Protective Services (CPS), 288
Cigarette burns, 121–122, 137–138; *see also*
    Burns
Circular red lesions, 121–122; *see also* Skin
    conditions
Classic metaphyseal lesion (CML), 52
Clitoral hood enlargement, 113–114; *see also*
    Genitourinary injury
CML, *see* Classic metaphyseal lesion
Coagulation tests, 96; *see also* aPTT,
    coagulopathy, PTT
Coagulopathy, 70
Complementary and alternative medicine
    cupping, 131–132
    garlic, 133–134
    maqua, 31–32
    moxibustion, 155–158
Complete blood count (CBC), 70
Computed tomography (CT), 91, 204
Condyloma acuminatum, 150; *see also*
    Infections
Congenital dermal melanocytosis, *see*
    Mongolian spot
Contact burns, 122; *see also* Burns
Cord marks, 40; *see also* Dermatologic injury
CPS, *see* Child Protective Services
Craniofacial injury; *see also* Dermatologic
    injury, Injury, Ocular injury, Oral
    injury
    blunt trauma, 215–218
    cephalohaematoma, 211–212
    drowning, 289–290
    facial bruises, 239–240
    multiple bruises, 167–168
    perinatal, 299–302
    skull fracture, 75–76, 91–92, 107–110
    strangulation, 15–16
    subdural, 203–204
    subgaleal, 161–162
    sudden infant death, 307–308
Crohn's disease (CD), 276, 291–292; *see also*
    Granulomatous lymphangitis
Crush injuries, 225–226; *see also* Wringer
    injuries
CT, *see* Computed tomography
Cupping therapy, 131–132; *see also*
    Complementary and alternative
    medicine
Cutting, 183–185; *see also* Self-mutilating
    behaviours, Dermatologic injury

Darier sign, 46; *see also* Skin conditions
Dental neglect, 221–222; *see also* Oral injury
Dermal melanosis, *see* Mongolian spot
Dermatitis artefacta, 171–172; *see also*
    Dermatologic injury
Dermatologic injury; *see also* Skin conditions
    abdomen, 49–50
    caused by bamboo, 1–2
    cord marks, 40
    cutting, 183–185
    dermatitis artefacta, 171–172
    iatrogenic, 111–112
    leg bruises, 249–250
    loop marks, 65–68, 105–106
    sentinel bruise, 35–36
    sibling, 141–142
    subcutaneous haemorrhage, 16
    suction mark, 83–84
    trichotillomania, 17–18
Diastatic fracture, 110; *see also* Fractures
Drowning, 289–290; *see also* Craniofacial injury

ED, *see* Emergency department
Emergency department (ED), 187, 297
Erythema nodosum, 71–72; *see also* Skin
    conditions

Facial bruise, 35–36, 239–240; *see also*
    Craniofacial injury; Dermatologic
    injury
Failure to thrive, 229–231; *see also*
    Malnutrition, Neglect
Femur fractures, 173–174, 179–180; *see also*
    Fractures
Fissure in anal mucosa, 47–48; *see also* Anal
    injury
Fixed drug eruption, 123–124; *see also* Skin
    conditions
Foot lesions, 61; *see also* Bites
Forced feeding, 95–96; *see also* Oral injury
Fractures
    burns with, 261–264
    femur, 173–174, 179–180
    humerus, 223–224
    hypophosphatasia, 159–160
    metabolic, 85–86
    multiple, 19–22
    osteogenesis imperfecta, 53–56,
        235–238
    osteopenia, 245–248
    parietal fracture, 299–302
    prematurity, 255–256
    ribs, 143–144

rickets, 187–188, 259–260
right femur diaphysis, 23, 26
skeletal survey, 57–58
skull, 75–76, 91–92, 107–110
spiral, 23–26
tibia, 51–52, 271–272
ulna, 119–120
Frena injuries, 13–14; *see also* Oral injury

Genetic anomalies, 70
Genitourinary injury; *see also* Sexual abuse
    buried penis, 103–104
    clitoral hood enlargement, 113–114
    hymenal septum, 283–284
    hymenal tag, 11–12
    hymenal transection, 43–44
    labial adhesion, 305–306
    labial haemangioma, 97–98
    lichen sclerosus, 139–140, 277–278, 295–296
    normal exam, 33–34
    penile injury, 279–280
    penile laceration, 297–298
    scrotum, 153–154
    straddle, 69–70
    thin hymenal rim, 63–64
    ulcer, 213–214
    urethral prolapse, 145–146, 193–194
Granulomatous lymphangitis, 275–276; *see also* Anal injury; Crohn's disease

Haemangioma, 93–94; *see also* Dermatologic injury
Haemoglobin decomposition into biliverdin, 49–50
Head; *see also* Burns; Infections; Injury
    injuries, 9–10
    lice infestation, 27–28
Henoch-Schönlein purpura (HSP), 115–116
Herpes infection, 269–270; *see also* Infections
Herpes simplex type 2 (HSV-2), 270
HIV, *see* Human immunodeficiency virus
HSP, *see* Henoch-Schönlein purpura
HSV-2, *see* Herpes simplex type 2
Human bite mark, 189–190, 243–244; *see also* Bites
Human immunodeficiency virus (HIV), 166
Humerus fracture, 223–224; *see also* Fractures
Hymen; *see also* Genitourinary injury
    hymenal findings, 98
    hymenal septum, 283–284
    hymenal tag, 11–12
    hymenal transection, 43
    thin hymenal rim, 63–64

Hyperpigmented marks, 7–8; *see also* Burns, Skin conditions
Hypophosphatasia, 159–160; *see also* Fractures

Iatrogenic, 111–112; *see also* Dermatologic injury
Imaging, *see* Skeletal survey, Computed tomography, Magnetic resonance imaging
Immersion, 191–192, 265–266, 285–288; *see also* Burns
Impetiginous lesions, 267–268; *see also* Infections
Infections
    carbuncles, 281–282
    herpes, 269–270
    human papillomavirus, 149–150
    impetigo, 267–268
    lice, 27–28
    Molluscum lesions, 150
    streptococcus, 37–38
    tinea versicolor, 206
Inflicted injury, 106
Ingestions; *see also* Neglect
    heroin, 89–90
    lidocaine, 29–30
Injury; *see also* Anal injury; Craniofacial injury; Dermatologic injury; Genitourinary injury; Neglect; Ocular injury
Intraoral injuries, 96; *see also* Oral injury
    frena, 13–14
Iron, 125–126, 151–152; *see also* Burns
Isoniazid, 124

Koebner phenomenon, 296; *see also* Skin conditions

Labia; *see also* Genitourinary injury
    labial adhesion, 305–306
    labial haemangioma, 97–98
Laceration, 175–176, 251–252; *see also* Anal injury, Dermatologic injury
Leg bruises, 249–250; *see also* Dermatologic injury
Lesions; *see also* Skin conditions
    asymmetric skin, 233–234
    circular red, 121–122
    foot lesions, 61
    impetiginous, 267–268
    Molluscum, 150
    oval blistered, 121–122

Lichen sclerosus (LS), 139–140, 277–278, 295–296; *see also* Genitourinary injury

Lidocaine intoxication, 29–30; *see also* Ingestions

Linear abrasions, 73–74; *see also* Blunt trauma, Dermatologic injury

Linear burns, 209–210; *see also* Burns

Loop marks, 65–68, 105–106; *see also* Dermatologic injury

LS, *see* Lichen sclerosus

Magnetic resonance imaging (MRI), 204

Malnutrition, 39–40; *see also* Neglect

Maquas, 31–32; *see also* Complementary and alternative medicine

Mastocytomas, 45–46; *see also* Skin conditions

Molluscum lesions, 150; *see also* Infections

Mongolian spot, 5–6, 241–242, 273–274; *see also* Dermatologic injury

Moxibustion, 155–158; *see also* Complementary and alternative medicine

MRI, *see* Magnetic resonance imaging

Multiple bruises, 167–168; *see also* Craniofacial injury

Multiple erythematous lines, 183; *see also* Skin conditions

Multiple fractures, 19–22; *see also* Fractures

Neglect; *see also* Injury
    crush, 225–226
    dental neglect, 221–222
    failure to thrive, 229–231
    malnutrition, 39–40
    opiate intoxication and, 89–90
    supervisional, 293–294

Neonatal intensive care unit (NICU), 255

NICU, *see* Neonatal intensive care unit

Non-accidental burns, 82; *see also* Burns

Non-scald intentional burns, 122; *see also* Burns

Ocular injury; *see also* Injury
    black eyes, 79–80
    subconjunctival haemorrhages, 3–4, 99–100
    vitreous, 147–148

OI, *see* Osteogenesis imperfecta

Opiate intoxication, 89–90; *see also* Ingestions

Oral injury; *see also* Injury
    caries, 221–222
    forced feeding, 95–96

frena, 13–14
intraoral, 96
palate, 253–254

Osteogenesis imperfecta (OI), 22, 53–56, 235–238; *see also* Fractures

Osteopenia, 245–248; *see also* Fractures

Oval blistered lesion, 121–122; *see also* Skin conditions

Paediatric bite, 117–118; *see also* Bites

Palatal bruising, 253–254; *see also* Oral injury

Palatal expansion, 254

Parathyroid hormone (PTH), 188, 255

Parietal fracture, 299–302; *see also* Craniofacial injury

Partial thromboplastin time (PTT), 168, 240

Patterned bruises; *see also* Dermatologic injury
    cupping therapy, 131–132
    erythema nodosum, 71–72
    human bite mark, 189–190, 243–244
    inflicted injury, 106
    moxibustion, 155–158
    physical abuse, 8, 40
    without supporting history, 70

Penis; *see also* Genitourinary injury
    buried, 103–104
    injury, 279–280
    laceration, 297–298

Perianal streptococcal dermatitis, 37–38; *see also* Infections

Perineal injury, 70; *see also* Genitourinary injury

Pharyngitis, 38; *see also* Infections

Physical punishment, 68; *see also* Injury; Trauma
    countries exercising, 126
    injuries from, 1–2

Phytophotodermatitis, 195–196; *see also* Skin conditions

Plant-induced photosensitivity reactions, *see* Phytophotodermatitis

Poisoning, *see* Ingestions

Post-inflammatory hypopigmentation, 206

Prematurity, 255–256; *see also* Fractures, Osteopenia

Prothrombin time (PT), 70, 168, 240

PT, *see* Prothrombin time

PTH, *see* Parathyroid hormone

PTT, *see* Partial thromboplastin time, Activated partial thromboplastin time

Rectal prolapse, 227–228; *see also* Anal injury

Rib fractures, 143–144; *see also* Fractures

Rickets, 187–188, 259–260; *see also* Fractures, Osteopenia

Scald burns, 219–220; *see also* Burns

Self-mutilating behaviours, 138

Sexual abuse, 11–12; *see also* Genitourinary injury
    anal dilation, 165–166
    anal trauma, 135–136
    boys, 104
    herpes infection, 269–270
    hymenal septum, 283–284
    hymenal transection, 43–44
    laceration, 175–176
    multidisciplinary evaluation, 33–34
    palate, 253–254

Sexually transmitted infection (STI), 166

SIDS, *see* Sudden infant death syndrome

Skeletal survey, 57–58; *see also* Fractures

Skin conditions; *see also* Burns, Dermatologic injury
    circular red lesions, 121–122
    erythema nodosum, 71–72
    extensive unexplained bruising, 70
    fixed drug eruption, 123–124
    haemangioma, 93–94
    Henoch-Schönlein purpura, 115–116
    hyperpigmented marks, 7–8
    Koebner phenomenon, 296
    lesion, 233–234
    mastocytosis, 45–46
    Mongolian spot, 5–6, 241–242, 273–274
    phytophotodermatitis, 195–196
    slippage, 290
    striae, 77–78
    vitiligo, 59–60, 205–206

Skull fracture, 75–76, 91–92, 107–110; *see also* Craniofacial injury; Fractures

Spider bites, 181–182; *see also* Bites

Spiral fracture, 23–26; *see also* Fractures

STI, *see* Sexually transmitted infection

Straddle, 69–70, 280; *see also* Genitourinary injury

Strangulation, 15–16; *see also* Craniofacial injury

Streptococcal pharyngitis, 38; *see also* Infections

Striae, 77–78; *see also* Skin conditions

Subconjunctival haemorrhages, 3–4, 99–100; *see also* Ocular injury

Subcutaneous haemorrhage, 16; *see also* Dermatologic injury

Subdural haemorrhage, 203–204; *see also* Craniofacial injury

Subgaleal haematoma, 161–162; *see also* Craniofacial injury

Suction mark, 83–84; *see also* Dermatologic injury

Sudden infant death syndrome (SIDS), 307–308; *see also* Craniofacial injury

Thin hymenal rim, 63–64; *see also* Genitourinary injury

Tibia, 51–52, 271–272; *see also* Fractures

Tinea versicolor, 206; *see also* Infections

Tourniquet syndrome, 265, 266; *see also* Burns

Trauma; *see also* Blunt trauma; Craniofacial injury, Ocular injury
    abdominal, 163–164
    anal, 135–136

Trichotillomania, 17–18; *see also* Dermatologic injury

Ultraviolet radiation, 196

Urethral prolapse, 145–146, 193–194; *see also* Genitourinary injury

Venous distension, 303–304; *see also* Anal injury

Vitiligo, 59–60, 205–206; *see also* Skin conditions

Vitreous haemorrhage, 147–148; *see also* Ocular injury

Whisker burn, 127–130; *see also* Burns

Wringer injuries, *see* Crush injuries; *see also* Neglect